The Woman Fantastic in Contemporary American Media Culture

THE WOMAN FANTASTIC
in Contemporary American Media Culture

Edited by Elyce Rae Helford, Shiloh Carroll,
Sarah Gray, and Michael R. Howard II

University Press of Mississippi / Jackson

www.upress.state.ms.us

The University Press of Mississippi is a member
of the Association of American University Presses.

First printing 2016

Library of Congress Cataloging-in-Publication Data

Names: Helford, Elyce Rae, 1962– editor. | Carroll, Shiloh, 1980– editor. |
Gray, Sarah, 1977– editor. | Howard, Michael R., 1972– editor.
Title: The woman fantastic in contemporary American media culture / edited by
Elyce Rae Helford, Shiloh Carroll, Sarah Gray, and Michael R. Howard II.
Description: Jackson : University Press of Mississippi, 2016. | Includes
bibliographical references and index.
Identifiers: LCCN 2016016556 (print) | LCCN 2016029277 (ebook) | ISBN
9781496808714 (hardback) | ISBN 9781496808721 (epub single) | ISBN
9781496808738 (epub institutional) | ISBN 9781496808745 (pdf single) |
ISBN 9781496808752 (pdf institutional)
Subjects: LCSH: Women in mass media. | BISAC: SOCIAL SCIENCE / Women's
Studies. | SOCIAL SCIENCE / Media Studies. | SOCIAL SCIENCE / Popular
Culture.
Classification: LCC P94.5.W65 W615 2016 (print) | LCC P94.5.W65 (ebook) | DDC
302.23082—dc23
LC record available at https://lccn.loc.gov/2016016556

British Library Cataloging-in-Publication Data available

Contents

Part I. The Making of Today's Woman Fantastic

Part II. Expanding the Horizons of the Woman Fantastic

Part III. The Woman Fantastic in Social and Theoretical Context

Acknowledgments

As with any project of this size and complexity, many individuals have helped and inspired us along the way.

First, we thank Katherine Kittredge of Ithaca College, whose 2011 "Pippi to Ripley" conference on science fiction and fantasy heroines inspired a 2012 follow-up conference at Middle Tennessee State University (MTSU), organized by (then) graduate students Shiloh Carroll, Sarah Gray, and Michael R. Howard II, titled "Catwoman to Katniss" and added female villains to the focus. We are grateful to all who presented at that conference and inspired the beginnings of this volume, long before Elyce became actively involved.

We thank MTSU's College of Liberal Arts and Dean Mark Byrnes, as well as the English Department and graduate director David Lavery, who offered his experience and advice. The university provided a supportive home as we undertook this adventure together.

At the University Press of Mississippi, we thank all who contributed to the production of the book. The anonymous external reviewers shared both praise and precise, detailed critiques that helped us make the work stronger in ways both large and small. Editorial assistant Lisa McMurtray patiently kept us on track and informed throughout the process. Copyeditor Michael Levine provided additional feedback and helped sharpen the writing. We also thank production manager Todd Lape and editorial associate Katie Keene. Above all, we offer our gratitude to acquiring editor Vijay Shah, who provided enthusiastic support throughout the process and kept our four-editor team productive and positive from start to finish.

Many thanks also go to all the authors in the volume—from senior scholars to graduate students—who shared their excellent work and made great use of feedback. We quite literally couldn't have done it without you.

Finally, although unconventionally, we editors wish to share our appreciation for one another. Shiloh, Sarah, and Michael (aka Mick) learned much about writing for publication from Elyce's guidance. Elyce values the strong team the four editors made together, each working from her or his areas of strength while learning others. And she looks forward to watching the academic careers of "the Trio" blossom.

The Woman Fantastic in Contemporary American Media Culture

Introduction

—Elyce Rae Helford, Shiloh Carroll, Sarah Gray,
and Michael R. Howard II

Who or what is the "Woman Fantastic," and what does it mean to engage critically with this figure in today's American media landscape? Just positing this question offers the beginnings of an answer. As the contrast between "women" and "woman" suggests, the Woman Fantastic is a gendered textual and cultural construction. Hence, "she" is entirely fantastic—less projection, stereotype, or imago than symbol, sign, or trope, an always already artificial creation. Within the realm of the popular, "she" is a sales pitch, the offer of a model or mask through which the feminine and/or female can be reified. Woman always denies the emperor has no clothes, and in this way Woman is always fantastic.

From this perspective, our insistence as editors on the concept of the Woman Fantastic signals our focus on textual constructions that foreground artificiality—through futuristic contexts, fantasy worlds, alternate histories, or the display of super powers that challenge the laws of physics, chemistry, and/or biology. We ask such questions as "How does the figure of the Woman Fantastic signify within overtly impossible, improbable, or alien textual spaces?" and "How do feminist concepts such as 'agency,' 'power,' and 'heroism' resonate through the Woman Fantastic in the fun-house mirror reflections and refractions of today's media?"

Certainly, this is not the first book to engage this type of figure. Early fans, authors, and scholars of women in science fiction and fantasy (e.g., Joanna Russ, Beverly Friend, Susan Wood) concentrated on literary representations. They encouraged appreciation for literature beyond the developing feminist "canon," illustrating the potential for nonrealist writing to provide a new perspective on cultural expressions of gender. Through small presses and fan gatherings, focus was placed on individual authors who had relative freedom to explore radical perspectives and challenges to social norms and the cultural status quo.

By contrast, our focus on contemporary American media culture shifts the context of both production and reception. Popular media texts are far less the products of individual minds. Auteur theory notwithstanding, television and mainstream comics are produced by teams within corporate structures, often with conflicting perspectives on the content, production, and goals of their final products. Radical innovation is antithetical to the business of the media and its investment in the top-down creation and control of popular culture. Even with more traditional forms, such as the novel, there can be severe formal constraints, as in paranormal romance or epic fantasy, where even relatively empowered/active female characters are relegated to traditional heteronormative endings and/or subjected to the dictates of the male gaze.

Of course, fans and critics may intervene in the interpretation and, occasionally, elements of production, and this should not be underestimated as one of the central pleasures of popular culture, as scholars from John Fiske and Henry Jenkins to Janice Radway have illustrated. This stated, the Woman Fantastic as we envision her for this collection is above all a figure of tension between feminist ambitions and economic and textual realities.

This collection also emerges alongside academic feminism and the fields of women's studies and popular cultural studies. In 1981, for example, Marleen S. Barr offered *Future Females*, a simple and audacious (for the era) edited exploration of images of women in science fiction, from the writing of Ursula K. Le Guin to female characters in the original *Star Trek*. Like the liberal and radical feminism from which the collection sprung, here woman is tied to women, where the search for role models and exploration of "herstory" to challenge history offers justification for the volume's existence. In the preface, Barr (1981) notes that the critical study of women in science fiction "is especially suited for speculation about women's future roles" (1). Two decades later, when Barr's edited follow-up collection, *Future Females, The Next Generation* (2000), was published, the radical feminist emphasis remained on the importance of strong female figures in science fiction; however, she added a focus on the widening sphere of textual spaces in which a more diverse group of fantastic women could be engaged, from postcolonial to queer studies and from cyberpunk to cyborg feminism.

Just before Barr's second collection emerged, Sherrie Inness (1998) was also challenging genre boundaries within image studies with her book *Tough Girls*. Through consideration of such characters as Emma Peel of *The Avengers*, Xena Warrior Princess, and Dana Scully of *The X-Files*, Inness explores the limits of proscribed gender roles, as female media figures of the 1990s demonstrated their toughness without fully challenging feminine norms. The importance of hegemonic negotiation—pushing boundaries without breaking them—drove studies such as *Tough Girls* as well as Inness's *Action Chicks* (2004), and as with Barr's work, inspires considerations of women in the media—particularly fantastic women—to the present day.[1]

The Woman Fantastic in Contemporary American Media Culture proceeds from both the pioneering efforts of 1970s feminists and the tradition as it has continued to develop. For this collection, the Woman Fantastic may appear in speculative or realist text, but her presence is always recognizable. She is neither second- or third-wave role model nor "positive" representation to counteract something identified first as "negative" image. Instead, she is an artificial construction of womanhood that "does" gender (as well as race, class, sexual orientation, age, ability, nation, and other factors of identification) in ways that reflect back to us what we mean when we talk about gender. Inspired by perspectives of feminist theorists including Donna Haraway and Judith Butler, we read the Woman Fantastic as herself a text. The various chapters in this book name, claim, and engage her meanings and methods of meaning-making, even as they contextualize the figure and her feminist potential through attention to economic and formal pressures.

Just as this book owes its existence to studies that came before it, so the volume you are reading owes its existence to two conferences that sparked its conceptualization. In 2011, Ithaca College held "Pippi to Ripley: Heroes in Science Fiction and Fantasy," organized by Katherine Kittredge. On the basis of this conference, (then) graduate students Shiloh Carroll, Sarah Gray, and Michael R. Howard II organized "Catwoman to Katniss: Villainesses and Heroines in Science Fiction and Fantasy." This sister conference broadened the scope of "Pippi to Ripley," including focus on both female heroes and female villains. The idea of a conference volume attracted a publisher, with the stipulation that a senior editor be added. This brought Elyce Rae Helford on board.

Reviewing the manuscripts submitted by conference presenters, we soon realized that just as broadening the scope of the conference had drawn greater critical attention to the project, broadening our scope in this collection would not only draw still more critical attention but would also address certain gaps and lags in scholarship regarding what we would come to call the Woman Fantastic. Although the past three decades have offered a growing and changing body of scholarship on images of fantastic women in popular culture, these studies tend to focus either on one particular variety of fantastic female (i.e., the action or sci-fi heroine) or on her role in a particular genre (villain, hero, temptress, etc.). Hence, "Villainesses and Heroines" became the "Woman Fantastic," and "Science Fiction and Fantasy" became "Contemporary Media Culture." As we broadened our focus, we also broadened our list of contributors and deepened our critical perspective. At the same time, lest the project become unwieldy, we narrowed our focus to popular literature, television, and comics, leaving such media as film and video games to volumes that fully attend film and video game studies methodologies.

To reflect and comment upon current trends in American media culture, the collection is divided into three subsections, each offering insight into the textual and contextual spaces in which she can be found. We begin with four chapters on "The Making of Today's Woman Fantastic." The characters of study within this section offer a starting point for establishing definitions within expected speculative settings. From heroic to villainous figures and from science fiction to comic book fantasy context, the chapters consider the easily identified Woman Fantastic where she is most often found.

J. Richard Stevens, who begins the collection with "Of Jungle Queens and Amazons: Marvel's She-Hulk as Poststructural Feminist Icon," considers the contemporary transformation of another action heroine, She-Hulk, from the jungle queen archetype. Stevens emphasizes her humanitarian mission, the strength of her voice against the masculine conventions of superhero narratives, and the ways in which her visual image challenges traditional sexual objectification.

Shifting from textual to audience studies, Alex Naylor's "'My Skin Has Turned to Porcelain, to Ivory, to Steel': Feminist Fan Discourses, *Game of Thrones*, and the Problem of Sansa" explores debates on Tumblr over the sword-fighting, gender-bending figure of Arya Stark and her princess-turned-stoic-survivalist sister, Sansa. Fan perspectives on Sansa, Naylor finds, take the form of intense appreciations of her, reflections on how her narrative refracts issues of young women's victimization and survival, and "defenses" that confront her detractors and implicate the role of sexism and misogyny in some fans' vocal dislike of the character. Because for many young women this kind of online popular culture critique is their first introduction to feminist ideas, argues Naylor, it is most productively explored within the context of a wider debate in both feminist and fandom social media spaces about what a modern feminist ethics of media consumption might look like.

In "The Dragon Lady of Gotham: Feminine Power, the Mythical East, and Talia al Ghul," Tosha Taylor returns us to the world of comics to consider the gender and race politics of Batman's most complex enemy and ally. The chapter explores patterns of Orientalist fantasy in the character's actions and appearance. Working from the initial Orientalist inspiration for Talia's villainous family as related by the character's creators, Taylor posits that Talia's chief function in the DC universe has been to embody the stereotype of the Dragon Lady, an exotic temptress capable of unconscionable acts of betrayal. The chapter examines Talia's forty-year struggle between being a villainess and heroine and argues that her presentation and level of agency often rely on her conformity to Western myths about Arabic and East Asian woman. The study concludes with consideration of whether Talia might at times serve as a metatexual indictment of Western heterosexist fantasy, craftily appropriating stereotypical images of Orientalism in order to manipulate heterosexual male characters.

Finally, Ewan Kirkland's "Situating Starbuck: Combative Femininity, Figurative Masculinity, and the Snap" studies the action heroine in the reimagined *Battlestar Galactica* (2004–2009) television series. He argues that Starbuck exemplifies a transformation of the 1970s male action hero in post-*Alien* action adventure science fiction and fantasy, where women warriors increasingly feature as a generic staple. Situating Starbuck in relation to action heroines from film, television, and digital games as well as the academic arguments that circulate them affords an understanding of the gender politics of the character and the extent to which she challenges dominant representations in popular culture.

Taken together, this first section illustrates new directions and familiar obstacles for figures readily identifiable as examples of the Woman Fantastic in predictable places. The second group of chapters, in the "Expanding the Horizons of the Woman Fantastic" section, posits the possibility of tracing similar figures in less expected textual spaces or the subversion of expected traits. When we do not find ourselves in fantasy worlds or science fictional futures, how does the Woman Fantastic signify? Moreover, are there characteristics deserving attention beyond strength and physical prowess?

The first chapter explores the race and class politics of today's Woman Fantastic in Frank Miller and Dave Gibbons' limited series comic *Give Me Liberty* (1990). In "From SuperOther to SuperMother: The Journey toward Liberty," Nicola Mann studies the character Martha Washington, a single mother from Chicago's Cabrini-Green public housing project, as she rises to the status of lauded war hero. As an African American woman, argues Mann, Washington not only re-scripts the familiar trope of the white male superhero, but also offers an alternate vision of the children of urban single mothers. Her success story speaks to contemporary real-world political claims-to-agency for young black women. In particular, the chapter explores the formal voyeurism implicit in *Give Me Liberty*'s panel sequences. Through the gutter—the blank white space between comic book panels—the reader becomes a silent accomplice in deciphering and linking the singular moments described in the panels into a series of topological connections, and eventually, a continuous unified whole. Deconstructing fields of objective linearity, readers participate in an intimate act of reconstruction, rebuilding one-note readings of African American single mothers.

Rhonda Nicol's "'Don't Underestimate Her Ability to Talk, It's Her Super-power': Epistemic Negotiation and the Power of Community in Carrie Vaughn's Kitty Norville Series" interrogates the action heroine of the urban fantasy genre. By contrast to most authors of the genre, Carrie Vaughn, posits Nicol, highlights her protagonist's interpersonal skills and community-building abilities, making them equal in value to physical power. The series thus posits a heroine easily identifiable to female urban fantasy readers while she questions the value of toughness for female empowerment.

Extending the significance of race and class in the first two chapters, Elyce Rae Helford adds attention to sexuality in "Positioning Parker: Negotiating the Hegemonic Binary in *Leverage*." Through a queer feminist lens, Helford explores popular culture's reliance on the doctrine of natural kinds and hegemonic binarism—where the human world is divided into two mandatory, privileged, distinct, and nonoverlapping categories. She posits the character of Parker in TNT's action-drama *Leverage* (2008–2012) as exemplification of the Woman Fantastic through attention to the ways in which character history and superheroic (or antiheroic) thieving abilities challenge gender absolutes. Simultaneously, argues Helford, Parker's romantic relationship with the series's African American computer hacker character challenges the combined effects of incest and miscegenation taboos. This case study illustrates hegemonic negotiation of the theory of natural kinds that continues to dominate popular culture.

Marleen S. Barr's "Hillary Orbits an Alternative Universe Earth: Interpreting the USA Network's *Political Animals* as Science Fiction" concludes the section with an exploration of Sigourney Weaver's character, Secretary of State Elaine Barrish Hammond, as a fantasy figure. Weaver resonates contextually through the science-fictional heroines she portrayed in *Aliens* and *Avatar* while her character in *Political Animals* (2012) echoes the life of Hillary Rodham Clinton. Through such parallels, argues Barr, the series exemplifies a power fantasy, recasting Clinton as an alternative history superhero.

In the final section of the volume, "The Woman Fantastic in Social and Theoretical Context," authors employ particular theoretical approaches to their subjects. Identifying the figure is less central in such studies than considering how particular perspectives elucidate her potential meanings and significances.

Joan Ormrod begins the section with "Body Issues in *Wonder Woman* 90–100 (1994–1995): Good Girls, Bad Girls, Macho Men." In an era that saw the emergence of violent, silicone-breasted, wasp-waisted bad girls, DC's *Wonder Woman*'s sales dropped. In response, Diana/Wonder Woman was reconceptualized to fit the new mold. Study of this shift to elongated, muscular bodies in fetishized clothing and soft-core porn poses, argues Ormrod, is productively achieved through application and critique of Laura Mulvey's concept of the male gaze. Then, positing an alternative model based on Turner's notion of the "somatic society," Ormrod reads the superhuman body as a metaphor for the body within wider culture, offering a historically contextualized commentary on women's changing place in society in the 1990s.

Katherine A. Wagner and Megan McDonough turn to issues of intersectionality and young adult literature in "Claiming the Throne: Multiplicity and Agency in Cinda Williams Chima's *The Seven Realms* Series." The authors find that possession of agency dominates female protagonists in the young adult fantasy genre but that complexity of character is equally vital, offering a blurring of rigid gender, ethnicity, and class boundaries. Through the concepts of multiplicity and intersectionality, Wagner and McDonough study sixteen-year-old Raisa *ana'*Marianna, heiress to a realm that has been ruled by women for centuries. Rather than having to challenge patriarchal rule, Chima's protagonist must come to understand identity as irreducibly multiple, as seen in feminist intersectionality, in order to claim agency.

Concluding the section and the volume is Rhonda V. Wilcox's "Forced Glory: Katniss Everdeen, Bella Swan, and Varieties of Virginity," which originated as the keynote lecture for the "Catwoman to Katniss" conference that inspired this volume. Through application of Janice Radway's conception of the romance heroine, Wilcox contrasts *Twilight*'s Bella Swan and *The Hunger Games*'s Katniss Everdeen. The chapter focuses on the differing representations of the characters' virginities, which Wilcox argues suggest disparate models of heroism and degrees of agency within contemporary literature for teens. There are many parallels between the characters, from triumph despite low self-esteem within a first-person narrative to being forced to wear elaborate outfits that serve as signs of power. In early repudiation of marriage and the mother, they reflect the pattern of independence illustrated in Radway's conceptualization of the romance heroine. Virginity is also central to this pattern, where mental impermeability, argues Wilcox, offers a metaphoric echo. Ultimately, where the characters most differ is in agency. Bella's protection from (mental) penetration is an inborn ability that helps assimilate her into patriarchy. Her virginity is of Edward's making, not her own. By contrast, Katniss pretends to have sex while being able to choose virginity. She purposefully and much later chooses procreation, while Bella and Edward, who experience an unplanned pregnancy, assert that in their love, they had no choice.

Without question, there are other ways one might organize a collection such as this. Medium, genre, and chronology, for example, offer different perspectives on the contemporary American Woman Fantastic. The particularities of production emerge when one separates television from comics or even adult genre literature from young adult fantasy. The generic boundaries between fantasy and science fiction encourage exploration of variances in means and methods between magical females and tomorrow's space pioneers—not to mention the speculative elements of realist texts. And differences in America's mediated cultural landscape between 1990 and the present day enable valuable historical study. This acknowledged, we as editors found most value in assessing the state of the contemporary American Woman Fantastic across related media, genre, and chronology. Whether evident and overtly delineated, contextually defined, or illuminated within specific theoretical context, we intend this volume as a contribution to the value of ongoing discussions of gender and feminism in popular culture.

Notes

1. It is no surprise that this same era saw also saw the publication of Elyce Rae Helford's (2000) *Fantasy Girls: Gender in the New Universe of Science Fiction and Fantasy Television*, which studies images of women in 1980s and 1990s speculative television within a multicultural feminist framework.

References

Barr, Marleen S., ed. 1981. *Future Females: A Critical Anthology*. Bowling Green, KY: Bowling Green State University Press.
———, ed. 2000. *Future Females, The Next Generation: New Voices and Velocities in Feminist Science Fiction Criticism*. Lanham, MD: Rowman & Littlefield.
Helford, Elyce Rae. 2000. *Fantasy Girls: Gender in the New Universe of Science Fiction and Fantasy Television*. Lanham, MD: Rowman & Littlefield.
Inness, Sherrie. 1998. *Tough Girls: Women Warriors and Wonder Women in Popular Culture*. Philadelphia: University of Pennsylvania Press.
———, ed. 2004. *Action Chicks: New Images of Tough Women in Popular Culture*. New York: Palgrave Macmillan.

PART I

The Making of Today's Woman Fantastic

Of Jungle Queens and Amazons: Marvel's She-Hulk as Poststructural Feminist Icon

—J. Richard Stevens

In most early comic books, female characters were presented in inferior roles: "Women were seldom presented as tough and independent. Instead, they were apt to require men to rescue them from all sorts of mishaps" (Inness 1999, 143). This status quo was challenged by the introduction of two iconic characters that would each spawn an archetype for future superheroines. The first was Sheena the Jungle Queen. In 1938, Fiction House published a story in *Jumbo Comics* #1 featuring Sheena, a sexy blonde woman who had been orphaned in the jungle and subsequently raised by animals. Able to speak with animals and fighting with weapons like knives and spears, Sheena became the first female character to receive her own title in 1942. The "jungle queen" motif was soon adopted and exploited by several other publishers. Sheena represented the pre–Pearl Harbor isolationist position, safeguarding her jungle against invaders without venturing beyond her community's boundaries, but the comic explored female sexuality at length:

> Sheena was drawn in provocative poses that best showed off her ample breasts carefully concealed by strategically placed leopard skin. Long shapely legs broke out of the panel borders in High Baroque style to arch across the page. Sheena swung from vines or leapt across the page, prominently showing off a spotted rump or widely spread legs. Her long blond hair was wild and free flowing. Stories mixed shades of Eros and Thanatos by showing the erotically drawn Sheena locked in combat with a wild snarling beast or writhing in the tentacles of a giant squid. Sheena was the untamed fantasy, the wild sensual creature that was not confined by polite society's idea of how a woman should dress or act. (Madrid 2009, 44–45)

The second iconic character was Wonder Woman. In 1941, she made her first appearance in *All-Star Comics* #8 and in the following decades became the prototype for all female superheroes. In her origin story, Diana must complete a string of physical trials to prove her skills, concluding with a test dubbed "bullets and bracelets," in which she is forced to deflect gunshots with her wristbands (O'Reilly 2005, 273). Once she passes the trial, her mother, the Queen of the Amazons, deems her fit to enter the man's world to fight for womankind in a manner that demonstrates power but is "loving, tender, maternal, and feminine in every other way" (Daniels 2000, 23). Unlike Sheena, Wonder Woman assumes an interventionist spirit, seeking to champion oppressed females in a foreign land, and in that capacity she minimizes her sexuality.

These two characters proved extremely popular, and each spawned a particular archetype after which every female hero for decades would be patterned:

> One was a beautiful blonde, the other a striking brunette. One was a savage fighter, who could deal death with her bare hands. The other had been trained since childhood in the art of war, but preferred to think that love was the true solution to conflict. One had only the strength of her body and her dagger to protect her. The other was blessed by the gods with amazing powers and was girded with fantastic weapons. They were both comic book royalty—one was a queen, the other merely a princess. The queen was the first of her kind, but the princess outlived her in life, and in legend. The queen was named Sheena, and the princess was called Wonder Woman. As different as they were from one another, these two sovereigns ruled the early days of comic books as the medium's two most popular heroines and the archetypes that would define the female superhero. Sheena was the passionate, savage beauty who embodied the erotic fantasies of men, while Wonder Woman was a powerful female who served as a role model for young girls. (Madrid 2009, 31)

Marvel Comics' She-Hulk would eventually come to represent a fusion of these two seminal archetypes to create a character that pursues a mission more consistent with the feminist ideal than either. To arrive at that point, she would first adopt the traits and narratives consistent with each before combining the two together and would do so following key transitions within feminist discourse. This chapter examines 557 comic books, beginning with the character's initial adventures in the early 1980s series *The Savage She-Hulk*, finding consistency with the Jungle Queen archetype. Next, She-Hulk's exploits in the pages of the *Avengers* and the *Fantastic Four* are considered alongside the late 1980s series, *The Sensational She-Hulk*, in which the Amazon-like archetype can be found. The first and second volumes of *She-Hulk* (2004 and 2005–2009, respectively) are then examined to locate a more consistently recognizable poststructural feminist model.

She-Hulk originated as a 1980 derivative text of the Incredible Hulk, both literally and structurally. The Hulk had become one of Marvel's most popular characters during the time the company was experimenting with licensing characters for cartoon animation, and Stan Lee worried that Universal would create a cartoon around female versions of some of the company's more popular characters (Howe 2012, 220). As a result, comic book titles for *Spider-Woman* and *The Savage She-Hulk* were rushed into production to secure the copyrights to those characters (Raphael and Spurgeon 2003, 205). Though a She-Hulk cartoon never materialized, *The Savage She-Hulk* was an unexpected smash hit, selling 250,000 copies of its first issue (Howe 2012, 236).

She-Hulk was one of the last characters Stan Lee created for Marvel. Lee (1977, 57) had already consistently argued for female roles to be more in comic narratives, and his previous efforts had been considered by some as "an unprecedented world of gender equality" for its time (Housel 2009, 85).

In some ways, the early She-Hulk was an exemplar of 1980s feminism. Her alter ego is lawyer Jennifer Walters, a defense attorney representing a man falsely accused of being a mobster. Her aggressive litigation style earns her the ire of unsavory figures, and it is because of her career that she is shot at her home, forcing her cousin—Bruce Banner (the Hulk)—to give her an emergency transfusion (Lee, Buscema, and Stone, February 1980). As a lawyer, Walters constantly struggles against the sexism displayed by her male colleagues, who worry that she cannot handle the stress of a "high-pressure man's world" (Kraft and Vosburg, July 1980, 6) and bombard her with verbal slights. For example, District Attorney Buck Bukowski dismisses perceived mistakes on her part as merely an indicator of "how flighty you females are!" (Kraft, Vosburg, and Bulanadi, October 1980, 8).

In her career, Walters embodies the struggle of second-wave feminism, fighting to have a successful career on her own terms. But as She-Hulk, that embodiment looks quite different as she struggles to adjust to the empowerment her new abilities give her. Upon her initial transformation, She-Hulk remarks, "I never felt like this way before! I can do anything! I'm throbbing with power!" (Lee, Buscema, and Stone, February 1980, 26). Later, she would exclaim that her transformation "hurts more . . . every time I become . . . the She-Hulk! But with the pain—comes the power! Power! That means no one can push me around! No one!" (Kraft and Vosburg, July 1980, 7).

Though She-Hulk is empowered enough to physically right the wrongs she must simply endure as Walters, there are a number of ways in which her character contradicts actual female empowerment. The structural origin of *The Savage She-Hulk* (as a derivative of the Hulk) was also mirrored within the comic text origin: whereas Wonder Woman received an Adam origin, created from the earth (Fingeroth 2004, 85), She-Hulk's origin is more consistent with that of Eve, in that she receives a transfusion from the Hulk which grants her the mutation. Even her name is given to her by a male, as one of the thugs trying to kill her yells out immediately after her initial transformation that she looks like some kind of "She-Hulk" (Lee, Buscema, and Stone, February 1980, 19).

From the beginning, She-Hulk varied from the Hulk in several key ways and more closely resembled the jungle queen archetype, which Savage (1990) describes as "the male criteria for the ideal woman: long hair, long legs, large breasts, physical agility, and proclivities rather more emotional than intellectual" (78). Whereas the Hulk's book is described as "incredible," She-Hulk's is "savage." Where Hulk is simpleminded, She-Hulk is intelligent but "in a perpetual state of PMS" (Madrid 2009, 255). Her constant struggle, both as Walters and She-Hulk, is to fight down her temper. When she loses her temper as Walters, she transforms into She-Hulk, and when she loses her hair-trigger temper as She-Hulk, she reacts impulsively and physically, the result being large-scale property damage. In contrast to her cousin, She-Hulk is largely successful in maintaining her rational faculties in physical confrontations. For example, when she encounters a destructive device called the Silver Serpent, she initially tries unsuccessfully to use brute force to stop its rampage. Calming herself, she tries using the length of the serpent and the conservation of momentum to bear: "Instead of pounding away at it mindlessly with her naked fists—the She-Hulk has used her awesome strength in an even more effective way—to bring the stupendous mass, weight and size of the silver serpent to breaking point!" (Kraft, Vosburg, and Stone, June 1980, 19–20). The use of her reasoning abilities would be a core trait of future She-Hulk narratives.

The jungle queen archetype is also present in She-Hulk's appearance. When she transforms, her height increases from the five-feet-ten Walters to the six-feet-seven She-Hulk, and she gains more than five hundred pounds of muscle. As a result, Walters's clothing stretches and tears, clothing She-Hulk in a short, white dress with frayed hems.[1]

The early adventures of She-Hulk featured the heroine in physical confrontations more consistent with a jungle queen, a break with conventional superhero narratives of that era, in which acts of heroism were primarily associated with masculinity (Polster 1992, 8), but the focus on female heroes tended to emphasize their bodies instead of their actions (Heinecken 2003, 1). However, one key difference between She-Hulk and Sheena would pivot on sexuality: the early She-Hulk was considered an ugly brute by at least some of the characters she encountered, even as she was overtly sexualized by others.

But the construction of the text itself should also be examined. Most female characters drawn by men are drawn to appeal to heterosexual appetites of male readership (Zimmerman 2004, 74), and when one considers Mulvey's (1975) conception of the male gaze, in terms of dress and body position, She-Hulk's presentation is no exception.

Throughout *The Savage She-Hulk* series, She-Hulk is portrayed as taking provocative stances. Her shredded dress barely covers her nether regions, her poses frame her body so that usually shreds of cloth are all that rest between the male gaze and nudity. When she faces the viewer, her shoulders are generally thrown back (with her pelvis thrust forward), or her shoulders are hunched forward to provide a better view of her cleavage. When she faces away from the viewer, her legs are generally spread apart in a wide crouch, with the shreds of dress barely covering her intergluteal cleft. No matter what position she assumes, the reader sees the full lines of her figure, with flesh usually exposed right up to the point of her genitals, which are narrowly covered by a strip of fabric. Beyond her clothing and stances, She-Hulk also engages in suggestive action, such as when she tears a strip of cloth from the portion covering her crotch in *The Savage She-Hulk* #5.

Finally, the use of submissive posture appears frequently in *The Savage She-Hulk*. Such posture is one of the subtle "signs of pornographic discourse" (Reynolds 1992, 34) frequently appearing in Good Girl art that titillates by implying sexual access through bondage, unconscious helplessness, or other compromising circumstances (Savage 1990, 124). She-Hulk experiences many such circumstances in her adventures, including a peculiar recurring position she often collapses into in which her legs spread wide apart as she appears helpless to safeguard her own body. A female character spreading her legs generally emphasizes sexuality (Inness 1999, 145). Such portrayals are consistent with Madrid's description of Sheena's posture and attire described above (see Figure 1.1).

The narrative also undermines feminist discourse, particularly in the portrayals of She-Hulk's relationships to other characters. One of the core tests of feminism discourse in entertainment narratives is the presence of the Bechdel Rule, which declares a text is subject to gender bias unless female characters interact in same-sex groupings, talking to each other about topics other than men or relationships (Stuller 2012, 238; Ulaby 2008). In the *Savage She-Hulk*, few competent females appear with whom She-Hulk can converse, much less confide in. The primary candidate for such a role, Jen Walters's friend Jill, is killed by mobsters in the second issue, robbing She-Hulk of her lone female confidante (Kraft and Vosburg, March 1980, 26). Walters also

Figure 1.1: The She-Hulk's torn "uniform" leaves little to the imagination, and she is often drawn in vulnerable and submissive poses. Clockwise from top left, images from *The Savage She-Hulk* #2 (Kraft and Vosburg, March 1980, 1, 15, 19, 18), *The Savage She-Hulk* #12 (Kraft, Vosburg, and Springer, January 1981, 1), and *The Savage She-Hulk* #11 (Kraft and Vosburg December 1980, cover).

repeatedly bemoans the absence of her mother, murdered many years before by a mob hit intended for her father. Walters feels this loss deeply and visits her mother's gravesite to "talk" with her, a symbol of her lack of female companionship. Even so, her "talks" with her mother often embolden her to stand up for herself (Kraft, Vosburg, and Springer, February 1981, 17–18).

But in fact, many of the subplot narratives in *The Savage She-Hulk* revolve around the role of men in her life. Jen Walters's professional adversary, Buck Bukowski, verbally jousts with Walters and uses sexist jargon to demean her and yet is revealed to be working from both a sexual tension and a desire to "save" Walters "from herself" (ibid., January 1981, 5). Much of the series revolves around Walters's strained relationship with her father who, as a sheriff, objects to his daughter's defense of alleged criminals in the justice system. Walters is anxious to earn the approval of her father, but misunderstandings related to her She-Hulk transformations and the tension stemming from Walters's legal career continually come between them, even resulting in her father once telling her, "I wish you had never been born!" (ibid., 12).

Romantic aspirations consume much of the series, as Walters is torn between two suitors, Danny "Zapper" Ridge and Richard Rory. Zapper is attracted to Walters, and when she is in her She-Hulk persona, she prefers his company as the more aggressive male, while in her human form, she prefers the more thoughtful company of Rory (ibid., April 1981).

Her struggle to reconcile and maintain both relationships serves to illustrate her own identity crisis, both as her preferences to live as Walters or She-Hulk but also in terms of her own empowerment. As She-Hulk, she is more impulsive and retains more voice and agency, while as Walters she often quietly endures sexism and injustice.

The Savage She-Hulk draws heavily on the Jungle Queen motifs, which revolve around the presence of a white female struggling to redeem a hostile, uncivilized world (Wright 2001, 36–37). *The Savage She-Hulk* reverses this formula even as it embraces its themes. Whereas the classic Jungle Queen narrative presents the Anglophile as outsider, She-Hulk is presented as the "savage" who is trying to cope with the sexism embedded within civilization, which as Jen Walters she for the most part quietly endures. As She-Hulk, she is free of the civilizing conventions that diminish her female voice, and as the series continues, the character increasingly expresses a desire to remain in She-Hulk form permanently, in part because of her physical empowerment and autonomy, but also in part because of the escape she receives from the social pressures that are imposed upon Jen Walters because of her gender. As Walters, she is derided for her gender in the pursuit of her professional duties and is called an "uppity feminist" (Kraft, Vosburg, and Springer, May 1981, 17)

Figure 1.2: The She-Hulk finds her male acceptance and "family" in *The Savage She-Hulk* #25 (Kraft and Vosburg, February 1982, 40).

and worse, but quietly accepts such attacks without response. As She-Hulk, Walters possesses the power to respond with force, and her struggle becomes one of restraint, of holding her emotions in check to respond rationally (ibid., November 1980, 3–4). While confronting the hostile world of Los Angeles society, the savage She-Hulk is often the only character who shows restraint and civility in the face of the frequent unprovoked attacks launched at her because of her gender.

But the feminism displayed by She-Hulk is mostly superficial. She doesn't bond with any female characters in any significant way and continues to define herself against the judgments of her male colleagues and her desire for male companionship. She often laments that such a focus is contrary to her personal autonomy, saying that though she is "trying to convince myself that I don't need anyone" (Kraft and Vosburg, December 1981, 4), she secretly longs for acceptance, and specifically from the males in her life. And in the series finale, the story resolves with She-Hulk finding this acceptance: she repairs her relationship with her father and chooses Zapper as her love interest (thereby choosing her She-Hulk identity's preferences over those of her Jen Walters identity). The final splash page wraps up with the verbalizations of these acceptances and the achievement of a pseudofamily status (ibid., February 1982, 40). For all of her struggle against the sexist structures and behaviors presented by the hostile society, it would appear in the end it is the Savage She-Hulk who is domesticated, aspiring to a family model revolving around the approval of her father and the love of a man (see Figure 1.2).

She-Hulk's Superheroic Struggles

A few months after her initial series ended, She-Hulk was invited to join the Avengers because the team decided it needed "more girls" (Shooter, Michelinie, and Hall, July 1982, 2). From that comic issue onwards, She-Hulk's attire changed. Gone were the torn white dresses reminiscent of Jungle Queens. In the following issue, She-Hulk is trying on designer clothing at the behest of the Wasp when supervillains appear near Avengers Mansion and a battle breaks out. She-Hulk runs towards the conflict but is stopped by the Wasp, who orders her to take her expensive clothes off before engaging in combat. She-Hulk complies and fights her first major battle with the Avengers wearing lingerie (Shooter, Grant, and LaRocque, August 1982, 20–22).

The She-Hulk who joined the Avengers evolved away from the Jungle Queen motif and toward a superficial Amazon frame. Within the pages of *The Avengers*, She-Hulk's attractiveness began to be emphasized as she became more of an established superheroine than a monster. Conventional physical attractiveness is a general requisite for a female superhero; she must be "ultimately be glorified as [a] sexual being; i.e., capable of attracting men and bearing children. Women who break that mold threaten social order" (Magoulick 2006, 749). Even when the character mutates away from convention in some profound way, she remains sexually viable. For example, although She-Hulk is significantly larger than most of her male counterparts and sports bright green skin and hair, she is still intensely sexualized: "The new 'kick-ass' girl heroines could not possibly be heavy, or large-boned, or extremely muscular: such bodies could not be situated as desired objects of the audience's gaze. Their physical potency must be rendered safely and recognizably feminine" (Durham 2003, 26). While She-Hulk is both heavy and extremely muscular, she is drawn proportionally in a way that accentuates her feminine form rather than detracting from it.[2] During her stint with the Avengers, She-Hulk began to wear form-fitting workout clothes as a costume, outfits that emphasized her feminine shape while alluding to the superhero costume. Instead of the barefoot presentation consistent with Jungle Queens, She-Hulk began to wear boots. Her attire more closely resembled Amazon outfits than the jagged and torn Jungle Queen dresses; it resembled Wonder Woman's uniform, clothing which maintains a delicate balance faced by most female superheroes: "The myth could be described as an unearned state of post-feminism, and carries the message for both male and female readers: 'you can have your cake and eat it.' For women, the subtext might be read as 'You can still dress sexy and still be taken seriously and hold a position of power.' For men: 'Just because you like her to wear sexy clothes doesn't mean you're degrading her status and equality'" (Reynolds 1992, 81). Amazons differ from the typical female in their focus on female relationships and their (usual) sexual purity, a sexual unattainability that often leads to a fetishization among their readers (Brown 2011, 237). She-Hulk doesn't follow this part of the archetype, and her sexuality became a part of the narrative, such as when, in *Avengers* v1 #234, She-Hulk asks one of her teammates, Starfox, on a date, and later the two are presented together in postcoital circumstances (Stern and Milgrom, August 1983, 3, 7). She-Hulk's sexual exploits, her lack of connections of sisterhood, and her close proximity to the dominant culture (as opposed to standing apart from it) undermine She-Hulk's role as a true Amazon, even as she comes to superficially resemble one and is frequently called one by her peers.

At the conclusion of Marvel's "Secret Wars" event, She-Hulk joins the Fantastic Four, a move that she privately muses should give her legitimacy as a superhero (Byrne, June 1984, 2). *The Fantastic Four* was written and drawn by John Byrne, who would have a significant hand in She-Hulk's development. Perhaps the most significant development would revolve around the character's struggles with exploitations of her sexuality.

In *The Sensational She-Hulk* graphic novel, She-Hulk is arrested by corrupt factions within the antiterrorism group S.H.I.E.L.D. and is strip-searched in front of the leering male agents. Her nudity occurs off-panel, but the reader is presented with a view of her removing her clothes and then sees the male gaze reflected through the ogling reactions of the agents (ibid., January 1985, 26–27). Later in the same book, She-Hulk is hit with gunfire that doesn't harm her but shreds her clothes (ibid., 50–51), leaving her torso and breasts exposed (though strategically shielded from the reader). This would be a recurring convention for Byrne and later writers as She-Hulk would struggle to keep her clothes on during battles.

In *Fantastic Four v1* #274, She-Hulk is caught on film sunbathing topless on the roof of the Baxter building by a tabloid publisher and struggles unsuccessfully to keep the photos from seeing print (ibid., February 1985), though a processing error publishes the photos color corrected for normal skin tones. Byrne would later say the inspiration for this plot originated from seeing a provocative pinup drawing of She-Hulk in *Marvel Fanfare v1* #18. These portrayals signal the growing fascination with She-Hulk as a sex object, a theme that would permeate her narrative during her second solo series.

Created by John Byrne, *The Sensational She-Hulk* would offer an unusual narrative for superhero comics: one in which the lead character knew she was in a comic book. In the first issue, She-Hulk breaks the fourth wall to converse with the reader about the plot (ibid., May 1989, 21), and in the second issue she does so again to complain to the author about a twist in her story she didn't favor (ibid., June 1989, 13). This allows She-Hulk to gaze directly at the reader, which is important, for "even a cursory survey of contemporary comic book covers reveals women's faces drawn facing away from the camera, suggesting their passivity in relations to the male protagonist—whose gaze strongly faces the reader" (Stuller 2012, 237).

This metafiction awareness would also allow for a greater aptitude for social commentary (Palumbo 1997), as She-Hulk could act within character or step outside of her own character to critique how certain conventions of comic books functioned in her stories, and particularly matters related to her sexual mores. The pages of *The Sensational She-Hulk* (and the two solo series that would follow) would present the "first major female superhero to be openly, and explicitly sexual and engage in sex with men in comics" (Beerman 2012, 204). This sexuality would take many forms. She-Hulk herself would daydream and dream about sexual encounters with masculine figures like Hercules (Byrne, November 1989, 8–9; ibid., December 1989, 9–10) and would pursue many others.[3]

Following the lead established in *The Avengers*, it would be a running convention that She-Hulk would often find herself in a situation in which she needed to strip to her underwear to fight (or have her regular clothes torn off during the fight).[4] In addition, at times She-Hulk would appear completely naked,[5] though as she explained in *The Sensational She-Hulk* #4, the presence of the Comics Code would prevent her from appearing indecently (ibid., August 1989, 27).

Because she could interact with readers within her narrative, and because she "knew" that female superhero comics were perpetually at risk of cancellation, She-Hulk began to explicitly flaunt her sexuality in the name of attracting ogling male readers. For example, on the cover of *The Sensational She-Hulk*

#39, she sprawls in a vulnerable pose wearing a bikini, saying, "Don't get the wrong idea . . . I'm only doing this because it makes a good cover!!" (ibid., May 1992). In the following issue, She-Hulk stands awkwardly on the cover, trying to cover her nakedness with a Comics Code seal as her writer hands her a jump rope (ibid., June 1992). The jump rope gag had been born in the letters page of issue #36 as a suggestion by readers to boost sales. Within the comic, She-Hulk does indeed (seemingly) jump rope while naked (ibid., 1–6).

This behavior, and the sexual activity in which She-Hulk boldly celebrated, prevents her from actually adopting the Amazon archetype. Amazons are typically framed as sexually pure and unattainable, whereas the Jungle Queen archetype frequently sexualizes the female body as possessable. She-Hulk's continued embodiment of certain Jungle Queen attributes allowed her to address the social consequences of women being known to have sex. In the 2004 Dan Slott series *She-Hulk*, she must wrestle the uncomfortable "next morning" consequences of waking up with a stranger in Avengers Mansion (Slott and Bubillo, May 2004, 4–5). She-Hulk is eventually asked to leave Avengers Mansion by Captain America and the Wasp because of the security risks posed by her frequent overnight guests (ibid., 15).

When the 2005 second volume of *She-Hulk* begins, the character continues to struggle against her growing reputation with men. After sleeping with S.H.I.E.L.D. agent Clay Quartermain, she wrestles with the existential crisis of her choices: "I'm Jen Walters and I'm She-Hulk. Only Jen wouldn't have done that. When I'm She-Hulk I do what I want, when I want. And with who I want. I have fun. I have adventures. I've got it all. So tell me . . . why don't I feel grounded anymore?" (ibid., January 2006, 22). This dichotomy would allow She-Hulk to explore different components of her femininity. One of the outcomes of *The Sensational She-Hulk* graphic novel had been a loss of her Jen Walters identity. When Reed Richard tried to gently break the news to her that massive radiation exposure had robbed her of her ability to transform, She-Hulk paused and then asked "So what's the bad news . . . ?" (Byrne, January 1985, 71).

Though she eventually regained her ability to transform at will, She-Hulk continued to grapple with balancing the power of her heroic stature against the accomplishments of her meeker alter ego, usually with a resolution to remain She-Hulk as much as possible. But the differences in her sexual mores in the two states served as an internal conflict surrounding her empowerment. Exploring her identity crisis, she makes a list of the strengths of each personality, decided that Jen Walters was "smart, resourceful, accomplished, dresses well for work, considerate, polite," while She-Hulk was "outgoing, brave, determined, dresses well for clubbing, funny, confident" (Slott, Templeton, and Burchett, July 2007).

Sexual reputation would continue to define She-Hulk to others as well. After a rumor of She-Hulk having a past sexual encounter with the supervillain Juggernaut, She-Hulk sees her advances towards Wolverine rebuked in *She-Hulk v2* #16 because he doesn't want "Juggernaut's sloppy seconds" (Slott and Burchett, April 2007, 23). This slut-shaming outrages She-Hulk, and she brings up the different standards for men and women with Tony Stark (Iron Man) after spending the night with him. The two begin to discuss why his male sexual prowess earns him the celebrated status as a player, while hers earns her the reputation of being a skank (ibid., May 2007, 9). The conversation is interrupted before its conclusion, but such portrayals led to an ongoing feminist critique of the double standard that sexual activity holds for one's reputation between the genders.

Eventually, She-Hulk would profess her tiredness at "being a sexual pinball" (David and Moll, February 2008, 14) but soon would bed Hercules again (David and Cucca, September 2008) and struggle to reconcile that choice against her sensibilities (ibid., 19). But She-Hulk would not resolve this internal conflict, at least not until she stopped measuring herself against the men in her life and begin to look for validation and support from the women she knew.

The Feminism of She-Hulk

Though she bore many of the outward traits, it is difficult to consider She-Hulk a representation of feminist ideals in her first twenty-eight years of existence. While she uses her power to embrace her identity, she consistently judged her self-imposed legitimacy against the acceptance of male heroes, even as she continued to seek acceptance through male-dominated family structures (first through her father and boyfriend, later from the Avengers and the Fantastic Four). Throughout her career, She-Hulk had often yielded to male authority, such as the circumstances that led her to throw an arm-wrestling contest with Hercules for fear it would damage his ego (Slot and Pelletier, January 2005, 24).

Because of her career as a lawyer, She-Hulk had come to outwardly represent a model of the 1990s professional woman. As one character described her, "You're perceived as intelligent, independent, strong but non-threatening to men, emotionally vulnerable—yet professional enough to manage dual careers, as an attorney and an Avenger, no less" (Gerber and Hitch, January 1990, 21). But She-Hulk never seems to feel secure of her standing in either of her identities. Though Jennifer Walters's identity is accomplished in her career, She-Hulk dislikes her quiet reserve and enjoys the bold empowerment at her fingertips and the supermodel-like status her superhero career affords. And yet, though Walters's progressiveness is evident in her expressed values and actions, the more empowered She-Hulk seemed to frequently resort to a more superficial lifestyle of parties and sexual exploration, often to the detriment of her reputation and even her ability to help others in ways outside of her superhero activities.

Robinson (2004) argued that She-Hulk is not a feminist icon because "she is so one-of-a-kind that she does not—cannot—share her strength with other women and thereby empower them" (104). But Wonder Woman, who is also unique, became a feminist icon not because of her powerlessness—in fact, Gloria Steinem successfully lobbied to have DC Comics reverse the 1970s narrative that depowered Wonder Woman to restore her costume and powers because she saw a powerful Wonder Woman as more of a symbol for feminism (Steinem 1995, 7). Empowerment itself was not the determining factor, but rather Wonder Woman's approach to her mission: "This was an Amazon super-hero who never killed her enemies. Instead, she converted them to a belief in equality and peace, to self-reliance and respect for the rights of others. If villains destroyed themselves, it was through their own actions or some unbloody accident" (ibid., 9). What made Wonder Woman a second-wave feminist icon was her relationships with other women and her refusal to adopt men's behavior to solve problems (Steinem 2013, 204). Though the term *Amazon* literally means "without a breast"—legend has it that Amazons cut off their breasts to improve their accuracy with a bow (Danna 2006, 72)— Amazons generally connote "strength, independence, power, and sisterhood" (Stuller 2010, 18), and it is the lack of general female companionship in She-Hulk's life that most causes her to fall short of the ideals in question.

She-Hulk does bond with a few female heroes, but she subverts her identity politics to those around her. For example, when planning an outing with Sue Richards of the Fantastic Four and Janet Van Dyne of the Avengers, the trio decide to spend the day on traditional female activities:

SHE-HULK: "What better opportunity for girl-talk than a trip to the beauty parlor? I wonder if they have the latest issue of 'Modern Movie Star'"?
JANET VAN DYNE: "Ha ha! Careful now, Jen. Much more of that kind of talk and you'll have to surrender your N.O.W. membership!" (Byrne, February 1986, 4).

Though this statement was offered as playful teasing, the truth is that She-Hulk does not appear to hold many of the values and convictions conventionally associated with feminism. The one time she is asked her views on reproductive rights, she responds by saying "the subject of abortion poses a real moral quandary for me" (McDuffie, Chaplik, and Brigman, October 1989, 13). In that same publication, She-Hulk struggles with her desire to have a child (ibid., 14).[6] Other issues seem more consistent with feminism, such as her outrage at the prospect of date rape (Slott and Conrad, June 2006, 18).

However, beginning in 2008, the character underwent a shift toward a portrayal more consistent with the feminist ideal. In that year, a new comic series for the Hulk launched, featuring a new Red Hulk as an antagonist. The character formally appears for the first time by assaulting She-Hulk from behind and knocking her unconscious (Loeb and McGuinness, April 2008, 2–5). Later, chaffing at the indignity of the assault, She-Hulk calls a list of her closest female friends in the superhero community for help (Loeb and Cho, December 2008) but initially recruits only two heroes, Thundra and the Valkyrie. Setting out for revenge, the trio struggle against the Red Hulk until six other female heroes arrive (ibid., January 2009), and these Lady Liberators work together to incapacitate him (ibid., February 2009).

The Liberators disband following the encounter, and the story returned to the question of the antagonist's secret identity. However, in the pages of *She-Hulk*, the main group of Lady Liberators is gathered again by She-Hulk, this time to consider a mission of mercy. She-Hulk is frustrated by the plight of the citizens in the fictitious nation of Marinmer, a Middle Eastern country in which the government was known to be blocking aid in relief of a famine affecting regions in which antigovernment sentiments existed. She-Hulk bristles at the inaction of the international community, held in check because Russia has strategic interests in the country. With the Valkyrie, Thundra, the Invisible Woman, and the shape-shifting Jazinda assembled, She-Hulk begins a group discussion about the situation:

> SHE-HULK: "It's insane. Money intended to help the people is going right into the pockets of the government . . . especially the president-for-life, Darqon Par."
> Sue Richards: "What do you want to do, Jen? Audit them?"
> SHE-HULK: "We can't do squat about the money, Sue . . . but there's medicine . . . food . . . all manner of necessary supplies that the Red Cross and other organizations have already shipped in. None of it's getting to the population. The produce is rotting in warehouses at the airport. Medicine and construction materials are being sold to the black market. Darqon's pockets are being lined while people are dying. Teams of heroes spend most of their time fighting villains or other heroes. Meantime, humanitarian causes are being ignored."
> RICHARDS: "Because Russia and China both have strategic and financial interests in the Marinmer government. The U.N. makes resolution to go in, but they keep being ignored."

SHE-HULK: "WE don't need resolutions."

VALKYRIE: "Why do you require our aid? To arrange transportation?"

SHE-HULK: "I have a means of getting over there. The thing is, if it's just me, then it's one woman sticking her nose in where it doesn't belong. At least, that's how they'll spin it. But if it's a group ..."

RICHARDS: "Then it becomes an organized protest in the face of inhumanity."

SHE-HULK: "Exactly." (David and Cucca, December 2008, 12–13)

This conversation is significant in its varying critiques of the masculine superhero formula. First, it abandons the isolationism embedded within the Jungle Queen archetype in favor of the interventionism embedded in the Amazon archetype. However, the women acknowledge that typical masculine intervention would not result in permanent outcomes (a critique often ignored in superhero stories), and so they seek to use their collective reputations to draw attention to the facts on the ground to garner international public opinion. In addition, such exchanges exemplify the Bechdel Rule (two or more women who talk to each other, and not about men or relationships), as the women discuss the political ramifications of their errand of mercy, as well as the implications for various individuals and groups.

In *She-Hulk v2* #35, the group enters the country and begins to transport food and supplies to the affected areas. But they are confronted by the Winter Guard, a team of Russian heroes that opposes their mission on the orders of their country. The two groups fight until civilians enter the conflict zone and beg for help. She-Hulk shames the Red Guardian, who then orders the others to join the Liberators' mission to deliver food and supplies to those in need (David and Qualano, January 2009). Though the two groups do engage in the stereotypical physical conflict, it is resolved through debate, emotional appeals, and compromise.

She-Hulk and the Invisible Woman next visit President Darqon Par to attempt to negotiate with him. He drugs the women and attempts to rape them, but the arrival of Jazinda turns the tables and places the dictator at the women's mercy. She-Hulk decides not to kill him and instead has her shapeshifting friend provide the illusion that the president had a change of heart about his policies and then committed suicide, while in reality he is banished to a sparsely populated region of Australia (ibid., February 2009). Much in the spirit of Steinem's praise of the 1970s Wonder Woman, She-Hulk and her companions find a way to reach their goals without bloodshed, drawing upon the same Amazon expression of the equality and peace that seeks to preserve life.

Upon her return to the United States, She-Hulk is arrested by the Justice Department for her actions. However, she is later released after public opinion

Figure 1.3: The Lady Liberators, as they appeared on the cover of *She-Hulk v2* #34 (David and Cucca, December 2008).

and media coverage proves favorable to her team's actions in Marinmer (ibid., March 2009).

She-Hulk's poststructural feminist approach to the international crisis is ultimately successful without the usual fisticuffs dictating the final outcome, and the internal outcomes reify the empowerment and bonds of sisterhood at the heart of feminist discourse. She-Hulk had been disillusioned by her role in the Civil War conflict between Iron Man and Captain America (two core Avengers, one of her two superheroic families). After serving as a government agent, she experienced personal betrayal when she discovered her cousin, the Hulk, had been duped to go into a rocket and was launched into deep space to remove him from Earth. These events had combined to push She-Hulk away from the system, leaving her jaded and resentful (and largely returning her to be more like the Jungle Queen archetype for a time). But her experiences with the Lady Liberators reinvigorates her spirit and restores her faith in both the system and her heroic mission: "I love these women. I love the whole hero thing. But because of the events of Civil War, and finding out what Tony and his pals did to Bruce . . . I turned my back on it all. I hated it and all it stood for. But I couldn't sustain the hatred. Instead I'm re-embracing the life I thought I'd left behind . . . because I can't get enough of it" (David and Asrar, February 2009, 23). But the feminist models were not merely constrained to the in-text narrative. The art and presentation of the Lady Liberators also conformed closely to the empowerment themes (see Figure 1.3). Whereas earlier She-Hulk comics had frequently presented her as a sexual object and had drawn her in many panels as fractured body parts that focused on her sexuality, the depictions of the Lady Liberators emphasized their power and musculature, often in poses more reminiscent of their masculine counterparts.

The females on the team all possess agency, they reason with one another, and they each respect and are respected by their teammates. Perhaps most notably, during this particular story arc, She-Hulk is not once portrayed without her clothing, not even when she was tied to bed in her human form about to be raped by Darqon Par. When one considers the male gaze as a vantage point, there is simply little titillation on display. Though Reynolds (1992, 79–80) notes it is typical for female heroes to consistently act like male heroes in terms of aggression and violence, the Lady Liberators demonstrate that ability but for the most part refrain from using it to achieve their goals. When all of these observations are combined, the Lady Liberators and She-Hulk appear unusually consistent with the poststructural feminist formula in many ways.

Analyzing She-Hulk

This evolutionary arc into the leadership of the Lady Liberators completes She-Hulk's integration of the Amazon archetype into the existing Jungle Queen archetype. By combining elements of each (the mutual empowerment from the Amazons, the emotional outrage at injustice from an outsider's perspective from the Jungle Queens), She-Hulk is placed into a role in which she uses her power and status to empower other women, uses her compassion to intervene in the world without violence, explores her own sexuality on her own terms, and serves as a symbol of womanhood apart from and alongside her male colleagues. Thus, She-Hulk and the Lady Liberators appear more consistent with the general formula of Poststructural Feminist Icons than either the Jungle Queen or Amazon archetypes. A key difference common to both archetypes is the rejection of masculine violence and utilization of female companionship to reach goals. After establishing their physical abilities, the Lady Liberators use their other abilities (negotiation, reputation, and political pressure) to resolve conflict and achieve their goals within a system of mutual support for one another.

Of course, part of the difficulty in maintaining a nonviolence resolution strategy in a medium built around hypermasculine expressions is embedded within the superheroic formula. Pearson and Pope (1981) state that "the study of the heroic pattern reveals that the treasure of wholeness and selfhood is the same for both the male and the female hero and encompasses both 'male' and 'female' qualities. However because society denigrates 'feminine' qualities, a woman is not likely to value her female attributes" (14). And though there has been an increase in female readership of comic books in recent years, the superhero genre is still consumed by a largely male audience (Brown 2004, 16).

Female superheroes acting like socially conscious females instead of hypermasculine vigilantes is certainly a rarity. And of course, it remains to be seen whether the Lady Liberators will continue to collaborate, or if this model would prove viable in the long term. Comic book stories about women tell us stories about ourselves (Barker 1989, Dubose 2007, Emad 2006, Klock 2002, Reynolds 1992, Taylor 2007, Wanzo 2009), but those stories still appear to tell us more about how males think about female stereotypes than anything else. Though the number of female superhero characters has grown, "any feminist critic could demonstrate that most of these characters fail to inscribe any specific female qualities: they behave in battle like male heroes with thin waists and silicone breasts" (Reynolds 1992, 80).

Female superheroes are still largely squeezing into the roles created by the idealized male stereotype of intervention and leadership: "The superhero is first and foremost a man, because only men are understood to be protectors in US culture and only men have the balls to lead" (Stabile 2009, 87). Part of that focus is the historic formula, but the larger part is the concentration on male readership.

During the run of *The Sensational She-Hulk*, the letters columns regularly reported the presence of female readers, yet it was obvious that male readers greatly outnumbered their female counterparts. As She-Hulk explored her gender, she did so squarely within the boundaries of the male gaze (and explicitly, as she often made clear when addressing the readers directly).

But what of those female readers? Research shows that an increasing number of young girls are attracted to superhero texts and play and actively position themselves as females within a heroic discourse when the opportunity is presented (Marsh 2000). How females are presented in comic books stands to matter a great deal when one considers the ramifications for social learning and modeling.

One final structural concern considers authorship. It should be noted that of the 557 comic books reviewed for this chapter, only two She-Hulk stories were written by women. This is significant because male authors tend to write female characters as males: "The comicbook industry was so dominated by men for so long and so little attention was paid to the polysemy of comicbook texts that most of the differentiation of female characters remained at the visual level; the code, message and way of thinking were clearly male and simply transposed into the mouths and minds of heroines" (Bongco 2000, 111). It should also be mentioned that in the first of those issues, She-Hulk had her clothes torn off by a supervillain while she was in court, and that a protracted fight in her lingerie ensued (Simonson and Morgan, July 1991).

To conclude, the evolution of She-Hulk represents a complex compilation of contradictions usually present when considering a female character in a hypermasculine genre: she begins as a derivative character who superficially represents positive embodiments of her sex in American society while at the same time demonstrating a worrisome need for male validation. Unlike her cousin the Hulk, She-Hulk rejects the loner tendency in favor of relationships and the juggles that come with balancing her superhero status with her professional career. Through the years, She-Hulk moves through different creative hands and treatments, but along the way she acquires qualities from the previous flawed attempts at representing empowered female characters (most notably the Jungle Queen and Amazon archetypes) and combines the best of those qualities alongside definitions gained from a female community of peers into a new configuration of female hero that pushes her closer to becoming a post-structuralist feminist icon than either of her source archetypes generally allows.

In 2014, a new volume of *She-Hulk* appeared. The opening line of the comic stated, "No one is only one thing" (Soule and Pulido, April 2014, 1), an allusion to the narrative's attempt to show the inherent contradictions and challenges in balancing a career, duty to one's community, personal relationships, and a devotion to equality for individuals regardless of status. These competing tensions represent the challenge women face in American society and signal She-Hulk's likely continued status as a unique location for exploring possible solutions to such challenges.

Notes

1. Sometimes to comical effect, She-Hulk's frayed dress looked the same no matter what Jen Walters had been wearing before her transformation. Her initial transformation occurred in a hospital room, and the hospital gown she wore became a short dress on She-Hulk's larger frame. And though Jen wore white blouses of varying kinds, the dress She-Hulk ended up in appeared uniform through *The Savage She-Hulk* run. For example, in issue #8, Jen is clearly seen wearing a white bathing suit with spaghetti straps after transforming from She-Hulk, but when she transforms again, She-Hulk ends up wearing the same frayed white dress she always wears (Kraft, Vosburg, and Stone, September 1980, 14, 18).

2. The exception would be the rare occasion in which She-Hulk would lose control, as in *The Sensational She-Hulk* #55 (Eury and Olliffe, September 1993). In such instances, She-Hulk gains additional muscle and loses part or all of her rational faculties. Eventually, she begins to refer to this state as her "savage" state, compared to the "sensational" normal She-Hulk state.

3. In 2007, She-Hulk would be asked in court to name each of her sexual partners, a process that would take more than twenty minutes and require reams of court reporter paper (Slott, Templeton, and Burchett, July 2007, 13).

4. For examples of She-Hulk disrobing to fight, fighting in her underwear, or having her clothes torn off during a fight, see Byrne, August 1989, 15; Gerber and Hitch, October 1990, 24–30; Gerber, Dixon, and Artis, November 1990, 23–28; Gerber, Dixon, and Artis, December 1990, 1–2; Simonson and Morgan, July 1991; Byrne, April 1992, 1–5; Zimmerman and Lopresti June 1991, 19; David, Moll, and Semeiks, April 2008, 19; David and Cucca, October 2008, 12; Byrne, April 1992, 13; Furman and Levins, May 1991; Simonson and Morgan, July 1991, 9; Byrne, January 1993, 29; Byrne, March 1993, 29; Eury and Britton, June 1993, 4; and Fisch and Jensen, December 1993, 27.

5. For examples, see Gerber, Dixon, and Artis, January 1991, 19–20; Furman and Hitch, April 1991, 26; and Byrne, September 1991, 2.

6. It should be pointed out that She-Hulk author John Byrne objected strongly to many of the plot elements and statements in *The Sensational She-Hulk in Ceremony* volumes, enough so that he was removed from *The Sensational She-Hulk* for nearly two years.

References

Barker, Martin. 1989. *Comics: Ideology, Power, and the Critics*. New York: Manchester University Press.

Beerman, Ruth J. 2012. "The Body Unbound: *Empowered*, Heroism, and Body Image." *Journal of Graphic Novels and Comics* 3 (2): 201–13.

Bongco, Mila. 2000. *Reading Comics: Language, Culture, and the Concept of the Superhero in Comic Books*. New York: Garland.

Brown, Jeffrey A. 2004. "Comic Book Fandom and Cultural Capital." *Journal of Popular Culture* 30 (4): 13–31.

———. 2011. *Dangerous Curves: Action Heroines, Gender, Fetishism, and Popular Culture*. Jackson: University Press of Mississippi.

Byrne, John. April 1984. "Home Are the Heroes." *Fantastic Four* 1 (265).

———. June 1984. "A Small Loss." *Fantastic Four* 1 (267).

———. January 1985. "Monster Mash, Part Two." *Fantastic Four* 1 (274).

———. January 1985. "The Sensational She-Hulk." *Marvel Graphic Novel: The Sensational She-Hulk* 1 (18).

———. February 1985. "The Naked Truth." *Fantastic Four* 1 (275).

———. January 1986. "Like a Phoenix." *Fantastic Four* 1 (286).

———. February 1986. "Prisoner of the Flesh." *Fantastic Four* 1 (287).

———. May 1989. "Second Chance." *The Sensational She-Hulk* 1 (1).

———. June 1989. "Attack of the Terrible Toad Men or Froggy Came Cavortin." *The Sensational She-Hulk* 1 (2).

———. August 1989. "Tall Dis-order." *The Sensational She-Hulk* 1 (4).

———. November 1989. "I Have No Mouth And I Am Mean." *The Sensational She-Hulk* 1 (7).

———. December 1989. "The World's Greatest Detective." *The Sensational She-Hulk* 1 (8).

———. September 1991. "Interrupted Melody." *The Sensational She-Hulk* 1 (31).

———. February 1992. "Plastic Snow and Mistletoe." *The Sensational She-Hulk* 1 (36).

———. April 1992. "Love in Bloom." *The Sensational She-Hulk* 1 (38).

———. May 1992. "Date Worse Than Death." *The Sensational She-Hulk* 1 (39).

———. June 1992. "One Potato, Two Potato." *The Sensational She-Hulk* 1 (40).

———. July 1992. "Rock & Ruin." *The Sensational She-Hulk* 1 (41).

———. September 1992. "Battle? Why?" *The Sensational She-Hulk* 1 (43).

———. January 1993. "Master Puppet!" *The Sensational She-Hulk* 1 (47).

———. March 1993. "Who is the New She-Hulk?" *The Sensational She-Hulk* 1 (49).

Daniels, Les. 2000. *Wonder Woman: The Complete History*. San Francisco: Chronicle Books.

David, Peter, and Mahmud Asrar. February 2009. "Cosmic Collision." *She-Hulk: Cosmic Collision* 1 (1).

David, Peter, and Vincenzo Cucca. September 2008. "He Loves You: Part 2." *She-Hulk* 2 (31).

———. October 2008. *She-Hulk* 2 (32).

———. December 2008. "Lady Liberators, Part 1." *She-Hulk* 2 (34).

David, Peter, and Shawn Moll. February 2008. "Jaded: Episode 3." *She-Hulk* 2 (24).

David, Peter, Shawn Moll, and Val Semeiks. April 2008. "The Whole Hero Thing Conclusion." *She-Hulk* 2 (26).

David, Peter, and Pasquale Qualano. January 2009. "Lady Liberators, Part 2." *She-Hulk* 2 (35).

———. February 2009. "Lady Liberators, Part 3." *She-Hulk* 2 (36).

———. March 2009. "Heroic Proportions; Part 1 of 2." *She-Hulk* 2 (37).

David, Peter, and Steve Scott. March 2009. "Heroic Proportions, Part 1." *She-Hulk* 2 (37).

———. April 2009. "Heroic Proportions, Part 2." *She-Hulk* 2 (38).

Danna, Elizabeth. 2006. "Wonder Woman Mythology: Heroes from the Ancient World and Their Progeny." In *The Gospel According to Superheroes: Religion and Popular Culture*, edited by B. J. Oropeza, 67–82. New York: Peter Lang.

Dubose, Mike S. 2007. "Holding Out for a Hero: Reaganism, Comic Book Vigilantes, and Captain America." *Journal of Popular Culture* 40 (6): 915–35.

Durham, Meenakshi Gigi. 2003. "The Girling of America: Critical Reflections on Gender and Popular Communication." *Popular Communication* 1 (1): 23–31.

Emad, Mitra C. 2006. "Reading Wonder Woman's Body: Mythologies of Gender and Nation." *Journal of Popular Culture* 39 (6): 954–84.

Eury, Michael, and Todd Briton. June 1993. "To Die and Live in L.A.! Part 1." *The Sensational She-Hulk* 1 (52).

Eury, Michael, and Patrick Olliffe. September 1993. "To Die and Live in L.A.! Part 4." *The Sensational She-Hulk* 1 (55).

Fingeroth, Danny. 2004. *Superman on the Couch*. New York: Continuum.

Fisch, Sholly, and Dennie Jensen. December 1993. "Shock of the Shulkie." *The Sensational She-Hulk* 1 (58).

Furman, Simon, and Bryan Hitch. April 1991. "Trash." *The Sensational She-Hulk* 1 (27).

Furman, Simon, and Rik Levins. May 1991. "Trash." *The Sensational She-Hulk* 1 (26).

———. January 1993. "Master Puppet." *The Sensational She-Hulk* 1 (47).

Gerber, Steve, and Bryan Hitch. January 1990. "Mass-market Menace." *The Sensational She-Hulk* 1 (10).

———. October 1990. "Dorkham Asylum." *The Sensational She-Hulk* 1 (20).

Gerber, Steve, Buzz Dixon, and Tom Artis. November 1990. "Atomic Secrets." *The Sensational She-Hulk* 1 (21).

———. December 1990. "Blondes and Bombshells." *The Sensational She-Hulk* 1 (22).

———. January 1991. "Las Vegas Mon Amour." *The Sensational She-Hulk* 1 (23).

Heinecken, Dawn. 2003. *The Warrior Women of Television: A Feminist Cultural Analysis of the New Female Body in Popular Media*. New York: Peter Lang.

Housel, Rebecca. 2009. "X-Women and X-istence." In *X-Men and Philosophy*, edited by Rebecca Housel and J. Jeremy Wisnewski, 85–98. Hoboken, NJ: Wiley.

Howe, Sean. *Marvel Comics: The Untold Story*. New York: HarperCollins, 2012.

Inness, Sherrie A. 1999. *Tough Girls: Women Warriors and Wonder Women in Popular Culture*. Philadelphia: University of Pennsylvania Press.

Klock, Geoff. 2002. *How to Read Superhero Comics and Why*. New York: Continuum.

Kraft, David, and Mike Vosburg. March 1980. "Deathrace!" *The Savage She-Hulk* 1 (2).

———. July 1980. "Enter: The Invincible Iron Man." *The Savage She-Hulk* 1 (6).

———. December 1980. "The Shadow of Death." *The Savage She-Hulk* 1 (11).

———. December 1981. "The She-Hulk War!" *The Savage She-Hulk* 1 (23).

———. February 1982. "Transmutations." *The Savage She-Hulk* 1 (25).

Kraft, David, Mike Vosburg, and Danny Bulanadi. October 1980. "The Power of the Word." *The Savage She-Hulk* 1 (9).

Kraft, David, Mike Vosburg, and Frank Springer. November 1980. "War of—The Word." *The Savage She-Hulk* 1 (10).

———. January 1981. "Reason and Rage!" *The Savage She-Hulk* 1 (12).

———. February 1981. "Through the Crystal!" *The Savage She-Hulk* 1 (13).

———. April 1981. "Delusions." *The Savage She-Hulk* 1 (15).

———. May 1981. "The Zapping of the She-Hulk." *The Savage She-Hulk* 1 (16).

Kraft, David, Mike Vosburg, and Chic Stone. June 1980. "Breaking Point!" *The Savage She-Hulk* 1 (5).

———. September 1980. "Among the Ogres!" *The Savage She-Hulk* 1 (8).

Lee, Stan. 1977. *The Superhero Women*. New York: Simon & Schuster.

Lee, Stan, John Buscema, and Chic Stone. February 1980. "The She-Hulk Lives." *The Savage She-Hulk* 1 (1).

Madrid, Mike. 2009. *The Supergirls: Fashion, Feminism, Fantasy, and the History of Comic Book Heroines*. Minneapolis: Exterminating Angel Press.

Magoulick, Mary. 2006. "Frustrating Female Heroism: Mixed Messages in *Xena, Nikita,* and *Buffy.*" *Journal of Popular Culture* 39 (5): 729–55.

Marsh, Jackie. 2000. "'But I Want to Fly, Too!' Girls and Superhero Play in the Infant Room." *Gender & Education* 12 (2): 209–20.

McDuffie, Dwayne, Robin D. Chaplik, and June Brigman. October 1989. "Part 1." *The Sensational She-Hulk in Ceremony* 1 (3).

Mulvey, Laura. 1975. "Visual Please and Narrative Cinema." *Screen* 16 (3): 6–18.

Nowlan, Kevin. "The Kevin Nowlan Portfolio." *Marvel Fanfare* 1 (18): 28.

O'Reilly, Julie D. 2005. "The Wonder Woman Precedent: Female (Super)Heroism on Trial." *Journal of American Culture* 28 (3): 273–83.

Palumbo, Donald E. 1997. "Metafiction in the Comics: *The Sensational She-Hulk.*" *Journal of the Fantastic in the Arts* 8 (3): 310–30.

Pearson, Carol, and Katherine Pope. 1981. *Female Hero in American and British Literature*. New York: R. R. Bowker.

Polster, Miriam F. 1992. *Eve's Daughters: The Forbidden Heroism of Women*. San Francisco: Jossey-Bass.

Raphael, Jordan, and Tom Spurgeon. 2003. *Stan Lee and the Rise and Fall of the American Comic Book*. Chicago: Chicago Review Press.

Reynolds, Richard. 1992. *Super Heroes: A Modern Mythology*. Jackson: University Press of Mississippi.

Robinson, Lillian S. 2004. *Wonder Women: Feminisms and Superheroes*. New York: Routledge.

Savage, William. W., Jr. 1990. *Commies, Cowboys, and Jungle Queens*. Hanover, CT: Wesleyan University Press.

Shooter, Jim, Steven Grant, and Greg LaRocque. August 1982. "A Gathering of Evil!" *Avengers* 1 (222).

Shooter, Jim, David Michelinie, and Bob Hall. July 1982. ". . . New Blood!" *Avengers* 1 (221).

Simonson, Louise, and Tom Morgan. July 1991. "The Fourth Wall . . . and Beyond." *The Sensational She-Hulk* 1 (29).

———. August 1991. "A Change of State." *The Sensational She-Hulk* 1 (30).

Slot, Dan, and Joan Bubillo. May 2004. "The Girl from Gamma Gamma Gamma." *She-Hulk* 1 (1).

———. January 2006. "Cause and Effect." *She-Hulk* 2 (2).

Slot, Dan, and Rick Burchett. March 2007. "Planet without a Hulk Part One: She-Hulk, Agent of S.H.I.E.L.D." *She-Hulk* 2 (15).

———. April 2007. "Planet without a Hulk Part Two: Gamma Flight." *She-Hulk* 2 (16).

———. May 2007. "Planet without a Hulk Part Three: Shock after Shock." *She-Hulk* 2 (17).

Slot, Dan, and Will Conrad. June 2006. "Beaus and Eros Part 2: Change of the Heart." *She-Hulk* 2 (7).

Slot, Dan, and Paul Pelletier. January 2005. "Strong Enough." *She-Hulk* 1 (9).

Slot, Dan, Ty Templeton, and Rick Burchett. July 2007. "The Gamma Defense." *She-Hulk* 2 (19).

Soule, Charles, and Javier Pulido. April 2014. "The Motion." *She-Hulk* 3 (1).

Stabile, Carol A. 2009. "'Sweetheart, This Ain't Gender Studies': Sexism and Superheroes." *Communication and Critical/Cultural Studies*, 6 (1): 86–92.

Steinem, Gloria. 1995. "Introduction." In *Wonder Woman: Featuring over Five Decades of Great Covers*, edited by Amy Handy and Steven Korte, 1–15. New York: Abbeville Press.

———. 2013. "Wonder Woman." In *The Superhero Reader*, edited by Charles Hatfield, Jeet Heer, and Kent Worchester, 203–10. Jackson: University Press of Mississippi.

Stern, Roger, and Al Milgrom. August 1983. "The Witch's Tale!" *Avengers* 1 (234).

Stewart, Andrew. 1995. "Imag(in)ing the Other: Amazons and Ethnicity in Fifth-Century Athens." *Poetics Today* 4 (16): 571–97.

Stuller, Jennifer K. 2010. *Ink-Stained Amazons and Cinematic Warriors: Superwomen in Modern Mythology*. New York: I.B. Taurus.

———. 2012. "Second-wave Feminism in the Pages of *Lois Lane*." In *Critical Approaches to Comics: Theories and Methods*, edited by Matthew J. Smith and Randy Duncan, 235–51. New York: Routledge.

Taylor, Aaron. 2007. "'He's Gotta Be Strong, and He's Gotta Be Fast, and He's Gotta Be Larger Than Life': Investigating the Engendered Superhero Body." *Journal of Popular Culture* 40 (2): 344–60.

Ulaby, Neda. September 2, 2008. "The 'Bechdel Rule,' Defining Pop-Culture Character." *All Things Considered* (National Public Radio). http://www.npr.org/templates/story/story.php?storyId=94202522

Wanzo, Rebecca. 2009. "The Superhero: Meditations on Surveillance, Salvation, and Desire." *Communication and Critical/Cultural Studies* 6 (1): 93–97.

Wright, Bradford. 2001. *Comic Book Nation: The Transformation of Youth Culture in America*. Baltimore: Johns Hopkins University Press.

Zimmerman, David A. 2004. *Comic Book Character: Unleashing the Hero in Us All.* Downers Grove, IL: InterVarsity.

Zimmerman, Dwight Jon, and Aaron Lopresti. June 1991. "Licensing Lunacy." *The Sensational She-Hulk* 1 (28).

"My Skin Has Turned to Porcelain, to Ivory, to Steel": Feminist Fan Discourses, *Game of Thrones*, and the Problem of Sansa

—Alex Naylor

Henry Jenkins (2006) has commented that a potent "balance between fascination and frustration" with the source text drives fan labor, sparking fannish critical and creative activities that seek to unpick the text and to refashion as well as celebrate it (247). The activist turn within social media–based fandom has tended to politicize this critical/creative process, especially in female-majority fandom spaces, such as the communities of LiveJournal and its successor, Tumblr. As Emily Regan Wills (2013, 0.2, 1.5) argues, online fandoms are often "discourse [communities] focused on contestation," whose interrogations and transformations of the media source material "make claims about issues of real world political importance, such as the relationship between gender, power and autonomy." Through a specific case study, I wish to contend that this kind of politicized fan critical and reflective labor can function as a form of feminist praxis—one which can be seen as distinctly fannish in the intensity of both textual immersion and critical engagement.

HBO's *Game of Thrones*, the highly successful TV adaptation of George R. R. Martin's *A Song of Ice and Fire* series of fantasy novels, is a lively locus of social media–based fan activity. Much *Game of Thrones* fan labor—critical commentary, art, graphics, and fiction—has focused upon the show's treatment of its more controversial female characters. In its reception, *Game of Thrones* as a TV adaptation arguably inherited and amplified the basic feminist critical dilemma posed by its source material. Feminist critics, consumers, and fans have applauded Martin's novels for their rich variety of complex, agentic female characters and critiqued them for issues including objectification, rape used as a plot device, and uncomfortable intersections of race and gender.

The resurgence and refashioning of second-wave feminist discourse by the fourth wave for twenty-first-century networked culture poses particular questions where media consumption is concerned. The second wave's "destruction

39

of pleasure as a radical weapon" (Mulvey 1975, 7) framed active critique as refusing and dismantling the media object and consumption and pleasure as inherently passive modes that allow the object to oppressively work upon the spectator. Fourth-wave or digital native feminism, shaped by and for a networked and hypersaturated social media culture, must necessarily find alternatives. In such a culture, a separatist position of wholesale media refusal and sabotage is arguably nearly impossible, and perhaps not even desirable. The new wave of feminist discourse thus displays a distinctively tangled, invested relationship with media critique and consumption, not dissimilar from the mixture of passion and frustration that characterizes fannish media engagement. *Game of Thrones* has proved a particularly attractive object of analysis for online fourth-wave feminists, and conversely. In some *Game of Thrones* fandom communities, fannish engagement with the text becomes a means of engaging with feminist discourse, for young women in particular.

Feminist fandom debate within Tumblr *Game of Thrones* fandom has coalesced around two characters in particular who are often opposed: Arya Stark, who learns sword-fighting and disguises herself as a boy, and her sister Sansa, whose initial princess fantasies give way to stoic endurance and cunning survival strategies in the hostile environment of a medieval court. Fan debate that intersects with the feminist blogosphere reaches past the initial question, "Arya or Sansa?," to a variety of often contradictory positions clashing in the open field of public social media. To her fans, the figure of Sansa, in particular, embodies tensions between feminist ethical ideals and more compromised realities both in the textual diegesis and in the text's reception. Through her character, Sansa's fans approach questions of feminist perspectives regarding representation and consumption. This discourse of political critique is marked by its fannishness: rather than the distancing of the critical self from the text in order to assess and unpick, we see an immersed and often highly identificatory personal engagement with text and character. This is a mode of criticism strikingly distinct from feminist approaches to the same topic and text in nonfan media.

Fan perspectives upon Sansa Stark as a character often thus take the form of affectively intense appreciations of her, reflections on how her narrative refracts issues of feminist concern around young women's victimization and survival, and "defenses" of Sansa that confront her detractors and implicate the role of sexism and misogyny in some fans' vocal dislike of the character. For many young women in their teens and early twenties, this kind of pop culture critique online is their first introduction to feminist ideas.

The passionate attentions of Sansa fan discourse, like other forms of feminist media criticism, are in outward motion from media to society: beginning in textual criticism, moving on to critique of reading, and from there reaching toward the effect of internalized sexism and misogyny on women's view of each other. In the process, such fan discourse feeds into wider debates in both feminist and fandom social media spaces about what a modern feminist ethics of media consumption might look like. To borrow some of the arguments Sansa's fans make regarding her, we should not dismiss this discourse as merely naïve or immature because many of its voices are those of teenage girls, and we should attend to its capacity for nuance and generative political insight.

Fourth-Wave Feminism, Media Critique, and Fandom

The advent of digital media and the increased popularity of online social platforms has led to a well documented convergence culture, in which mainstream consumers are increasingly expected to consume and discuss media across platforms in historically fannish ways (Jenkins 2006; Williams and Zenger 2012). This growth of networked participatory culture has led to the increased accessibility and cultural prominence, even mainstreaming, of geek subcultures.

The networked culture of social media also brings discourses of media fandom, feminist activism, and consumption into contact with each other in other ways. Progressive politics and activism are increasingly a prominent part of fandom spaces on platforms like Tumblr and Twitter, and performance of them increasingly bears cultural capital within these fandom communities as fan discourses become politicized. Fan activist groups like Racebending and the Harry Potter Alliance practice what the latter call "cultural acupuncture." This phrase connotes identifying and acting upon a wider cultural pressure point through the political transformation of elements from the "shared cultural mythology" of media that "people feel an immediate emotional connection with and have an impulse to share" (Jenkins, Ford, and Green 2013, 170, 222; Kligler-Vilenchik, McVeigh-Schultz, Weitbrecht, et al. 2012; Lopez 2012).

Numerous recent critics (for example, danah boyd 2011) argue that social media increasingly constitutes a new kind of public sphere, especially for the millennial generation: 41 percent of people aged eighteen to twenty-five have engaged in political discussion or action on social media (Martin and Valenti 2012). Bryce J. Renninger (2014) draws a distinction between boyd's notion of social media sites as networked publics and the affordances of certain social networking platforms, specifically Tumblr, for networked counterpublics to convene, address, and discuss. In outlining such a distinction between public and counterpublics, he draws upon Nancy Fraser's (1990) critique of Jürgen

Habermas's notion of a singular bourgeois public sphere. Fraser argues that marginalized groups sit radically outside a hegemonic public sphere which does not include their perspectives. Exchanges of ideas within such groups form their own smaller public spheres—subaltern counterpublics—with different social values, rules, and assumptions to those of the hegemonic public sphere. The feminist movement for Fraser constitutes one such counterpublic; I would contend that, particularly in 2014, it constitutes a *number* of intersecting counterpublics.

Fraser's (1990) analysis of subaltern counterpublics noted the importance of various spaces to communication and organizing within the twentieth-century women's movement, those being "journals, bookstores, publicizing companies, film and video distribution networks, lecture series, research centers, academic programs, conferences, conventions, festivals, and local meeting places" (67). The securing, marking out, and defense of separate and/or separatist feminist spaces in which to safely gather was a particular priority for second-wave feminism. However, as Ann Travers (2003, 231) notes, in the relatively public and visible spaces of online communication—and more so with modern social media—it becomes incrementally harder to convene and organize in private, or to strictly limit who can comment in a discussion, and so separatism often necessarily gives way to other structures.

The interconnected and public networked media environment of social media has helped feminism to resurge into the cultural mainstream and to gain increased prominence in subcultures such as media fandoms. When counterpublic communications gain greater exposure to a mass audience, there is both benefit, vastly increased reach for activism and campaigning, and harm, in the form of similarly increased pushback and personal harassment of activists, such as the feminist programmers and video games critics targeted in GamerGate. Online activity is now, for good and ill, central to much activist work.[1]

Many recent commentators (for instance, Schuster 2013; Munro 2013; Keller 2011; Martin and Valenti 2012) argue that this rise in online feminism as a networked counterpublic is not simply an extension of third-wave organizing, but in fact is a generationally distinct fourth wave with its own concerns, priorities, ideas, and methods.[2] Online participation itself creates to some extent a generational divide for feminists in the same way that the extent and kind of digital participation can mark out generational and other social gaps elsewhere in Western societies (Schuster 2013, 20). Courtney Martin and Vanessa Valenti (2012), feminist bloggers themselves, describe this networked counterpublic as distinct in that "it is decentralized and accessible, unapologetically intersectional, community-oriented, catalyzes

rapid, large-scale action, and is very often youth-led" (2). Fourth-wave feminist campaigners and organizers are often young, in their twenties and even
teens (Martin and Valenti 2012, 8, 12, 27), and for them online spaces are the
primary venue for much of the work that physical and print feminist spaces
hosted for the second and third wave. Martin and Valenti refer to "conversations on blogs and Tumblrs" as "the 21st century version of consciousness
raising" (3). The Pew Internet and American Life Project has observed more
generally that young adult women ages eighteen through twenty-nine "are
the 'power users' of social networking" (Madden and Zickhur 2011). This generation of young women is the one which drives this movement and whom it
seeks to engage.

Fourth-wave feminist discourse returns to many of the central concerns of
the second wave, including sexual victimization and the cultural centrality of
the male gaze. It also arguably rejects some aspects of postmodern feminism.
However, there are significant shifts in perspective with which it approaches
these issues, including the politics of cultural consumption and critique.
Laura Mulvey (1975) ends her seminal essay "Visual Pleasure and Narrative
Cinema" (18) by arguing that feminist critique should aim for the "radical
destruction of pleasure" and the ultimate destruction of narrative cinema.
Second-wave media critique often aimed at cultural sabotage, destruction,
and refusal. Third-wave feminism interested itself more in the subversion
and remixing of mainstream culture to feminist ends. The fourth wave, while
often critiquing the optimism of postmodern feminism, does not have the
option of a separatist cultural withdrawal to alternative feminist spaces and
cultures. That is because its activism fundamentally works and thrives within
the interpenetrating networked spaces of social media. If it cannot reject
media hypersaturation, then fourth-wave feminism must find its breathing
space within it.

By this token, fourth-wave feminism blogging often embraces forms of
pop culture critique that are not grounded in outright rejection but in com-
binations of fascination and frustration which are not so dissimilar in tone
to the invested and passionate discourses of fandom. Analysis and critique
of popular culture in fact forms an important part of the fourth-wave feminist blogosphere both on general blogs major and minor, some specifically
devoted to the analysis of popular culture and media through a feminist lens.[3]
Numerous commentators and feminist bloggers have noted that media and
pop culture critique often provides a gateway to feminist thinking for young
women isolated among their offline peers (Schuster 2013, 17; Nussbaum 2011;
Martin and Valenti 2012, 12), who might "Google 'Beyoncé' or 'Real House-
wives' and then get drawn into threads about abortion" (Nussbaum 2011).

Tumblr as a Fan/Political Counterpublic Platform

Bronwyn Williams and Amy AA Zenger (2012) note that pop culture provides the "rhetorical, linguistic and semiotic building blocks" through which young people engage with the world, material which they appropriate and reuse "to perform identities and make meaning in their own lives" (3). While this is not in and of itself a new phenomenon, digital culture allows them to engage with media in an "intense, autonomous, and interest-driven way" (Itō 2009, 28) unique to the modern new media environment. They rightly caution against being "naïvely celebratory" in discussing these practices; the online fan and political spaces discussed by this essay are often neither utopian nor "safe" (ibid.). Their users can be seen to engage in reflexive analysis and critique of their own spaces. However, one can also note passionate and even romantic celebrations and defenses of these platforms. These reflect their value and importance to users, both as alternative communities offering support, enjoyment, and comradeship and as sources of reflection, learning, and personal growth.

There is rich evidence upon Tumblr that many users see pop culture critique as a gateway drug to networked feminist counterpublic discussion. In a cartoon posted on her Tumblr blog that has over thirty-two thousand notes[4] at the time of writing (karapassey 2012), artist and musician Kara Passey pictures herself, head in hands, while a huge speech bubble proclaims in capitals, "I'm addicted to feminist media criticism," and below, in much smaller script, "I can never enjoy something quietly again." Smaller panels show her commenting upon media while consuming it: "that song is so sexist," "this video game is full of racist stereotypes," "this author is a misogynistic asshole." Thousands of reblogging users comment concisely in tags and text comments about how accurately she has nailed their predicament: "same," "about me," "same here," "literally me," "oh my god it's so true," "gpoy" ("gratuitous picture of yourself," an acronym meaning that something is so accurate to the user you could call it a selfie).

While Tumblr is a much smaller social networking platform than Facebook or Twitter, it is significantly more popular among the young: 13 percent of American eighteen-to-twenty-nine-year-olds online blog on Tumblr (Duggan and Brenner 2013, 13). It is also a locus for a rich variety of counterpublics and subcultures: "feminists, queers, trans* people, and alienated youth" among others from vegans to media fandoms (Renninger 2014, 8; Thelandersson 2013; Fink and Miller 2013; Cho 2011). The Pew Internet and American Life project, among others (Lenhart, Purcell, Smith, et al. 2010), has recently noted the relative discomfort of many youth at using Facebook, where they are observed by a large network of family, peers, and acquaintances, for certain kinds of communication and expression. Schuster (2013) reports that certain groups particularly value the anonymity offered by blogging and social media platforms that, like Tumblr, allow pseudonyms and control of how much real-life information users give out (18). Renninger (2014) cites many young bloggers' passionate declarations of Tumblr's personal importance to them as a space for alternative community, sparked by fears over Yahoo's purchase of the platform in May 2013 (8). In its pseudonymity, Tumblr offers these bloggers escape from the scrutiny of family and acquaintances, a place where they can "be themselves" and "speak their minds." Renninger (ibid. 2014, 2) further argues that pseudonymous social media platforms like Tumblr offer an attractive space for young people and counterpublics vulnerable to ridicule and disruption online (ibid.). While the pseudonym or pen name is far from a secure fortress against trolling and harassment, it constitutes a more ephemeral form of identity from which the user potentially has the power to step away.

The shift of media fan communities and their creative activity from older blogging platforms such as LiveJournal to Tumblr has inevitably led to numerous shifts in the way fans convene, discuss, and share information. One such notable shift has been an increase in mobility and permeability. The many communities upon Tumblr often encounter each other due to the platform's specific affordances. The blurring of public and private that characterizes social media takes a particular form here (boyd 2011, 49). All blogs are pseudonymous and bloggers share personal information such as names and photographs only by choice. However, blogs on Tumblr are either entirely private and password protected or entirely public and open to reblogging and commentary by any user of the site. Thus, most conversation on Tumblr takes place in public, and anonymity and obscurity often take the place of privacy.

In addition, commenting upon a post is in most cases only possible through reblogging and annotating it with further comment in the body or in new hashtags appended to the bottom of the post. Posts are viewed on an aggregated timeline news feed of blogs one follows, similar to Twitter and Facebook, or via browsing hashtags to see all posts tagged with a topic or phrase. The emphasis upon reblogging and sharing means posts are highly mobile within the platform and often subject to commentary that alters, adds to, critiques, or questions their meaning and import. Tumblr's affordances as a platform thus often render communications within specific communities highly visible outside that community. The dashboard format means that users encounter posts from the blogs they follow in a timeline that mixes users and subject matters: "[asexual identity politics] posts . . . show up . . . next to cat videos and fan art" (Renninger 2014, 4–5), and every user who sees a post on their dashboards will see it in a different, individualized, personal context.

Many users browse the tags for favorite media, characters, and romantic pairings. Since any user can tag a post however they like, tags are also often employed by hostile users to disrupt discussion. Thus, for example, a character name tag like #Sansa will often contain provocative "character hate" posts from bloggers seeking the attention of her fans, and political tags like #feminism also end up hosting antifeminist commentary. Pseudonymous platforms also offer an increased potential for confrontation and hostility: the freedom of expression Tumblr offers is also used for fierce and direct disagreement and criticism, sometimes to the extent of hostility and serious harassment (Schuster 2013, 19).

These factors—a user base that skews young, highly mobile, and spreadable posting, and the concomitant exposure of users to a wide variety of communities, topics, and discourses—mean that feminist pop culture critique on Tumblr often takes particular forms. As I shall explore, this is richly evident in responses to *Game of Thrones*.

Doylist Critiques and Watsonian Engagements

The TV series *Game of Thrones* and the novels by George R. R. Martin that it adapts have been a particularly strong source of mixed delight and frustration to feminist commentators online. Set in a pseudomedieval world with some elements of fantasy, the novels and series draw heavily upon the aspects of medieval European societies and cultures that fantasy and historical texts often gloss over. Both novels and show make a point of realism that presents not just privies and leechings but also a systemically brutal society, where life is cheap for even kings, but proportionally cheaper the less powerful and more marginalized a person is. The novel series *A Song of Fire and Ice* and the TV show *Game of Thrones* are both at core about power relations, more specifically about systemic and personal abuses of power and the efforts of many individual characters to survive in this toxic and dangerous environment. However, Martin's treatment of female characters is arguably the most important factor in the amount of feminist virtual ink spilled over show and books. This is also, arguably, the source of the book's and show's large female audience. In the show's third season, women made up 42 percent of its audience and 50 percent of its positive commentators on social media (Watercutter 2013).

Feminist discussion of *Game of Thrones* in nonfan media and the progressive blogosphere has tended to deploy close textual analysis of style and representation to unpack issues of gender and power. I outline some of the discursive characteristics of this discussion in order that we may note both the commonalities of concerns and the distinct difference of approach displayed within Sansa fandom.

Feminist viewers of *Game of Thrones* must wrestle with issues including the reproduction of a heterosexual male gaze through camerawork, including "sexposition" scenes where gratuitous sexualized female nudity livens up talky plot exposition; with the depiction of a culture where rape and abuse are utterly normalized; and the extent to which Daenarys's status as female leader and general comes at the cost of a generous application of the "white savior" trope. Rebekah Owens (2013) critiques the camera's objectification of women and further argues that the depiction of this intensely misogynist society carries a "subliminal message" of "fantasies of female subjugation." Sady Doyle (2011) has similarly argued that the books are a "fundamentally conservative" sexist fantasy aimed at men.

Much feminist commentary upon *Game of Thrones*, however, voices "fascination and frustration" rather than outright condemnation. *Game of Thrones* contains an unusually large, diverse, and complex set of female characters within its cast for modern Western television, particularly within the SF/fantasy genres. Its women and girls are for the most part agentic and complex; their actions often drive the plot; and in the case of many, including Sansa, we are invited to see events from their perspective. For instance, while voicing discomfort with the show's relentless depiction of abuse and violence toward its female characters, Andi Zeisler (2013) of *Bitch* magazine comments upon the "sheer numbers" and variety of women in its cast: "not an army of super-human, you-go-girl ass-kickers with no complicating romantic lives or moral failings, but a glorious array of faceted, complex, problematic, not-sure-if-they-can-be-trusted human beings." *Game of Thrones* offers potential for both a validation of and a challenge to a basic Mulveyan critique of the objectified woman-as-spectacle, who stands opposite the camera- and viewer-identified male protagonist.

Laurie Slavin of *Feminspire* comments similarly that while "many women have been unable to read or watch because of the heavy presence of rape and what often feels like gratuitous nudity, George R. R. Martin's female characters play the hands dealt to them to the best of their ability in a patriarchy that subdues them at all costs" (Slavin 2013). Alyssa Rosenberg (2011) defends the choice of women and feminists to engage with the show, suggesting that the "endemic sexual violence" of Westeros invites politicized reading and consideration of the relation of fictional world to real. Fantasy "fiction that has some tie to, amplifies, or inverts our current problems is actively useful" for feminists and other progressives, requiring as it does from the reader "active consumption and debate."

The "glorious array" of flawed and interesting women that appeal to many commentators in the series is in itself a point of feminist contention. Doyle and Owens both argue that none of the female characters successfully "represent[s] feminist values" (Owens 2013). Owens considers only the HBO show's two queen figures: Cersei, who fails to adequately handle her power as regent, and Daenarys, who "has to make too many compromises in order to be powerful." Rosenberg takes issue with the underlying assumptions of this stance. Arguing first that its male and female characters are similarly complex and flawed, she continues that a putative feminist standard that female characters be both idealized and embedded in a nonsexist world would mean that "we can't tell any very interesting stories about women's struggles and women's liberation" (Rosenberg 2013).

Feminist critics' difficult relationship with the show often generates broader reflections upon the dilemmas of media consumption. Latoya Peterson (2011) of *Racialicious*, noting the "race and gender issues" of the show, reflects on the dilemmas of consumption for black feminist fans posed by the general prevalence of racism and sexism within SF/fantasy. Peterson locates her "informed choice" to consume and enjoy *Game of Thrones* and its source novels with a consciousness of their flaws as an experience common to "fen [fans] of color." Peterson's self-identification as a fan as well as a black feminist is not uncommon in more pop-culture-focused online feminist spaces, reflecting both a geekification of some feminisms and the increasing phenomenon of feminist voices speaking up in geek spaces.

Fan discussion of *Game of Thrones* on Tumblr and nonfan feminist media critiques circulated within fandom (although such a distinction is hard to draw cleanly) sometimes take similar approaches to media criticism to those in the wider feminist blogosphere, amplifying the feminist dilemma of speaking out as fans in the intensity of their engagements and disengagements. However, much of the fandom takes another route to engaging with the show's and books' problematics, and it is this I wish to examine. The community within *Game of Thrones* and *A Song of Ice and Fire* fandom that identifies specifically as Sansa fans is founded in a deep investment and empathy with Sansa and her situation, experiencing both validating empathy with her suffering and celebration of her endurance and survival.

The difference between the two critical discourses might usefully be referred to using a vernacular theoretical distinction common in online media fandoms: *Doylist* versus *Watsonian.*[5] Doylist approaches to a text seek to understand and analyze it as a constructed fictional artifact, for example, a 1903 short story written by Arthur Conan Doyle. Watsonian analysis, on the other hand, accepts the story's premise that it is a documentary record of actual events recorded by Dr. John Watson and seeks explanation for aspects of the work by looking purely within the fictional diegesis. Watsonian fan discussion is by its nature immersed and highly imaginatively engaged. It is also often speculative and creative, seeking to plug unexplained narrative gaps or contradictions with creative speculation, where a Doylist analysis would expose them. Watsonian fan discussion often attends to the unseen aspects of a text where reader and viewer imagination is invited regarding such matters as romantic subtext and character motivation.

The Defense of Sansa in Fandom

The line of Sansa's from Martin's *A Storm of Swords* that titles this chapter is one of the most popular Sansa quotations for her fandom, which often uses it as a slogan emblematic of her character and her development through the books and show, despite the fact that this line never appears in the show, only the source novel.

After the murder of her former fiancé, the abusive, cruel, and foolish young King Joffrey, at his own wedding, Sansa immediately finds herself a prime suspect, but Ser Dontos, a former knight whose life she talked Joffrey into sparing, offers to help her escape into hiding overseas. As she prepares to flee the city, she notes her own "numb and dreamy" dissociative state, but also an uncontrollable overflowing of affect, even "tears of joy" at her abuser's demise: "The gods are just, thought Sansa. . . . The gods heard my prayer, she thought. She felt so numb and dreamy. My skin has turned to porcelain, to ivory, to steel" (Martin 2000, 565).

While the last line could be taken as a poetic evocation of her numbness, it also has other implications. Sansa has survived her abuser and is about to finally escape her prison. Although her fate is uncertain, her options are still limited, and her survival is dependent upon trusting others, there is an undercurrent of unsteady triumph in this passage—and even a sense of transformation. The materials evoked, all hard, are progressively less fragile and more durable. The line implicitly suggests a shift in the quality or uses of Sansa's numbness: from a decorative and fragile hollowness to armor protecting a living body.

Fan-made GIF sets (image series, often animated short moving clips) and graphics featuring Sansa often use this line as a slogan emblematic of Sansa's endurance and survival and of her growth throughout the series. Several

typical GIF sets accompany the phrase with stills from the show depicting
moments of testing, trauma, and resistance for the character, while the ageing
of Sophie Turner, the teenage actor who plays Sansa, over four seasons provides a visual index of her journey from innocence to experience (cosmiclara
2014; asongoficeandfiregraphics 2012; theperksofbeinggiullia 2014). Perhaps
the most popular moment of all is a shot from the last episode of season
1: a close-up of Sansa, head lowered and looking upwards, eyes glowering,
lip bloodied, newly an effective prisoner within the court. Her fiancé, King
Joffrey, has just forced her to view her father's and nurse's decapitated heads
displayed on pikes on the battlements. As she is held in place and ordered to
look, her mood shifts from hysterical crying to a chilly calm. Joffrey threatens
to decapitate her rebel brother Robb, too; she coolly suggests Robb might
offer her Joffrey's. He slaps her; she responds by silently considering pushing
him from the battlements to his death (indicated through point-of-view camerawork in the show and narration in the novel). The scene is a marked step
forward for Sansa, suggesting she possesses reserves of character, shrewdness,
and endurance much deeper than so far seen.

Sansa's fans are emphatic that her appeal and iconicity to them are not
diminished by her vulnerability, her victimization, or the constant attempts
of others to manipulate her and remove her agency. In fact, her endurance
and quiet resistance in a hostile and dangerous environment is often cited
as a source of this appeal. As one blogger comments in tags to a reblogged
image post:

> #this is the evolution of one girl's descent into reality #she is being ripped from
> childhood and told 40 different things about who to trust and what to do #and
> her knight in shining armor turns out to be a horrible person #and her father
> doesn't even understand her #this loving man she adores doesn't even know she
> doesn't like dolls #i mean haven't we all had that? #where we expect someone to
> know and love us completely #and then it turns out they expect us to be someone
> else? #it's hard okay #and for sansa it means rebelling in little ways (fuckyeah-
> sansastark 2012)

Another blogger responds to the same image post: "#The way she begins to
understand how the world around her works and #how she learns to play the
game in the only way she knows how #Her progression and ability to continue
growing emotionally physically and mentally in a world where she's being
thrown every single punch #is just absolutely beautiful to me" (ibid. 2012).

Sansa's "descent into reality" is for both these bloggers, and for many others,
a revelation of—and a head-on confrontation with—the gendered violence

underlying the princess narrative. Bloggers emphasize and appreciate Sansa's endurance and growth in conditions of abuse and danger, in terms that move from "her" to "we" and "me." This movement toward affective identification also displays reflection upon the parallels between Sansa's experiences of oppression and survival and fans' own experiences.

Some fans express admiration too for a trait of Sansa's that marks her out as unusual among the series's characters and their means of survival. Despite her disillusionment, her growing necessary cunning, and her immersion in an amoral environment, Sansa's own moral code remains unchanged and uncorrupted. One blogger comments in tags to a reblogged image post that "#after all she is made to go through #she can still find it within herself to be kind . . . #that's a strength few people could barely dream of #it's sansa's kindness that defines her #the fact that she can live through what she's lived through and still look for goodness in people #it's remarkable" (whoistorule 2014). One blogger's close reading of the "porcelain, ivory, steel" line argues that it refers to the integrity she retains through her development, "[drawing] attention to the fact that the changes—though great—do not signify her metamorphosis into an entirely different person; the body is the same, merely enclosed in a different skin" (littlesteelbird 2012). Most *Game of Thrones* characters who begin with principles and ideals find them gradually sheared away by the dystopian world of the text; Sansa is one of the few who contravenes this textual tendency to moral drift. As well as identifiable and sympathetic, she is framed as admirable, even iconic.

As for her fans, the text is refocused into Sansa's bildungsroman; she remains steely despite her kindness and agentic despite others' attempts to control her: "She is not a force to be ignored, and anyone who thinks she's weak or useless needs to sit down and reassess their view of this girl who's been robbed of the life she used to know, who has come out of the other side with winter in her bones" (floydlawton 2013).

If a defensive thread can be detected in these passionate fannish celebrations of Sansa's qualities, there is arguably reason for it. Sansa's appreciators find themselves in a combative social media environment where browsing activity exposes them to tagged public denunciations of the character they are seeking to celebrate. One such tagged post complains that Sansa is "totally shallow, selfish, and she fails to take responsibility. She's apathetic and passive" (drinkingtea-and-readingbooks 2014). Another Sansa fan blogger comments that "I have seen all sorts of accusations laid at Sansa's feet: 'she's whiny,' 'she's naïve,' 'she's a snob,' 'it's her fault Ned died'" (queencersei 2014). This issue is vastly amplified outside the female-majority fandom spaces of Tumblr—including on the novels' and show's semiofficial fan forums endorsed by

George R. R. Martin, westeros.org. Tumblr's young female fans often comment that they have found such forums an uncomfortable space to inhabit as female geeks, in part because of misogynistic commentary leveled at female characters.

Fan defenses of Sansa tend to approach their subject from two angles, often within the same post. Reflections and analysis focusing upon "Sansa hate" offer point-by-point rebuttals and argue for an appreciation of the character. One such post is subtitled "A rage post, brought to you by an enraged eighteen (almost nineteen!) year old feminist who . . . gets pissy when people tag their hate and/or leave Sansa off their lists of 'strong women'" (ofhouseadama 2012).

However, "defense of Sansa" posts also often move beyond this approach, attempting to unpick the gender-based narratives underlying character hate. Just as Sansa appreciators foreground her identity as a teenage girl, their appreciation is grounded in the notion that to be a teenage girl is to be embattled and attacked; their appreciation is already a defense. Sansa antifandom becomes another source of reflection and insight into the condition of being a teenage girl within our fiction, our culture, our society. Commenting upon "frequent hate in the Sansa tag," one blogger notes that "much of the hate Sansa receives is indeed sexist or misogynist in tone" (fyeahsophieturner 2012). In a post titled "In Defense of Sansa Stark," one of many on Tumblr by different authors so titled, another blogger argues that her "crime" for fandom is really "the unforgivable fact that she is a pre-teen girl" (aquanautic 2012).

One recurring concern of Sansa defenses is the comparison of Sansa and her story to that of her younger sister, Arya. Arya is introduced in books and the TV show as an archetypal pre-teen tomboy, requesting archery and sword-fighting lessons and deriding her sister's naïve dreams of marrying a prince. However, Arya's narrative departs from its stereotypical course once she becomes a fugitive after their father's execution. She stabs another child to death during her initial escape, and her embrace of the sword as a means to survival leads her to repeated murders and to apprenticeships under assassins and mercenaries. Within the bloody and brutal "realist fantasy" diegesis of Westeros, Arya's fantasies of knighthood are shown to be as naïve as Sansa's dreams about the life of a princess. Both court lady and swordswoman are trapped in their positions and fighting for survival within the same toxic system.

Fan comparisons of Arya and Sansa often, perhaps predictably, treat the characters as competitors and seek to establish which is "better," flattening the characters into "badass" tomboy and "weak" princess. Meanwhile, self-labeled feminist fan analysis of the two girls often picks apart the sexist undercurrents of such comparisons and reaches past the competitive model to argue that the two sisters can be seen in more fruitful ways than as rivals for the audience's sympathy. Here again the media text object provides material to explore an issue with wide and recognizable real world implications for girls and young women.

One blogger comments, in response to an anonymous question from a commentator who confesses "she really [dislikes] Sansa," that although "[a lot of] people throw Sansa to the street because they compare her to Arya and somehow find her wanting. . . . Sansa and Arya mirror each other textually" (apriki 2012). Another blogger comments she finds it "unfortunate" that sexism causes some fans to miss out on the fact that Sansa and Arya are "meant to be taken together, and appreciated together as deconstructions of two fantasy tropes: the tomboy and the princess." She further argues that "it is completely understandable to prefer one character to another, but if your reasons for doing so are because Arya embodies traditionally masculine qualities while Sansa survives with traditionally feminine qualities then be prepared to get called out on your deeply flawed logic" (fyeahsophieturner 2012). Arguing against the stereotyping of both characters by competitive comparisons, a third post explores the sisters' parallels in detail, arguing that "Arya and Sansa actually use the same strategy to survive." The same post points out that they both idealize knights and become brutally disillusioned, both change disguises and names, both have moments when they react similarly to trauma, both survive abuse and brutality, both have potential for compassion, and both have relationships with the violent but morally ambiguous Sandor Clegane (jeynewaters 2013). Watsonian emotional engagement in these analyses leads not to playing favored characters off each other in competition. Instead, these bloggers put forth an alternative route that feminists of all waves would recognize: toward political analysis, toward a sense of solidarity (which here doesn't seek to undo difference or impose a norm), to Woolf's "Chloe liked Olivia." Sansa fandom itself can be seen as a source of identification and solidarity. Who are we? We are fans of Sansa, united by appreciating and defending this fictional character.

One way of communicating this parallelism graphically is through animated GIF sets using a series of screen captures from the show, which by showing images of the sisters next to one another both suggests the similarities under their contrast and gives both characters equal weight. These often use a descriptor for the sisters popular within fandom: two sides of the same coin. One such GIF set juxtaposes images of Arya dirty, short-haired, and on the run and Sansa in court getup, facing each other, both appearing to turn and look towards the viewer (dgrays 2012). Another, again with the same caption (gloriouslilyevans 2014), which accumulated over 11,156 notes in its first two weeks of circulation, shows images of the two girls smiling next to close-ups of Arya's sword and Sansa's necklace (used, although without her knowledge, to smuggle the poison that murders Joffrey). A third popular GIF set (14,387 notes at the time of writing), again using parallel images of each sister, depicts their journeys: showing them in motion, running away and growing up (catofthecanals 2013). The final images of the set show them both staring out to sea, backs to the viewer, eyes implicitly to the horizon. The GIF set locates them both as heroes of their own unfinished stories, and like the others, it suggests to the viewer that they are characters to be appreciated together.

Some posts critique the fandom rivalry between Sansa girls and Arya girls in feminist terms. One post argues that this fandom rivalry is a synecdoche of a wider societal sexism, "false dichotomies set up and perpetuated by a society that thinks girls can only be one thing" (deanisthenewcain 2014). She goes on to couch a feminist rallying cry in fandom terms:

> We have to come to the realization that the distinction between us and the Sansa-girls is a fairy tale, if we're ever going to find the strength to survive in a world that is dedicated to keeping women in boxes and binders, and trapped under glass ceilings. . . . We have to learn that we all have strength in different forms and guises, and use that strength to put an end to the social structures and cultural attitudes that encouraged us all to conform to stereotypes, and hate each other for it. We have to learn to direct our ire at the right things and people instead of uselessly expending it fighting each other. . . . When it comes down to it, we're all Starks being slowly killed off by Lannisters. (ibid.)

The writer invites fellow fans to let their passionate identification with Arya or Sansa lead them towards wider reflection upon the power structures that constrain and oppress both girls within the text—and from there, to reflect upon their own experiences of oppression, to transform their interactions with other female fans, to consider the potential power of solidarity. Here, the feminist fan's Watsonian emotional immersion in the diegesis and attachment to a single character does not lead to escapism or a narrow and selective engagement with the text. Instead, the writer argues, it returns the fan to her own experience with oppressive structures in the real world, now with new insight.

Conclusions: "For all the women I have loved who were dragged through the mud"

It is perhaps unsurprising that a platform with a large blogging community of young women in their teens and twenties, often feminist-minded, should produce so much lively discourse in defense of a character derided for being too much like a teenage girl. Through their engagement, Tumblr's young feminists discover old problems, unpleasantly familiar to every generation of feminists: the cultural deprecation of what is coded feminine and the notion that all women must be in perpetual competition with one another.

Sansa, of course, is not the only fictional teenage girl subjected to vitriolic character hate and impassioned defenses. In fact, the defense of Sansa Stark can be located in terms of a wider youth feminist discourse on Tumblr that seeks to unpack and problematize the cultural deprecation of real and fictional teenage girls, including their use as whipping girls for sexism and misogyny in media. Elsewhere on Tumblr, a phenomenally popular nonfandom post, with over 150,000 notes accrued over two months, reads as follows in its entirety: "What men don't understand is that women are FIERCELY PROTECTIVE of underage girls because we remember when we were young and some adult man made us uncomfortable or manipulated us or was inappropriate with us and we were powerless" (foxtrotsky 2014). Tags added by another blogger and frequently reblogged read "#teenage girls are so important #all young girls are so important #i will kill a thousand men to protect young girls #with my bare hands" (beahleah 2012).

Much recent public and mainstream discussion of appropriate media icons for young women has tended to directly pit heroines in competition against one another, as with Arya and Sansa. There is also Katniss versus Bella Swan. If Katniss is better than Bella Swan, though, why turn denunciations towards Bella herself rather than critique the troubling sexual politics underlying the text in which she is embedded? In a lengthy Tumblr essay, "For all the women I have loved who were dragged through the mud," aiffe (2013) unpacks potential reasons underlying the misogynistic character hate she sees leveled at female characters within female-dominated fandom spaces. aiffe argues that "it's always that the female characters aren't good enough, even when they obviously have a double standard, and they're measuring women on an impossible scale full of contradictions and no-win binds." She urges fellow feminist fans to self-examine regarding internalized misogyny in their attitudes to female characters: "We've all got fucking toxic shit in our heads from living in this toxic world. No one is immune."

I think every woman hates women a little, even the ones who fiercely love women harder just to fight that. This world hates women and we're part of this world" (aiffe 2013).

Visible, too, in the defense of Sansa Stark are the attempts of young feminists to both validate and unpack the self: the experiences and traumas of female adolescence, the passionate consumptions and productions of media fandom, the revelations of feminist ideas in new and old forms. Feminist fans invite each other to treat the creative and critical discourse through which they interact, the "doing of fandom," as praxis. Through these intensities of engagement with a beloved character and the insights these generate, they ultimately propose to transform the fan communities they inhabit. Consciousness-raising for the twenty-first century, indeed.

Notes

1. To give some examples: a vibrant feminist blogosphere, many of whose writers bring their voices to the mainstream media; activist organizations like Hollaback! (which tackles street harassment); grassroots campaigning, debate, and sharing of stories on Twitter through retweeting and hashtags like #everydaysexism; the rapid mobilization of a large international cohort through social media publicity in campaigns like #Delhibraveheart or No More Page Three; and the use of social media to organize and publicize offline actions, consumer boycotts, and protests.

2. In this chapter, I draw a distinction between this recently emerged new generation of young digital-native feminists and the Generation X-adjacent Third Wave generation as coined by Rebecca Walker in her 1992 article for *Ms.* magazine (Walker 1992, 39–41). Twenty-two years separate the 1970 Miss World feminist protest and Walker's article; twenty-two years separate her article and this year. However, in this stance I acknowledge that the validity of the "fourth wave" as a concept is not uncontroversial. See Cullen and Fischer (2014) and Nicholson (2010) for fuller discussion of the validity and drawbacks of the wave metaphor to draw generational distinctions within feminism.

3. A few examples of influential and well-known general blogs include *Feministing*, the more commercial *Jezebel*, and in the United Kingdom, *The F Word*. Well-known blogs and online magazines that focus exclusively on or mainly examining pop culture from intersectional feminist perspectives include *Feminist Frequency* (subtitled "Conversations with Pop Culture"), *Racialicious* ("the intersection of race and culture"; "a hip-hop feminist and anti-racist view on culture"), *Crunk Feminist Collective* (a "space of support and camaraderie for hip hop generation feminists of color"), *Autostraddle* (a "progressively feminist online community for a new generation of kickass lesbian, bisexual & otherwise inclined ladies," which grew out of a fan blog for the lesbian TV show *The L Word*), and *The Border House* ("Our goal is to bring thoughtful analysis to gaming with a feminist viewpoint").

4. On Tumblr, notes are the total number of likes and reblogs. They are the measure of the popularity of a post.

5. These terms, coined within Sherlock Holmes fandom in the 1980s or earlier, spread to general use in online fandom during the early 2000s (Fanlore 2012).

References

aiffe. 2013. "For all the women I have loved who were dragged through the mud." *Tumblr*. February 21. http://aiffe.tumblr.com/post/43660300604/for-all-the-women-i-have-loved-who-were-dragged-through (accessed April 30, 2014).

apriki. 2012. "I really really dislike Sansa. Are you judging me or do you get where I'm coming from even though you like her?" *Tumblr*. March 13 (accessed April 23, 2014). http://apriki.tumblr.com/post/19229537463/i-really-really-dislike-sansa-are-you-judging-me-or-do (accessed April 23, 2014).

aquanautic. 2012. "In defense of Sansa Stark." *Tumblr*. June 17. http://aquanautic.tumblr.com/post/25272505949/in-defense-of-sansa-stark-sansa-stark-must-be-one (accessed April 23, 2014).

asongoficeandfiregraphics, 2012. "my skin has turned to porcelain, to ivory, to steel." *Tumblr*. August 23. http://asongoficeandfiregraphics.tumblr.com/post/30048182322/my-skin-has-turned-to-porcelain-to-ivory-to (accessed April 22, 2014).

beahleah. 2012. Untitled post. February 28. *Tumblr*. http://beahbeah.tumblr.com/post /782 64897104/foxtrotsky-what-men-dont-understand-is-that (accessed March 20, 2014).

boyd, danah. 2011. "Social Network Sites as Networked Publics: Affordances, Dynamics, and Implications." In *Networked Self: Identity, Community, and Culture on Social Network Sites*, edited by Zizi Papacharissi, 39–58. New York: Routledge.

catofthecanals. 2013. Untitled post. *Tumblr*. November 18. http://catofthecanals.com/post /67410818448/they-are-the-daughters-of-winter-the-children (accessed April 23, 2014).

Cho, Alexander. 2011. "Queer Tumblrs, Networked Counterpublics." Paper presented at the annual meeting of the International Communication Association, Boston, MA, May 25.

cosmiclara. 2014. "Game of Thrones character evolutions 2/?" *Tumblr*. March 16. http://cosmiclara.tumblr.com/post/79790111297/game-of-thrones-character-evolutions-2-sansa (accessed April 22, 2014).

Cullen, Pauline, and Clara Fischer. 2014. "Conceptualising Generational Dynamics in Feminist Movements: Political Generations, Waves, and Affective Economies." *Sociology Compass* 8 (3): 282–93.

deanisthenewcain. 2014. "Falling under Friendly Fire: Arya Girls vs. Sansa Girls." *Tumblr*. April 18. http://deanisthenewcain.tumblr.com/post/83125665569/falling-under-friendly-fire-arya-girls-vs-sansa-girls (accessed April 21, 2014).

dgrays. 2012. Untitled post. *Tumblr*. March 12. http://dgrays.tumblr.com/post/19183760804 /two-sides-of-the-same-coin (accessed April 23, 2014).

Doyle, Sady. 2011. "Enter Ye Myne Mystic World of Gayng-Raype: What the 'R' Stands for in 'George R. R. Martin.'" *Tiger Beatdown*. August 26. http://tigerbeatdown.com/2011/08/26

/enter-ye-myne-mystic-world-of-gayng-raype-what-the-r-stands-for-in-george-r-r
-martin (accessed April 4, 2014).

drinkingtea-and-readingbooks. 2014. "Sansa Rant." *Tumblr.* January 27. http://drinkingtea
-and-readingbooks.tumblr.com/post/74775624130/sansa-rant (accessed April 23, 2014).

Duggan, Maeve, and Joanna Brenner. 2013. "The Demographics of Social Media Users—
2012." *Pew Internet & American Life Project.* http://www.pewinternet.org/2013/02/14/the
-demographics-of-social-media-users-2012 (accessed April 23, 2014).

Fanlore. 2012. "Watsonian vs. Doylist." *Fanlore.* Organization for Transformative Works.
http://fanlore.org/wiki/Watsonian_vs._Doylist (accessed April 23, 2014).

Fink, Marty, and Quinn Miller. 2013. "Trans Media Moments: Tumblr, 2011–2013." *Television
& New Media.* Doi:10.1177/1527476413505002.

floydlawton. 2013. "That's not how you play the game. You don't just blurt out the right answer."
Tumblr. April 1. http://deadshot.co.vu/post/46817571079 (accessed March 4, 2014).

foxtrotsky. 2014. Untitled post. *Tumblr.* February 28. http://foxtrotsky.tumblr.com/post/780
82639234/what-men-dont-understand-is-that-women-are (accessed March 20, 2014).

Fraser, Nancy. 1990. "Rethinking the Public Sphere: A Contribution to the Critique of Actually Existing Democracy." *Social Text* 25 (26): 56–80.

fuckyeahsansastark. 2012. Untitled post. *Tumblr.* February 11. http://fuckyeahsansastark.
tumblr.com/post/17433559560/glasslightss-aragorns-oh-sorry-you-cant (accessed March
15, 2014).

fyeahsophieturner. 2012. Untitled post. *Tumblr.* October 21. http://fyeahsophieturner.tumblr
.com/post/34043802148/it-seems-like-there-is-more-frequent-hate-in-the (accessed
March 29, 2014).

Game of Thrones. 2011– . HBO. Television.

gloriouslilyevans. 2014. Untitled post. *Tumblr.* April 12. http://gloriouslilyevans.tumblr.com
/post/82524856040/two-sides-of-the-same-coin (accessed April 23, 2014).

Itō, Mizuko. 2009. *Living and Learning with New Media: Summary of Findings from the Digital Youth Project.* Cambridge, MA: MIT Press.

Jenkins, Henry. 2006. *Convergence Culture: Where Old and New Media Collide.* New York:
NYU Press.

Jenkins, Henry, Sam Ford, and Joshua Green. 2013. *Spreadable Media: Creating Value and
Meaning in a Networked Culture.* New York: NYU Press.

jeynewaters. 2013. "The parallels between Sansa and Arya Stark's storylines." August 22.
http://jeynewaters.tumblr.com/post/59063243925/the-parallels-between-sansa-and-arya
-starks-storylines (accessed April 22, 2014).

karapassey. 2012. "Everything makes me grumpy." February 18. http://karapassey.tumblr.com
/post/17857832011/everything-makes-me-grumpy (accessed March 31, 2014).

Keller, Jessalynn Marie. 2011. "Virtual Feminisms." *Information, Communication, and Society*
15 (3): 429–47.

Kligler-Vilenchik, Neta, Joshua McVeigh-Schultz, Christine Weitbrecht, et al. 2012. "Experiencing Fan Activism: Understanding the Power of Fan Activist Organizations through
Members' Narratives." *Transformative Works & Cultures* 10. Doi:10.3983/twc.2012.0322.

Lenhart, Amanda, Kristen Purcell, Aaron Smith, et al. 2010. "Social Media & Mobile Internet
Use among Teens and Young Adults. Millennials." *Pew Internet & American Life Project.*

http://www.pewinternet.org/2010/02/03/social-media-and-young-adults. (accessed April 23, 2014).

littlesteelbird. 2012. "Sansa Stark." *Tumblr*. June 5. http://littlesteelbird.tumblr.com/post/2444 6379001/sansa-stark (accessed March 14, 2014).

Lopez, Lori Kido. 2012. "Fan Activists and the Politics of Race in The Last Airbender." *International Journal of Cultural Studies* 15 (5): 431–45.

Madden, Mary, and Kathryn Zickuhr. 2011. "65% of Online Adults Use Social Networking Sites," *Pew Internet and American Life Project*. http://pewinternet.org/Reports/2011 /Social-Networking-Sites.aspx (accessed April 23, 2014) (accessed April 23, 2014).

Martin, Courtney, and Vanessa Valenti. 2012. "#Femfuture: Online Revolution." *Barnard Center for Research on Women*. http://bcrw.barnard.edu/publications/femfuture-online -revolution (accessed April 23, 2014).

Martin, George R. R. 1996. *A Game of Thrones*. New York: Random House.

———. 1999. *A Clash of Kings*. New York: Random House.

———. 2000. *A Storm of Swords*. New York: Random House.

———. 2007. *A Feast for Crows*. New York: Random House.

———. 2011. *A Dance with Dragons*. New York: Random House.

McDougall, Sophia. 2013. "I Hate Strong Female Characters." *New Statesman*, August 15. http://www.newstatesman.com/culture/2013/08/i-hate-strong-female-characters (accessed April 4, 2014).

Mulvey, Laura. 1975. "Visual Pleasure and Narrative Cinema." *Screen* 16 (3): 6–18.

Munro, Ealasaid. 2013. "Feminism: A Fourth Wave?" *Political Insight* 4 (2): 22–25.

Nicholson, Linda. 2010. "Feminism in 'Waves': Useful Metaphor or Not?" *New Politics* 12: 48.

Nussbaum, Emily. 2011. "The Rebirth of the Feminist Manifesto." *New York Magazine*. October 30. http://nymag.com/news/features/feminist-blogs-2011-11 (accessed April 4, 2014).

ofhouseadama. 2012. "Why Sansa Stark Is a Strong Woman (TM)." *Tumblr*. May 9. http://ofhouseadama.tumblr.com/post/22679344694 (accessed April 23, 2014).

O'Neill, Elaine. 2011. "Game of Thrones." *The F Word*. July 22. http://www.thefword.org.uk /reviews/2011/07/game_of_thrones (accessed April 4, 2014).

Owens, Rebekah. 2013. "A Fantasy of Female Subjugation." *The F Word*. December 27. http://www.thefword.org.uk/reviews/2013/12/game_of_thrones_subjugation.

Peterson, Latoya. 2011. "Can I just watch *A Game of Thrones* in peace? [brown feminist fan rant]." *Racialicious*. April 19. http://www.racialicious.com/2011/04/19/can-i-just-watch -a-game-of-thrones-in-peace-brown-feminist-fan-rant (accessed April 4, 2014).

queencersei. 2014. "ifallontragedy: I went through your FAQ and saw that you like Sansa but couldn't find a link: What's your opinion about her?" *Tumblr*. February 3. http://queenc ersei.tumblr.com/post/75475617964/i-went-through-your-faq-and-saw-that-you-like -sansa-but (accessed March 29, 2014).

Regan Wills, Emily. 2013. "Fannish Discourse Communities and the Construction of Gender in 'The X-Files.'" *Transformative Works & Cultures* 14. Doi:10.3983/twc.2013.0410.

Renninger, Bryce J. 2014. "'Where I can be myself . . . where I can speak my mind': Networked Counterpublics in a Polymedia Environment." *New Media & Society*. Doi:10.1177/1461444814530095.

Rheingold, Howard. 2012. *Net Smart: How to Survive Online*. Cambridge, MA: MIT Press.

Rosenberg, Alyssa. 2011. "Feminist Media Criticism, George R. R. Martin's A Song of Ice and Fire, And That Sady Doyle Piece." *ThinkProgress.* August 29. http://thinkprogress.org /alyssa/2011/08/29/305723/feminist-media-criticism-george-r-r-martins-a-song-of-ice -and-fire-and-that-sady-doyle-piece (accessed April 4, 2014).

Schuster, Julia. 2013. "Invisible Feminists? Social Media and Young Women's Political Participation." *Political Science* 65 (1): 8–24.

Slavin, Laurie. 2013. "Game of Thrones and the Red Wedding: What the Hell Was That?" *Feminspire.* June 3. http://feminspire.com/game-of-thrones-and-the-red-wedding-what -the-hell-was-that (accessed April 4, 2014).

Thelandersson, Fredrika. 2013. "Tumblr Feminism: Third-Wave Subjectivities in Practice." MA thesis, New York University.

theperksofbeinggiullia. 2014. "4th season is coming." April 5. Web. http://theperksofbeinggi ullia.tumblr.com/post/81745066200 (accessed April 22, 2014).

Thomas, Kayley. 2013. "Revisioning the Smiling Villain: Imagetexts and Intertextual Expression in Representations of the Filmic Loki on Tumblr." *Transformative Works & Cultures* 13. Doi:10.3983/twc.2013.0474.

Travers, Ann. 2003. "Parallel Subaltern Feminist Counterpublics in Cyberspace." *Sociological Perspectives* 46 (2): 223–37.

Walker, Rebecca. 1992. "Becoming the Third Wave." *Ms.* January/February, 39–41.

Watercutter, Angela. 2013. "Yes, Women Really Do Like *Game of Thrones* (We Have Proof)." *Wired.* June 3. http://www.wired.com/2013/06/women-game-of-thrones (accessed April 23, 2014).

whoistorule. 2014. Untitled. *Tumblr.* April 29. http://skipdiprazzdoo.tumblr.com/ post/84236452146/sansa-endures-its-what-she-does-shes-tortured (accessed April 30, 2014).

Williams, Bronwyn, and Amy AA Zenger, eds. 2012. *New Media Literacies and Participatory Popular Culture across Borders.* New York: Routledge.

Zeisler, Andi. 2013. "Does It Matter Whether Game of Thrones is Feminist?" *Bitch.* June 7. http://bitchmagazine.org/post/does-it-matter-whether-game-of-thrones-is-feminist (accessed April 4, 2014).

The Dragon Lady of Gotham: Feminine Power, the Mythical East, and Talia al Ghul

—Tosha Taylor

Debuting in *Detective* #411 in 1971, Talia al Ghul has fulfilled more roles than are typically assigned to female characters in comics. She has been Batman's lover, mother of his only biological child, daughter of immortal ecoterrorist Ra's al Ghul, partner to Lex Luthor, foil to Superman, mentor to a former Robin, member of the Society of Super Villains, head of her own global crime network, and an independent agent of both good and evil. However, with her revealing costumes and curvaceous figure, Talia occupies an even more important role to the DC Universe's overarching narrative—that of the heterosexual Western male fantasy of the Eastern woman. In this essay, I will explore comics' treatment of Talia's ethnicity, which is often complicated by racial stereotypes and anxieties. Throughout her forty-year history, Talia has embodied both the Near Eastern Oriental described by Edward Said and the Dragon Lady who has become a problematic trope regarding depictions of East Asia. She serves as the site of convergence and contradiction, for while she embodies both, she rarely does so simultaneously. Her outward representations, this essay demonstrates, change to correspond to her actions, which in turn frequently correspond to Orientalist and Far Eastern archetypes in Western thought.

Though the exact ethnic origins of Ra's al Ghul are debatable, his origin story, *Birth of the Demon*, identifies Talia's mother as Arabic and Chinese (O'Neil and Breyfogle 1992, 92).[1] Thus physically characterized by Arabic and Asian ethnic heritages, Talia's body is a space on which both sexual desires and anxieties regarding Eastern women may be projected. Her cultural background as a mixed-race woman rarely seems to offer explorations of cultural fluidity. Rather than appearing as an Arabic-Asian woman, Talia is largely presented as exclusively Arabic *or* Asian *or* even Caucasian, with few intersections of these ethnic categories. The desires and anxieties inscribed upon her by other characters often correspond to distinct emphases on physical signs meant to identify a particular ethnicity. Talia the Arabic woman, dressed in sarongs and stereotypical harem girl costumes, is frequently portrayed as a distinctly different character from Talia the East Asian woman, who wears bright kimono or ninja attire. Both women have been a love interest for Batman for forty years, but the former is typically a subservient damsel in distress, victimized by her Arabic father and rescued by the American Batman, whereas the latter is a villain in her own right, a sly temptress who can kill as easily as she can seduce. Through the combined efforts of writers and artists, Talia has been established as an exotic femme fatale who threatens Batman not only through her actions but also through her very identity as an Eastern woman. Serving as both the submissive Arabic harem girl and the vindictive Asian siren, she embodies tropes of Orientalist thought, bridging colonial discourses and contemporary fears and fetishizations.

As Talia's East Asian heritage was not revealed until 1992, and the first comics featuring her explicitly point toward Near Eastern ethnicity, Edward Said's *Orientalism* provides an appropriate context for studying her. Though subsequent scholars have made alterations to Said's concept, his basic tenets of Orientalist thought are supported by the claims of many other gender and postcolonial critics. At its most basic level, Said's ([1978] 2003) Orient "was almost a European invention, and had been since antiquity a place of romance, exotic beings, haunting memories and landscapes, remarkable experiences" (1). He explicates, furthermore, that "the imaginative examination of things Oriental was based more or less exclusively upon a sovereign Western consciousness out of whose unchallenged centrality an Oriental world emerged, first according to general ideas about who or what was an Oriental, then according to a detailed logic governed not simply by empirical reality but by a battery of desires, repressions, investments, and projections" (ibid., 8). Yeğenoğlu (1998) describes Said's Orient "as the place of sensuality, corrupt despotism, mystical religiosity, sexually unstable Arabs, irrationality, [and] backwardness" (17). For the early Orientalist writers and artists, both those working from nonfiction and fiction, the Orient, as a phenomenon, did not exist on its own but was an embodiment of contrasts with the West, not a self but an eternal Other. Such characterizations were not limited to Oriental locations but extended to the inhabitants of Oriental places. The Oriental body became a means through which the Western man could identify himself and solidify his nature as a successful Westerner, as opposed to the flawed Oriental.

Said ([1978] 2003) describes Orientalism as a phenomenon comprising four dogmas:

One is the absolute and systematic difference between the West, which is rational, developed, humane, superior and the Orient, which is aberrant, undeveloped, inferior. Another dogma is that abstractions about the Orient, particularly those based on texts representing a "classical" Oriental civilization, are always preferable to direct evidence drawn from modern Oriental realities. A third dogma is that the Orient is eternal, uniform, and incapable of defining itself.... A fourth dogma is that the Orient is at bottom something either to be feared (the Yellow Peril, the Mongol hordes, the brown dominions) or to be controlled (by pacification, research and development, outright occupation whenever possible). (301)

These dogmas can be used to explicate and understand the treatment of the al Ghul family in the DC Universe (hereafter referred to as the DCU) and will here be examined individually.

Though the first dogma, the juxtaposition of East and West, might seem most applicable to the conflict between Batman and Ra's, it is no less applicable to Talia when juxtaposed against other women and even against Batman himself. For instance, in *Hush* (Loeb and Lee 2009), Selina Kyle is complicit with Batman in abducting Talia as a means of blackmailing Ra's, and yet it is Talia who is invariably presented as the more villainous of the two women, even though she is the kidnapping victim. Her face, in particular, appears sinister as she asserts her claim to Batman's love while undermining Selina's. Though her malice disappears at the end of the scene, when Selina has been grievously injured by the Chinese assassin Lady Shiva, Talia's Eastern-ness plays a key role; Western medicine cannot save Selina, but Talia's exotic remedies are guaranteed to heal her "within hours." Later, in *Gotham City Sirens* (2009–2011), Talia's relationship with Selina continues to emphasize the women's cultural differences. In the series's second issue, Talia summons Selina to her mountain base in Tibet, where she, sitting in a lotus position and through a fog of incense, offers to teach Selina an esoteric art. Her East Asian features are distinctly prominent in this scene (Dini and March 2009). Talia is rarely shown to interact with other Near Eastern and Far Eastern characters other than her father for longer than a few panels; the vast majority of her interactions are with Westerners, creating a constant juxtaposition of East and West.

The second dogma calls to mind Talia's untrustworthiness, which is not limited to her actions and loyalties but also extends to her level of agency— do other characters, and do readers, actually believe her, and should they? Talia's ability to deceive is an artful one; at any time, she may be revealed as having ulterior motives. A number of her first appearances see her engaging in treachery and subterfuge to serve her purposes.[2] Deceit and betrayal have continued to characterize her well into her recent appearances, and such acts are not limited to her dealings with Batman. She turns against her father after appearing to aid his quest for vengeance and domination; a notable and relatively recent example occurs in the *JLA* storyline "Tower of Babel," in which Ra's al Ghul comes close to destroying the Justice League but is thwarted when Talia leaks information to the heroes (Waid, Porter, Geraci, et al. 2000). As evidenced in *Batman: Our Worlds at War* #1, even Talia's simplest actions may be something more; in this comic, she, knowing Batman is near, touches the chest of one of Lex Luthor's men, surreptitiously dislodging the man's security badge and leaving it for Batman to find and use (Brubaker, Gaudiano, and Tewes 2001). Moreover, her entire tenure as CEO of LexCorp is shown to be something of a ruse in the conclusion of *Superman/Batman: Public Enemies*, when it is revealed that, while leading the company, Talia has secretly sold all of Luthor's assets to Bruce Wayne even as she worked as a villain (Loeb, McGuiness, Vines, et al. 2004).

The third dogma, which refers to the Orientalist tradition of presenting the East as timeless, a thing defined only by what has gone on around it, is echoed in the ahistorical settings in which both Ra's and Talia often work and live, settings that, despite the Demon's continued technological advancements, are distinguished in the texts by being neither Gotham nor any other modern city. The al Ghuls work out of elaborate Himalayan fortresses, exotic desert tents in Africa, and East Asian temples. Even when Talia takes up residence in Gotham, her home appears externally similar to a pagoda, a structural anomaly in the ultramodern, sleekly Western city. Batman first meets Talia in East Asia (*Detective* #411, 1971); her second appearance sees Batman traveling to the Himalayas, where she waits to marry him (*Batman* #232, 1971).[3] In both issues, Talia's dress evokes a romanticized Eastern past. Another forced marriage attempt occurs in international waters in 1978's *DC Special* #15, and Ra's al Ghul's dialogue emphasizes the nonconformity of the marriage with modern American standards: "In my nation, the consent of the female and her father are sufficient for marriage!" "The wedding would not be legal in the United States!" (O'Neil, Adams, Brown, et al. 1991, 137–38). In *Batman* #244 (1972), a change between the Swiss Alps and a generic southern desert is marked by omniscient narration as we see robed men leading camels: "This . . . is the desert!—A hellish panorama of blazing emptiness that defies living creatures . . . yet, men do live here! And stranger still, some men prosper" (ibid., 125).[4] The timeless Arabic setting is echoed more recently in Grant Morrison's *Batman and Son*, in which Talia and Batman are shown having sex in a fire-lit desert tent "above the Tropic of Cancer," in which the only seemingly contemporary artifact is Batman's discarded costume (Morrison and Kubert 2008, 54).

Finally, Said's fourth dogma succinctly describes Batman's relationship to the al Ghul family as a collective unit and as individuals. Ra's al Ghul is presented as an Arabic tyrant, seemingly limitless in his power and strength, and yet the American hero necessarily defeats him. In the conclusion of *Batman* #244 (1972), Batman defeats Ra's with a single punch; when he expresses shock at his enemy's defeat, Talia assures him, "Perhaps, Beloved, he recognized his . . . master!" (O'Neil, Adams, Brown, et al 1991, 130). Likewise, Talia is a fearsome warrior with unlimited resources, and she thus simultaneously serves as the site of anxiety and the object that Batman must conquer and claim. In the same issue, following her aforementioned line, Batman pulls Talia into a passionate kiss, claiming her physically and romantically before carrying her father's unconscious body away. Indeed, Batman's methods of disarming the al Ghuls often seem purposefully contrasted, matching violence and wits against Ra's and playing upon Talia's love for him. The latter method remains particularly notable in the *Final Crisis Companion* (2009), a supplementary book to the 2008 crossover epic, in which Talia appears as a member of Lex Luthor's Secret Society. The Society is mentally assaulted by Martian Manhunter, who causes all the individual members to hallucinate that they are being attacked by their most feared enemy. Talia is the lone exception—her hallucination is of Batman kissing her (Tomasi, Mahnke, Alamy, et al. 2008).

Said's dogmas each rely on the notion of difference. Drawing from the writing of Evelyn Baring, First Earl of Cromer, Said notes a system of binary contrasts that distinguish men of the West from those of the East: "The European is close reasoned . . . he is a natural logician . . . he is by nature sceptical [sic] and requires proof before he can accept the truth of any proposition; his trained intelligence works like a piece of mechanism. The mind of the Oriental, on the other hand, like his picturesque streets, is eminently wanting in symmetry" ([1978] 2003, 38). In this characterization, place of origin is mirrored in the human mind: the West may seem colder and more clinical, but from that hardness comes intellect, whereas the Easterner, constructed from exotic locales of great beauty and poetic language, lacks the faculties through which the Western man proves himself the true victor of the world. In terms of the DCU, a victory over the Joker may establish Batman as the savior of Gotham, but defeating Ra's al Ghul and Talia assure his physical and moral superiority on a global scale.

Global conflict was indeed the basis for the conception of the al Ghul family. Dennis O'Neil, who created both Ra's and Talia, intended his writing in the comics to react against the campy *Batman* television series of the 1960s, which boasted both heroes and villains that were far more laughable than dangerous: "We set out consciously and deliberately to create a villain in the grand manner, a villain who was so exotic and mysterious that neither we nor Batman were sure what to expect" (Hamm 1991, 7). The result of those efforts was the Demon's Head and his daughter. In his introduction to *Tales of the Demon*, Sam Hamm (ibid.) credits O'Neil with "[realizing] that the stock pulp figure of the nefarious Asian mastermind [as typified by Fu Manchu] could be neatly retooled to embody the anxieties of the second half of the twentieth century." No longer would Batman fight Nazis or supernatural creatures; now his international attentions turned to the Middle and Far East, where the United States had interests in oil and the spread of Communism. The "anxieties" the al Ghuls' creators wished to address, according to Hamm (ibid.), were those "of an America that, poised between the twin upheavals of Vietnam and Watergate, was beginning to question its own long- cherished cultural verities—as well as the morality of its own actions at home and abroad." Co-creator and artist Neal Adams sought to separate Ra's from any one specific ethnicity (ibid., 7–8), but with her epicanthic folds and revealing sarongs, Talia is immediately identifiable as an Eastern woman, coded as such by both Arabic and Asian signifiers.

In "Black Skins and White Masks: Comic Books and the Secret of Race," Singer (2002) emphasizes the importance of physical appearance in comics, which, he writes, "rely upon visually codified representations in which characters are continually reduced to their appearances." Superhero comics, Singer argues, are particularly dependent upon appearances, for their "characters are wholly externalized into their heroic costumes and aliases" (107). In such a world, Talia's racial fluidity may point not toward identity but unknowability. She has traditionally lacked a need for aliases until very recently. Feeling no fear of legal reprisal for any crime in which she may be implicated, Talia works in both East and West as Talia al Ghul, Talia Head, and Daughter of the Demon, a title that dramatically reveals her true identity rather than hiding it. Grant Morrison's recently concluded Batman epic sees Talia adopting a villainous alias, Leviathan, to prolong her horrifying game with Batman. As Talia herself notes to the World's Greatest Detective, Leviathan is even a partial anagram of her name, a fact she has taken no pains to conceal. On one hand, Talia's lack of artful aliases might be interpreted as an affirmation of her identity and role within the DCU, but Brown (2011) argues that the act of self-naming empowers the name bearer: "A central cliché in superhero stories is not just the iconic costuming but the opportunity to be identifiable. The importance of empowerment through self-declaration is crystallized in the clichéd use of decisive proclamations used in every superhero movie: 'I'm Batman!,' 'Who am I? I'm Spider-Man!,' 'The suit and I are one. I am Iron Man!,' 'I'm Kick-Ass!'" (80).

Brown's argument can be extended to villains as well. For example, it is through addressing Two-Face as Harvey that Batman continually shows concern and even pity for the former district attorney, and it is through the rearrangement of Harleen Quinzel's name into Harley Quinn that one of the most wildly popular DC women originated. Conversely, the Joker's ability to maintain the secret of his pre-criminal identity imbues him with unique agency. Returning to Brown's example, we can immediately infer that Batman invokes the symbolism of the bat as part of his heroic persona, that Spider-Man has a similar connection to his animal namesake, that Iron Man's strength lies in his suit, and that Kick-Ass means to kick ass, but what does it mean to be "Talia"? Through her name, we may suspect only her exoticism, but not her role. Likewise, the occasional title of Daughter of the Demon only positions her back into an Orientalist paradigm, one that continues to affect multicultural women. In her study of mixed-race women, Bettez (2010, 145) finds that women of multiple ethnic backgrounds tend to identify themselves not as what ethnic identity they feel describes them, but rather by listing the backgrounds of their parents. When Talia presents herself as the Daughter of the Demon, she is claiming not a personal identity but a parental one, and one which immediately calls to the readers' (and other characters') minds her coded Arabic-Oriental father. By name, Talia is identified only as the Oriental or daughter of the Oriental.

The importance of dress is noted by Calefato (2010): "The 'clothed' body is a place where tastes and fashions are represented and shared, a place of edification of the myth, where desires and values are expressed, where power is noticeably 'enforced' and manifested" (351). When it comes to dress as signifier, Talia is an unusual case. In a world in which most inhabitants boast unique costumes (even Lex Luthor's bald scalp makes him instantly recognizable to the reader), Talia seems to lack canonical criteria for her appearance. Her skin color changes from story to story (and sometimes even changes midstory), as does the color of her hair. She may appear distinctly Middle Eastern, distinctly East Asian, or distinctly white. She has no unique costume, appearing and working in a wide variety of outfits that may or may not suit the occasion. Some of her modes of dress are popular enough to denote a female character as *potentially* Talia—these most notably include her white harem girl dress and her black catsuit—but there is no single costume that necessarily delineates her from the other women who occupy similar roles in the DCU. The woman in harem dress lounging next to Ra's might be Talia, or it might be simply one of his servants. The woman in the black catsuit probably is not Selina Kyle (they have different hairstyles, after all) but is not necessarily Talia unless explicitly named or spotted in a location unique to the workings of the al Ghul family. The warrior woman in the Far Eastern costume might be Talia, but might just as easily be Lady Shiva. The difficulty of identifying Talia by dress, regardless of setting, seems emphasized in *Superman* #190, where, despite being the head of Lexcorp and thus the most powerful woman in the Western world, Talia prominently wears a nametag (Seagle, McDaniel, Owens, et al. 2003).

Nonetheless, it is through dress that we begin to see patterns of identity and agency formed by Orientalist discourse. If the Arabic woman is to be interpreted as a submissive object in need of rescue and through whom the American hero can prove the might of his Western will, as will be discussed in greater detail later, then we might expect Talia to appear in fantasy Arabic attire in stories in which she fulfills a submissive role. Another wardrobe is needed, however, to mark her occupation of a different space in a narrative—the treacherous East Asian femme fatale.

Talia's abrupt transformation from the beautiful Arab woman weeping in Batman's arms to the Asian vamp does not come without precedence. Originating in the weekly comic strip *Terry and the Pirates* in 1934, the Dragon Lady would quickly come to be recognized as an exciting trope in comics and film. She stood in stark contrast to the meek, compliant Asian woman in need of Western male love and protection as typified by Madame Butterfly and could be just as merciless as any male villain (Ma 2000, 5). Beautiful and skilled in the art of lovemaking, the Dragon Lady was perhaps a far greater danger to American heroes than were the typical male villains in that she alone wielded power over heroes' emotions—and libidos. However, despite her capacity for cruelty, the Dragon Lady had a unique weakness herself—her necessary attraction to the conquering American hero. "Onto the curvaceous body of the Dragon Lady," Ma (2000) writes, "the West projects its morbid narcissism. Fu Manchu's sadism and Charlie Chan's loyalty were fused and feminized in her, and she became a mere girl, vulnerable and vindictive, in the presence of the irresistible Pat Ryan" (16), the comic strip's American hero. Despite her regal pride and ferocity as a warrior, Talia experiences the same vulnerability in Batman's presence, weeping and forsaking her mission out of fear or acknowledgment of his rejection. Even when the Dark Knight has treated her cruelly, she cannot resist her own love for him. For perhaps the most iconic instance of Talia's undoing, we can return to the first kiss between her and Batman in *Batman* #244 (1972). Having bested Ra's in battle, Batman plans to turn his fallen enemy over to the authorities (in the '70s, though powerful, Ra's had yet to boast the kind of cruelty that would see him leading massacres of anyone who attempts to hinder him). Talia meekly approaches the conquering crusader: "And I?" she asks. "Am I also to be imprisoned?"

(O'Neil, Adams, Brown, et al. 1991, 130). Batman responds with a passionate kiss; their poses emphasize his enormous stature and Talia's seeming physical vulnerability. The issue ends with Batman carrying Ra's across the desert as Talia looks on in tears, rendered powerless by the loss of her father and the departure of her Beloved.

While comics, with their fantastic presentation of virtually every element of the body, notably the ability of men to walk off a gunshot wound and of women's spines to hold up the weight of their massive breasts without debilitating discomfort, may seem too fantastical to warrant serious concern for their depiction of ethnicity, Ma (2000) reminds us that the fantasies embodied in the medium are indicative of far more than character choices for convenience: "Far more important than entertainment, adventure comic strips [such as *Terry and the Pirates*] were, and still are, part of the stories a nation repeats to itself, out of which a national identity and myth arise" (3); he then goes on to note that the Oriental has long been the trope against which the protagonists of adventure comics are characterized as American. While Batman's American-ness is never in question, it must come to the forefront of conflict when he presents himself as the ultimate foil to Ra's al Ghul, a coded Arab Oriental man who tempts him with promised access to the Oriental woman. Indeed, just as the Oriental man creates the enemy against whom the American comic book hero stands, the Oriental woman serves as the reward for American victory: "In the case of adventure comic strips, the shortest route from boyhood to a 'moral' and 'intrepid' adulthood seemed to cut across the exotic terrain of . . . the erotic body of Chinese females" (ibid., 6). As a woman of both explicitly Arabic and Chinese ethnicity, Talia serves as enemy and reward for the explorative Batman comics of the 1970s.

Though Talia moves easily between the two contrasting character tropes, that fluidity is rarely mirrored in individual stories. Rather, as was briefly mentioned earlier, storylines in which Talia is prominently featured often seem to present her as *either* Arabic *or* East Asian, with a wardrobe and life-style markers that strictly correspond to the singular role she occupies. These costume changes and shifts of character tropes are made even more problematic by recent stories in which Talia has appeared as a Caucasian woman, for in addition to undergoing physical whitewashing, she moves outside of both of her traditional roles, becoming instead a neutral agent rather than the damsel in distress or femme fatale. (An exception to this may occur in the film *The Dark Knight Rises* [dir. Christopher Nolan, 2012], in which Talia is portrayed by French actress Marion Cotillard and is given the European name Miranda Tate through much of the film, only revealing her identity as Talia in the film's final minutes. However, it is notable that before Miranda reveals herself as Talia, she dons an East Asian robe-style coat modeled after Ra's al Ghul's in *Batman Begins*.[5]) These changes are not limited to specific writers or artists, as Talia's physical appearance and actions may change under the same creative team as her function in the story shifts. Indeed, a reading of her appearances in comics over the past forty years reveals that the relationship between Talia's role in a story and her appearance, with few exceptions, constitutes a pattern of dichotomous Orientalist fantasies. In the following section, I will discuss this pattern as it manifests in specific texts that provide highly visible examples of such fantasies.

"All I Desire Is Dead": The Submissive Arab Princess

As a precursor to the 1999 epic *No Man's Land*, in which Gotham would be destroyed first by a plague and then by a catastrophic earthquake, Chuck Dixon created a story that would pit Batman, Ra's al Ghul, and Bane against each other. However, its precursors, *Bane of the Demon* and *Batman: Legacy*, belong just as much to Talia as to the male warriors, for Dixon's story sees Talia moving from Dragon Lady to oppressed Arabic woman, a failed Scheherazade. Her journey is both visual and narrative, full of costume changes that herald her gradual loss of agency as she transforms from one Orientalist trope to the other. At the start of Dixon's story, *Bane of the Demon* #1 (1998), a League of Assassins ninja removes her mask to reveal the Demon's Daughter herself, a nightmarish commander as cruel as she is beautiful. When Bane attempts to take Talia hostage, the much smaller woman surprises the behemoth by disabling him with a kick and throwing him over her shoulder. "I do not have much experience of—umm—women," Bane admits when Talia voices amusement with his defeat (Dixon, Nolan, Palmer, et al. 1998a). Talia's reaction to Bane's violence and subsequent naïveté is to take him back to League headquarters with her and present him to Ra's.

However, Bane soon turns the tables on his captor. Finding Talia vulnerably exposed and threatened by a symbolically phallic moray eel, Bane rescues the fair maiden, and though at first Talia resists, she ultimately appears to reward Bane with sex (ibid. 1998b). But for Talia, an afternoon of passion does not mean love, and she soon rejects Bane's continued advances, unaware that Bane has learned the secret of the Lazarus pits and intends to kill Ra's, take the pits for himself, and make Talia his slave (ibid. 1998c). Talia's costumes become more revealing, exposing more and more of her body as they move from a ninja-inspired jumpsuit to the light, transparent dresses of a harem girl. Though revealing costumes on women are hardly rare in superhero comics, in the Orientalist artistic tradition, women's nudity "had a striking and titillating immediacy" not found in Western nudity; thus, Talia's costume changes are implicitly eroticized (MacKenzie 1995, 64). This gradual exposure therefore suggests a temptation to what she cannot suspect but which the reader already knows will happen: Bane will attack her sexually. Fulfilling the role of the oppressive Arabic father who would have his women subjugated, Ra's approves the match between Bane and his daughter, much to Talia's horror (Dixon, Nolan, Palmer, et al. 1998d).

When their story resumes in *Detective* #700,[6] Talia has lost all trace of the Dragon Lady within her, and this loss is reflected in her dress. Donning an elaborate fantasy-Arabic costume, she waits submissively upon her father, her skin darkened and her eyes distinctly almond-shaped with thick lashes to further suggest epicanthic folds. Thus Orientalized, Talia, the same woman who fearlessly overpowered and kidnapped Bane, now merely cowers in fear and revulsion as Bane reminds her at every turn that he is going to spend eternity raping her. However, even Bane voices astonishment at Talia's sudden weakness: "But what of your wishes, Talia?," he asks in a surprising moment of humanity. "What of your desires?," to which Talia, believing Batman has been killed, answers: "They are nothing. *Less* than nothing. All I desire is dead" (Dixon, Nolan, Hanna et al. 1996). Without the conquering American hero to serve as her love interest, Talia loses all sense of agency, resigning herself to spending the rest of her life as a slave.

Following *Legacy* (1996) and the subsequent story *Cataclysm* (1998), Talia appears in Washington to order Bruce Wayne, who has given up his mission as Batman in the wake of Gotham's complete destruction, to get back into the cape and cowl and perform his duties as a hero (*No Man's Land* #0, 1999). When Bruce shrugs her off with a flippant, and arguably misogynistic, comment, Talia slaps him hard enough to reopen the facial wounds he sustained in an earlier fight. "No one," she reminds him, "speaks to the daughter of Ra's al Ghul with such disrespect" (Rucka, Gorfinkel, Land, et al. 1999). Her fear of angry men and submissive nature seem to have disappeared with the elaborate harem girl costumes that characterized her as she was so graphically victimized. Under writers Greg Rucka and Jordan B. Gorfinkel and artists Greg Land, Drew Geraci, and Rob Schwager, post–*Cataclysm* Talia conducts her business wearing a simple gown, and her physical appearance boasts signifiers of both Arabic and East Asian ethnicity. In a rare treatment, her ethnicity is apparent but is neither emphasized nor fantasized.[7] Notably, though, there is no mention of her dealings with Bane in this issue, despite the fact that, the last Bruce knew of her, she was obviously endangered by Bane, and by proxy, Ra's, who desires her to marry her would-be rapist.

The Dragon Lady Reborn: Grant Morrison's Leviathan

Subsequently, Talia as the Dragon Lady has made a dramatic return, one that has resulted in highly polarized opinions among fans of the character. Talia arrives onto the scene of what has become Grant Morrison's multiyear Batman epic wearing a flowered kimono-style dress; reappears to remind Batman of her villainous nature by wearing the black bodysuit; and wages war against her own son, Damian, and new Batman Dick Grayson wearing yet another kimono. In each of these appearances, her face boasts prominently East Asian features, forming expressions that range from Eastern beauty to Eastern parody.[8] At the climax of "Leviathan Strikes!," the introduction to the final arc of Morrison's epic, Talia wears a monastic-style robe and a skull mask; once the mask is removed, a distinctly Asian face appears and the robe parts to reveal a seductively bare leg (Morrison, Stewart, Fairbairn, et al. 2012). Talia-as-Leviathan is presented as the ultimate global villain, the most powerful since Ra's al Ghul, and that global villain is unquestionably, and dangerously, East Asian—the Dragon Lady returned in full glory.

Talia's new and extreme villainy is a divisive topic. On one hand, it may appear that Morrison has simply played once more into Orientalist tropes by reviving the Dragon Lady. On the other, this usage of the Dragon Lady does sometimes stand in opposition to the Orientalist trope. Rajgopal (2010) notes that, when it has come to onscreen depictions of American heroes vs. Oriental villains, "no Asian actress could play a lead role opposite a white man. Thus Asian American actresses played only negative roles, such as the evil henchmaiden to the Asian villain" (149). Talia's role in Morrison's epic is inarguably negative, but in a medium in which villains often receive more appreciation from fans than secondary heroes, we should also note that by establishing Talia as Leviathan, Morrison has rejected the notion of an Asian woman serving only as a servant to the principal male villain. "Ra's al Ghul is dead," Talia tells Batman at the very beginning of Morrison's story, *Batman & Son,*[9] "This is my very own little magnum opus" (Morrison and Kubert 2008). Not only has a woman bested the Dark Knight to create a global criminal empire, but an Eastern woman, someone who, as a mixed Arabic-Chinese woman, boasts three identities that would traditionally deny her such power. In this regard, Morrison's epic may even be said to have feminist leanings, for Talia comes to replace Ra's as the most dangerous supervillain in Batman's world. That she is an Eastern woman becomes, then, simultaneously empowering and stereotypical.

Perhaps most problematic in terms of Talia's ethnic representation in Morrison's work are the implicit hints of Orientalism in his own thoughts on the character. In an interview with *USA Today* to promote *Batman Incorporated* #2, Morrison states that "she used to look so beautiful and exotic as drawn by Neal Adams."[10] Indeed, known for making specific requests of artists working with him, Morrison recommended that *Batman Incorporated* artist Chris Burnham base Talia on her 1970s appearances, in which she served as the beautiful, foreign prize for Batman. As Kim and Chung (2005) note, images of both demure Asian women and the Dragon Lady "stimulate the sexual voyeurism of White American males and the objectification of foreign, exotic Oriental women as their rightful property" (75–76). The second issue of the series serves as a Year One of sorts for the character, Talia's first real origin story in her forty-year history. Her East Asian attributes are prominent as Burnham draws her, but notably, distinct traces of her Arabic ethnic heritage have here been removed. Though the issue's re-envisioning of Talia's first appearance in 1971 does credit her with more agency, she remains the object of Batman's rescue mission, referencing the '70s comics in which the American hero battled against inferior Easterners. Morrison's Talia is an admitted mix of European and Asian physicality,[11] once more suggesting that the place of the Arabic woman in Batman comics is that of the submissive, sexually endangered maiden. Once empowered and made completely autonomous, she shifts into the East Asian siren, leaving behind her Arabic heritage and features.

Throughout the remainder of Morrison's run, which concluded on July 31, 2013, after seven years, Talia has continued wearing her kimono and her face has remained characterized by East Asian, but not Near Eastern, features. For Morrison's final issue, Talia enters the Bat-cave wearing a Bat-mask and cape, holding no weapon but a sword. "The house of al Ghul," she tells Batman, "needs no branding, no flags, no slogans. I trade in drugs, weapons, human lives, mind control—and I already rule the world" (Morrison, Burnham, and Fairbairn 2013). Casting the mask aside, she confronts Batman in the only costume she needs, a bright red catsuit, similar to the kimono she has worn for the past several issues.

Her association with the creature for which the Dragon Lady is named continues, not only in the form of Leviathan's name, but also with one of its frequently invoked symbols, the ouroboros, a snake devouring its own tail. The cyclical nature of the symbol foreshadows Talia's defeat, for as her final plan comes to fruition, it backfires upon her: Batman refuses to kill her, although her death will call off Leviathan's forces, and the former Robin, Jason Todd (who is also Talia's former lover), disables the "oroboro trigger" that will detonate a series of massive explosives.[12] Kathy Kane, the first Batwoman of the 1970s, arrives on scene in deus-ex-machina fashion and shoots Talia, killing her instantly. After slaying the Dragon Lady incarnation of Talia, the intrepid

American spy anonymously assists Batman in clearing Bruce Wayne's name of crimes attributed to him during Leviathan's war. Referencing Talia's draconic symbol, Kathy admonishes him, "It all comes full circle in the end, Bruce" (Morrison, Burnham, and Fairbairn 2013). In addition to co-opting Leviathan's standard, her words set the stage for an open ending to Morrison's epic, for Talia's body is stolen from its Gotham grave by Ra's al Ghul, who renews his vow to make war with Batman. Thus, Morrison's Talia is characterized not only by visual markers of the classic Dragon Lady, but by a serpentine symbol that doubles as literal plot device, and as if to emphasize her foreignness, her defeat is only finalized when her body is removed from Gotham.

Sarongs in the Boardroom: Racial Reminders

Currently, no comics storyline has offered an exploration into Talia's ethnic identity. Her existence as a woman of Arab and Asian ethnic heritage is often either taken for granted or ignored altogether. However, some comics have made a point to remind the reader that Talia is an ethnic Other; notably, she appears in these stories as a villain. *Action* #773 concludes a two-part story with Talia agreeing to work with Lex Luthor by becoming his handpicked CEO of LexCorp. As they come to their accord, Luthor discusses what he feels is the true reason for Ra's al Ghul's inability to dominate the Western corporate world: "Your father, savagely efficient businessman that he is, did not play well with others. It was, in part, I believe, because he hated to wear pants. Cloaks and sarongs have no place in the boardroom" (Kelly, Kano, Amancio, et al. 2001). Luthor's statement seems to have less to do with the actuality of their situation and more to do with asserting Western superiority in the corporate world. Ra's al Ghul does, in fact, command a number of corporate ventures and has at times foregone his signature cloak in favor of Western-style business suits, but Luthor, himself only vaguely familiar with the global supervillain, finds failure in what he has assumed of the man—being of Arabic and Asian descent and still primarily operating in those cultural spheres, Ra's is incapable of wielding the kind of power that a white, Western businessman does. Moreover, his use of "savagely" is a curious one. Luthor is himself a "savage" businessman, engaging in ruthless and illegal practices to maintain his power; however, his is the world of suits, and Ra's's characteristic costume would, in Luthor's opinion, deny him entry into a corporate world that privileges conformity over individuality. We should also note that "savage" may carry a more implicitly malicious racial message. His words, however, are not lost on Talia. Once she takes the helm of LexCorp, her characteristic wardrobe largely disappears, replaced by suit jackets, button-up blouses, and pencil skirts. Her name, too, is changed, as she Anglicizes and reduces her surname simply to Head, "pronounced," she tells Luthor, "in the British way" (Rucka, Eaglesham, and Kryssing 2001), evoking a colonial sense of British superiority. The immediate trappings by which a comics character is identified, their name and costume, are removed and replaced by those denoting Western-ness.

Talia's navigation of linguistic differences extends beyond accents. Comics have traditionally handled language barriers between characters (and between characters and the reader) through the use of English text enclosed in chevrons, sometimes accompanied by an editorial note identifying the language the characters are meant to speak. *Nightwing: Freefall*,[13] however, forgoes chevrons in favor of keeping Talia on hand to provide translations. When the Chinese-speaking Mother of Champions talks to Nightwing, Talia mediates their communication (Tomasi, Kramer, and Florea 2009). In this scene, all three characters overlook the fact that it was Talia who kidnapped the Mother of Champions in order to use the woman's supernatural womb as an incubator for her own personal army. Talia's position as a woman of Asian ethnicity takes precedence over her role as a villain in the story. Although she has spent the entirety of the multi-issue storyline antagonizing Dick Grayson and is the one who had the Mother of Champions drugged and repeatedly impregnated, she willingly assists Nightwing in communicating with her former captive. Given the brutality of what Talia has done previously in the storyline, the scene is almost awkward, serving little purpose but to remind the reader of Talia's ethnicity.

No Damsel in Distress

A surprising take on Talia's degree of autonomy comes in the form of J. M. DeMatteis's *Batman/Spider-Man* (1997). In this crossover, Talia easily negotiates Western and Eastern expectations, donning her Western business attire, a harem girl outfit, and a bodysuit reminiscent of her ninja-inspired black costume at various points. Her clothing changes according to each scene's setting rather than character tropes. Notably, her physical features boast Arabic and East Asian influences, including a darker complexion and epicanthic folds. Arabic cultural practices are also acknowledged; though the al Ghuls are not Muslims, Talia's refusal to drink alcohol calls to mind Islamic prohibition.[14]

The story's exploration of Talia's motivations and implicit indictment of Orientalist thought can be further understood through applying Said's work to Ra's al Ghul, for it is in Ra's's characterization that the establishment of Talia as an Oriental woman truly begins. While Talia signifies ethnic tropes primarily through such implicit means as dress, Ra's makes his Middle Eastern identity quite apparent to both comics characters and readers themselves. Indeed, it is his physical, social, and even spiritual difference from the West that provides a greater context for his actions. In his updated preface to *Orientalism*, Said (2003) characterizes the Western imperative to colonize the Orient in terms that anyone with an interest in the al Ghuls should find notable: "Every single empire in its official discourse has said that it is not like all the others, that its circumstances are special, that it has a mission to enlighten, civilize, bring order and democracy, and that it uses force only as a last resort"; he goes on to label such empires as "benign or altruistic" (xvi). The architect of his very own empire, Ra's antagonizes Western sensibilities through his rejection of even the false notion of force as a last resort. The earth, he believes, and as both his daughters agree at various points in their lives, must first be purged of iniquity before any other steps can be taken; for him, enlightenment and order may come only through the use of as much destructive force as possible. We see mirrored in his eternal war with Batman, a white upper-class hero of the West, an active resistance to such ideologies and an opposition that turns Western colonial discourse on its head. In *Batman/Spider-Man*, Talia joins her father in that antagonism. It is rare that we see Talia explicitly espousing her father's views, though often appearing to assist in his work out of a sense of duty, but in this comic, she expresses a pride in their mission that rhetorically and visually counters Batman's spoken condemnation of it: "Ra's al Ghul is a visionary—who seeks to usher in a golden age . . . so that all of humankind may live in peace and prosperity. Many times he has attempted to save this dying planet, transform his vision into reality. But he has been thwarted by men of limited intellect—and vengeful hearts. This time it will not be so"[15] (DeMatteis, Nolan, Kesel, et al. 1997). Talia's stated faith in her father's work becomes a crucial point at the story's end and serves as the context for her empowerment as it is gradually revealed, much to Batman's surprise.

Though it is easy to overlook DeMatteis's story as a novelty crossover, *Batman/Spider-Man* appears to make an indictment of Orientalist fantasies and anxieties. Indeed, much of the story credits Talia with an awareness of such Western ideas about her ethnic heritage, and in multiple scenes, she acts on that awareness, either arguing against such ideas or actively incorporating them into her plot to aid her father. She goes to Batman wearing a revealing sarong and feigns vulnerability as her assassins attack him. DeMatteis writes a telling description of Batman's thoughts as he battles for Talia's safety: "Raised in the shadow of Ra's al Ghul's corrupted soul, she has been a prisoner of his obsessions, of his need to control not just the fate of the world . . . but the fate of his only child. Do I think, [Batman] muses, that I can save her, *heal* her, even though I've never been able to heal myself?" (DeMatteis, Nolan, Kesel, et al.). Batman's belief in Talia's vulnerability recalls Rajgopal's (2010) indictment of Western discourses for "reify[ing] the Orientalist portrait of women from the global South as victims of their own cultures." In such discourses, women are "victims of their own hyper-patriarchal societies," which are themselves "desperately in need of intervention and the *mission civilisatrice*" (151).[16] Rather than requiring Batman's aid, however, Talia sets off a smoke bomb and uses its cover to disappear.

At the story's end, when Batman, having saved the day, seeks to liberate Talia from her father, Talia rejects his offer: "There is one thing you have never understood about me, Batman. I do not need . . . *rescuing*. I am here at my father's side for the same reason that I love you: not because I am compelled to—but because I choose to" (DeMatteis, Nolan, Kesel, et al. 1997). In the final panel of these lines, Talia looks directly at Batman and the reader, appearing to break the fourth wall as she argues against the notion of herself as an Arabic damsel in distress. The readers, too, are invited to reexamine their own expectations of Talia. It seems implicit that the reader will find Batman's views reliable—after all, the hero's views are implicitly correct—but Talia rejects that presumption of Batman's correctness by rejecting his desire to "rescue" her. Additionally, the expectation of Talia to become the Dragon Lady when betraying Batman is negated by the lack of an actual betrayal at the story's climax. Batman has been misled about Talia's intentions not by Talia herself, but rather by his own assumptions about the vulnerability of Eastern women.

Conclusion

Historical precedents for the character tropes Talia fulfills leave us with a seemingly simple question that ultimately boasts no easy answer: if Talia is the product of the same colonial discourses that brought us such characters as Madame Butterfly, the Daughter of Fu Manchu, and the Dragon Lady, is not her very existence somewhat problematic? O'Neil and Adams's establishment of the al Ghul family as Batman's major international nemeses would seem to prevent readers from divorcing Talia from her origin as an exotic femme fatale, intended, in part, to reflect American cultural anxieties. Often when her ethnicity is made prominent, it is fetishized, resulting in stereotypical depictions of a submissive, endangered Arabic woman or a cold and cunning

East Asian vamp. Storylines such as Grant Morrison's bring notions of female empowerment into conflict with postcolonial concerns. However, stories like those written by Rucka and DeMatteis, as well as others, have shown that it is possible to maintain Talia's traditional appearance, including her costumes, while rejecting characterizations that fall into these tropes. Such treatments offer readings of Talia as a dynamic character who transcends Orientalist stereotypes. Rather than being Arabic *or* East Asian, she becomes both Arabic *and* East Asian and performs actions that are not tied to the tropes that have popularly characterized Eastern women.

Dynamic depictions of Talia that acknowledge her ethnicity while resisting Orientalist tropes serve a greater purpose than the comics themselves. As the audience for comics grows to include global readers, representations of nonwhite characters gain both a personal and political importance. Particularly as a mixed-race woman, Talia boasts the potential to serve as a means of representation and identification for multicultural readers. In his study of media fan practices, Jenkins (1992) notes that "for female [comics] fans, Catwoman became a way of exploring issues of feminine empowerment, of resistance to male constraints and of the requirement to be a 'good little girl'" (35). Talia's refusal to live as the helpless woman dictated by Orientalist and sexist discourses offers readers the same model of resistance. Her potential for resistive readings is not limited to female readers, for her unique ethnic heritage positions her as the site of broader cultural discussion. Jenkins (ibid.) further contends that "fans are drawn to particular [objects] because they provide the materials most appropriate for talking about topics of more direct concern, because they continually raise issues the fans want to discuss," which may "offer insights not only into the fictional characters but into different strategies for resolving personal problems" (83). For the increasingly multicultural comics readership, Talia becomes a possible political fan object. Talia's empowerment as both a woman and a character of mixed ethnicity reaches beyond the fictional universe of the comics to serve as an exploration of contemporary Orientalist discourses and how they are deployed or rejected—both for readers and for media culture itself.

Notes

1. Through his title, frequent bases of operations, and occasionally his physical features, Ra's himself is generally coded as Arabic. Some stories suggest he may be a member of a Chinese nomadic tribe.

2. Many of these appearances are collected in *Tales of the Demon* (1991). Talia's deceitful acts in this collection include drugging a criminal whom Batman means to question with an amnesia-inducing serum, an act she claims was an accident. Her self-deprecating language in the scene and previously acknowledged medical training make it apparent that she is lying.

3. Collected in *Tales of the Demon* (1991).

4. Ibid.

5. As this article is concerned with comics, not mainstream film, *The Dark Knight Rises* falls outside of my scope. However, a postcolonial reading of Miranda Tate is certainly a worthy subject. Similarly, an interesting ethnic characterization of Talia occurs in the 2011 video game *Arkham City*.

6. *Detective* #700 was actually published two years prior to *Bane of the Demon*. However, both stories were written by Chuck Dixon, and *Bane of the Demon* tells the story of the events leading up to *Detective* #700, so they are presented here sequentially rather than by their chronological publication dates.

7. Rucka, who is known for his dynamic portrayals of female characters, would also write a Talia-centric story in *President Luthor* #0 (2001). In this issue, Talia's appearance is very similar to her appearance in *No Man's Land* #0.

8. Most notably, a panel of *Batman and Robin* (2010) features Talia pulling a grotesque expression that, with exaggeratedly slanted eyes and prominent teeth, seems to accidentally mimic Mickey Rooney's Yunioshi in *Breakfast at Tiffany's* (1961).

9. *Batman & Son* collects *Batman* #655–658 and #663–666. These issues originally appeared in 2006 and 2007.

10. http://www.usatoday.com/life/comics/story/2012-06-18/Batman-Incorporated -comic-book-series/55667438/1 (accessed February 19, 2016).

11. http://www.usatoday.com/life/comics/story/2012-06-18/Batman-Incorporated-comic -book-series/55667438/1 (accessed February 19, 2016).

12. Though nonstandard, "oroboro" is the spelling Morrison uses in this issue.

13. *Nightwing: Freefall* collects *Nightwing* #140–146. These issues originally appeared in 2008.

14. While the al Ghuls are not Muslims, they are frequently shown to be living and operating in predominantly Muslim areas, and several of their nameless allies appear to be Muslim. It seems likely that, despite not following the religion, the al Ghuls are nonetheless respectful of its customs.

15. Visual countering occurs through the page layout, as the page is split to juxtapose Talia's face against Batman's. The background behind Batman is a series of Bat symbols; behind Talia is a repeated Demon's Head. Batman's speech is also juxtaposed against Talia's: "Ra's al Ghul is a madman—whose dream of a 'better world' is one in which all wills are

subjugated to his. All men, all nations, under his control. Not long ago, he nearly murdered nine-tenths of the earth's population in the name of his 'holy' cause. I stopped him then—and I'll stop him again."

16. Said's 2003 preface to *Orientalism* similarly refers to the *mission civilizatrice* as the Western response to Eastern Empire (xvi).

References

Bettez, Silvia Cristina. 2010. "Mixed-Race Women and Epistemologies of Belonging." *Frontiers: A Journal of Women Studies* 31 (1): 142–65.

Brown, Jeffrey A. 2011. "Supermoms? Maternity and the Monstrous Feminine in Superhero Comics." *Journal of Graphic Novels and Comics* 2 (1): 77–87.

Brubaker, Ed, writer, Stefano Gaudiano and Roberta Tewes, illustrators. 2001. "Hidden Agenda." *Batman: Our Worlds at War* 1 (August). New York: DC Comics.

Calefato, Patrizia. 2010. "Fashion as Cultural Translation: Knowledge, Constrictions, and Transgressions on/of the Female Body." *Social Semiotics* 20 (4): 343–55.

DeMatteis, J. M., writer, Graham Nolan, Karl Kesel, and Gloria Vasquez, illustrators. 1997. *Batman & Spider-Man*. New York: DC Comics.

Dini, Paul, writer, and Guillem March, illustrator. 2009. "Girls Talk." *Gotham City Sirens* 2 (September). New York: DC Comics.

Dixon, Chuck, writer, Graham Nolan, Scott Hanna, and Gloria Vasquez, illustrators. 1996. "Legacy, Part One: Progeny of the Demon." *Detective* 700 (August). New York: DC Comics.

Dixon, Chuck, writer, Graham Nolan, Tom Palmer, and Noelle Giddings, illustrators. 1998a. *Bane of the Demon* 1 (March). New York: DC Comics.

———. 1998b. *Bane of the Demon* 2 (April). New York: DC Comics.

———. 1998c. *Bane of the Demon* 3 (May). New York: DC Comics.

———. 1998d. *Bane of the Demon* 4 (June). New York: DC Comics.

Hamm, Sam. 1991. "Introduction." In *Tales of the Demon*, by Dennis O'Neil, 5–8. New York: DC Comics.

Jenkins, Henry. 1992. *Textual Poachers: Television Fans and Participatory Culture*. New York: Routledge.

Kelly, Joe, writer, Kano, Aluir Amancio, Marlo Alquiza, et al., illustrators. 2001. "Kith & Kin Part Two." *Action* #773 (January). New York: DC Comics.

Kim, Minjeong, and Angie Y. Chung. 2005. "Consuming Orientalism: Images of Asian/American Women in Multicultural Advertising." *Qualitative Sociology* 28 (1): 67–91.

Loeb, Jeph, writer, Ed McGuinness, Dexter Vines, and Dave Stewart, illustrators. 2004. *Superman/Batman: Public Enemies*. New York: DC Comics.

Loeb, Jeph, writer, and Jim Lee, illustrator. 2009. *Batman: Hush*. New York: DC Comics.

Ma, Sheng-Mei. 2000. *The Deathly Embrace: Orientalism and Asian American Identity*. Minneapolis: University of Minnesota Press.

MacKenzie, John M. 1995. *Orientalism: History, Theory, and the Arts*. Manchester, UK: Manchester University Press.

Morrison, Grant, writer, and Andy Kubert, illustrator. 2008. *Batman & Son*. New York: DC Comics.

Morrison, Grant, writer, Cameron Stewart, Nathan Fairbairn, and Chris Burnham, illustrators. 2012. *Batman Incorporated: Leviathan Strikes!* 1 (February). New York: DC Comics.

Morrison, Grant, writer, Chris Burnham and Nathan Fairbairn, illustrators. 2013. "The Dark Knight and the Devil's Daughter." *Batman Incorporated* 13 (July). New York: DC Comics.

O'Neil, Dennis, writer, Neal Adams, Bob Brown, Dick Giordano, et al., illustrators. 1991. *Tales of the Demon*. New York: DC Comics.

O'Neil, Dennis, writer, and Norm Breyfogle, illustrator. 1992. *Birth of the Demon*. New York: DC Comics.

Rajgopal, Shoba Sharad. 2010. "The Daughter of Fu Manchu: The Pedagogy of Deconstructing the Representation of Asian Women in Film and Fiction." *Meridians* 10 (2): 141–62.

Rucka, Greg, and Jordan B. Gorfinkel, writers, Greg Land, Drew Geraci, and Rob Schwager, illustrators. 1999. "Ground Zero." *Batman: No Man's Land* (December). New York: DC Comics.

Rucka, Greg, writer, Dale Eaglesham and Ray Kryssing, illustrators. 2001. "The Most Suitable Person." *President Luthor: Secret Files and Origins* 1 (March). New York: DC Comics.

Said, Edward. (1978) 2003. *Orientalism*. London: Penguin.

Seagle, Steven T., writer, Scott McDaniel, Andy Owens, Tanya Horie, et al., illustrators. 2003. "Justice." *Superman* Vol. 2, 190. New York: DC Comics.

Singer, Marc. 2002. "Black Skins and White Masks: Comic Books and the Secret of Race." *African American Review* 36 (1): 107–19.

Tomasi, Peter J., writer, Doug Mahnke, Christian Alamy, Rodney Ramos, et al., illustrators. 2008. "Requiem: Caretakers of Mars." *Final Crisis: Requiem* 1 (September). New York: DC Comics.

Tomasi, Peter J., writer, Don Kramer and Sandu Florea, illustrators. 2009. *Nightwing: Freefall*. New York: DC Comics.

Waid, Mark, writer, Howard Porter, Drew Geraci, Ken Lopez, et al., illustrators. 2000. "Tower of Babel Part 3: Protected by the Cold." *JLA* 45 (September). New York: DC Comics.

Yeğenoğlu, Meyda. 1998. *Colonial Fantasies: Towards a Feminist Reading of Orientalism*. Cambridge: Cambridge University Press.

Situating Starbuck: Combative Femininity, Figurative Masculinity, and the Snap

—Ewan Kirkland

This chapter is an exploration of Kara Thrace, also known by her call sign Starbuck, in the reimagined *Battlestar Galactica*. With reference to a broad range of scholarship on this subject, the extent to which her character conforms to or transcends various tropes and stereotypes of the action heroine is considered in order to illustrate the continued structural limitations of fictional women in narrative popular culture, and science fiction fantasy in particular. To a significant extent, Starbuck managed to avoid the pitfalls of such potentially positive characters. However, it is also argued that the ending of the series, and the show's inability to find an appropriately heroic conclusion for the action heroine, reveals much about the continued failure of visual culture to meaningfully accommodate agented female characters.

Starbuck follows a clearly established type within recent science fiction film and television, one which has attracted the attention of numerous scholars concerned with the representations and constructions of women in the media. Her character is a polysemic figure (Kirkland 2008a, 347–48) open to a range of readings within the context of feminist criticism. At various stages, in various ways throughout the series, Starbuck might be considered an action heroine (Hills 1999); a combative female (Willis 1997); a tough woman (Inness 1999); an action babe (O'Day 2004); a maternal action heroine (Good 2007); and ultimately, a frustrating female hero (Magoulick 2006). None of the academic accounts cited here are wholeheartedly celebratory. Many studies engage with the extent to which these character types negotiate the active heroism required of their roles with the tendency for popular media to render women characters passive, incomplete, isolated, and marginalized. Recurring problems concern the extent to which traditionally coded female qualities such as to-be-looked-at-ness (Mulvey 1975), maternity, and submissive heterosexuality still circulate the bodies of these characters and function to curtail their otherwise progressive or transgressive aspects. The action heroine remains a figure of tensions within film and television, reflecting the limitations of female characters within the gendered visual grammar and storytelling structures of popular narrative cultures.

In many accounts, such figures are seen as relinquishing their femininity in assuming the traditionally male position. Militarized, hardbodied heroines are required to lose something of their womanhood in adopting a role traditionally reserved for male characters. Their effect is to reinforce associations between masculinity and activity, even though the active body is a female one. In contrast, when the femininity of the action heroine is emphasized, their confrontational potential is considered undone by the tendency for the camera to objectify, fragment, and fetishize the female body according to the gendered conventions of Hollywood filmmaking or to compromise their strength through their association with disempowering female stereotypes. Both critics and producers of action culture featuring strong, tough female characters are engaged in negotiating and navigating these polarized positions. Situating Starbuck in relation to comparable figures from film, television, sequential art, and digital games, and the academic arguments that circulate them, affords an understanding of the gender politics of the character and the extent to which she challenges dominant formations of visual culture.

Starbuck and the Action Heroine

Starbuck's existence on board the reimagined Battlestar *Galactica*, the transformation of the male action hero of the original 1970s series into the 2000s action heroine, is almost testimony to the extent to which the tough heroine has become a required presence within the ensemble science fiction action series (Kirkland 2008b, 132). Other examples of this type range from hardened warriors like Sarah Connor in *The Terminator* films (1991) and television series (2008–2009), *Tank Girl* (1995), *Farscape*'s (1999–2003) Aeryn Sun, and *Resident Evils*'s (2002) Rain Ocampo, to the more sexualized leads of *Barb Wire* (1996), *Tomb Raider* (2001, 2003) and the *Charlie's Angels* movies (2000, 2003). Earlier films to have attracted attention for their active female protagonists include *Thelma & Louise* (1991), *Silence of the Lambs* (1991), *Speed* (1994), *Twister* (1996), and *GI Jane* (1997). Like the *Bad Girls* (1994) and Charlie Baltimore from *The Long Kiss Goodnight* (1996), Starbuck is a character who manages to "transgress both cinematic genre codes and cultural gender codes which position female characters as the passive, immobile and peripheral characters of Hollywood action cinema" (Hills 1999, 38). Marc O'Day (2004) notes that many of these Girl Power film heroines have their roots in other media such as television, comic books, and video games (202), and Starbuck might be understood as a similarly adapted character, featuring in a deliberately revisionist rebooting of an older science fiction show.

Clearly, Starbuck is a character from television rather than cinema, and despite similarities between the forms, the two media have different ways of telling stories, representing characters, and engaging with audiences. As Nickianne Moody (2002) argues in a positive comparison between the movie *Starship Troopers* and *Space: Above and Beyond*, the lengthy format of the television series show allows significantly more scope for narrative and character development and the exploration of gender politics (65). The televisual medium also involves considerable collaboration, with teams of writers, rotating directors, and fluctuation in cast and crew, all compromising the possibility of a uniform voice imposing a single meaning across the text. In contrast with cinema, tyrannies of the author, the auteur, and the great male artist are comparatively absent in television, in practice and in popular discourse, opening the small screen text to a broader range of interpretations. Television is also less aligned with the grammar of the male gaze and its habitual objectification of the female body. Historically, the domestic medium has been associated with more female centered genres, such as the soap opera, talk show, and reality television. Anne Millard Daugherty's (2002) description of *Buffy the Vampire Slayer* as "'post-gaze' product" (149) highlights the significance of cinematic issues in the show, even as the author acknowledges that the male optical perspective has never enjoyed the same status in television. In addition to media format, there are issues of genre. While *Battlestar Galactica* is science fiction space opera, the screen texts listed above include westerns, espionage thrillers, and war films. It is important not to conflate what amounts to several decades of feminist studies circulating some very different texts, including film noir, rape revenge movies, horror films, and crime dramas. Nevertheless, an assessment of Starbuck in terms of recent feminist criticism serves to position her in terms of other active female characters across media cultures.

While conventionally attractive, Starbuck could not be easily characterized as "drop-dead gorgeous and outfitted in costumes that emphasize sexuality rather than muscle" (Waites 2008, 204–5). Although located in a science fiction universe, Starbuck does not mobilize the iconography of the sort of "curvaceous sex kittens" exemplified by Barbarella (Inness 1999, 102) or the fetishistic fantasy iconography of *Barb Wire*'s combination of comic books and softcore pornography (Tasker 1998, 69). With very few exceptions, Starbuck's body is not sexualized by or for the camera. This is a point of significance in terms of her maintaining power and authority when on screen. The moment when Ripley undresses at the end of *Alien*, Sherrie A. Inness (1999) argues, "does a great deal to limit the threat to gender norms posed by her tough persona," allowing the camera to linger on her rear, restructuring her body as a feminine one, and defining her as potential victim (107). There are scenes where we see Starbuck showering, boxing, and engaged in physical combat, but these moments largely emphasize her head, shoulders, and muscular arms, her fitness and her physical control (Kirkland 2008b, 140), much in the manner of Sarah Connor's depiction in *Terminator 2* (Inness, 1999, 125). The male gaze is significantly undermined by the show's documentary style, refusing clear visual alignment with any particular character. Across the show there is little of the "doubling up" of female bodies as both active narrative agent and erotic spectacle that O'Day sees throughout action babe cinema (2004, 203).

Distinguishing her from the stars of *Charlie's Angels* and *Alias* (Coon 2005), Starbuck is not required to dress up in a range of seductive costumes, masks, and disguises in order to do her job (3). In contrast to the "ridiculously impractical outfits" worn by Mary Magoulick's frustrating heroines (2006, 743), Starbuck's clothing is drab and utilitarian, while her hair is either functionally short or tied back during combat. The singlet over T-shirt guise in which Starbuck frequently appears might suggest the "outerwear, as underwear" as O'Day (2004) describes the costumes of Croft and *Resident Evil*'s Alice (214), but this appears to be standard military issue, worn by both male and female crew members. The only time Starbuck wears a dress, at the end of "Colonial Day" (1:11), her appearance is decidedly incongruous. In contrast to the film version of Lara Croft, Starbuck does not use her sexuality as a weapon, something which Kate Waites (2008) argues defines the videogame heroine as a female body for the male gaze, despite her action (210–11). Aspects of Starbuck's narrative revolve around her relationships with Lee Adama and Sam Anders, but this does not overwhelmingly define her as a sexual, sexualized, or romantic figure. Neither is Starbuck threatened by these men in her life, in the manner of Buffy who, Magoulick (2006) observes, "faces intense, overt hostility and danger from loved ones" (737). Contrasting with the infantilized Beatrix Kiddo of *Kill Bill* (Waites 2008, 205), Starbuck's name carries associations of power, majesty, and sexual aggression reflective of the fact that this was originally the property of a heteronormative male character. Starbuck is not isolated in the manner whereby active women in films are frequently marked as "'exceptional,'" such as the heroine of *Cut-Throat Island* (Tasker 1998, 82). Instead, she is surrounded by other strong and developed female characters, including President Laura Roslin, Boomer, Kat, and Racetrack, as well as the cylon women who run the enemy base ships and a range of female pilots who make up the Battlestar fleet. The feature length special *Razor* shows that military women are not particular to this ship. Like the action babes O'Day (2004) considers, Starbuck is largely concerned with doing her job, and doing it well (208). As is everyone else in the show, Starbuck may be motivated by a straightforward need to survive, but contrasting with the absence of such heroic tropes in the female-centered action heroine narratives discussed by Waites (2008, 207), a "higher purpose" to her action does indeed emerge as the show progresses, relating to her role in finding a planet for the remaining colonies to inhabit, a destiny she fulfils in the series' final episode.

Consistent with contemporary cultural studies' approaches to the screen industries, many authors interrogate the extratextual material that circulates images of strong women. Along similar lines as Jonathan Gray (2010), David Roger Coon (2005) argues that such "paratexts" are significant, presenting viewers with a "preferred reading" of film and television and impacting even on consumers who chose—possibly because of the nature of such material— not to watch a show or attend a screening. Coon demonstrates how promotional material for *Charlie's Angels* and *Alias*, texts about active, resourceful, professional women, focused on the central actors' sex appeal largely to the exclusion of all else. Similarly, Sara Crosby (2004) notes the ways mainstream media reviews responded to the sexualization of Jessica Alba in *Dark Angel* (157) and O'Day (2004) considers the extent to which publicity and behind-the-scenes material function to position the stars of action babe cinema according to traditional feminine structures (205–7), while Inness (1999) writes of the press attention paid to Kate Mulgrew's hairstyle as having a similar effect of emphasizing Captain Janeway's femininity (116–17). An extensive analysis of the publicity material for *Battlestar Galactica* is beyond the scope of this chapter, but images of Katee Sackhoff, who is associated with the show, depict her in the same military gear as her character, employing none of the feminizing and sexualizing extratextual practices of which Coon, Crosby, O'Day, and Inness are so critical.

While as flawed as any other character in *Battlestar Galactica*, Starbuck can be considered the most unambiguously heroic female of the show. Starbuck is the one tasked by the president with returning to Caprica to find the Arrow of Apollo, and she is the first to enter the Tomb of Athena. Starbuck alone flies Tyrol's stealth ship. She also runs the reconnaissance mission to the resurrection ship, after which she is effectively headhunted by Pegasus's Admiral Cain. Starbuck leads efforts to rescue hostages in the bar siege ("Sacrifice" 2:16) and to regain control of Galactica following the coup by Gaiter and Zarek in season four. Starbuck is the best pilot ("Miniseries") and the most accurate sniper shot ("Bastille Day" 1:3); she also can beat Caprica's best at pyramid ball ("Resistance" 2:4). More than a grunt, Starbuck is also educated and cultured, versed in religious knowledge, appreciative of Caprican poetry, and a skilled pianist. At the same time, Starbuck can be seen as reinforcing many aspects of the action heroine considered to limit and restrain her impact. Like Xena, Buffy, and Nikita, as considered by Magoulick (2006, 734–35), and Croft, Kiddo, and the Angels, discussed by Waites (2008, 205), Starbuck is subservient to a male figure in the form of Admiral Bill Adama, whose military authority frequently holds the upper hand over Roslin's government. Starbuck's problematic relationship with Leoben, a cylon who stalks her and holds her captive, suggests the threatening coupling Magoulick also considers.

As such, Starbuck remains a problematic figure, and understandably so. The troubled history of popular culture's representation of women, active or otherwise, combined with the rich and complex heritage of feminist criticism within which they can be positioned, means that any comparable character is unlikely to be without issues. Like previous film and television series, the narrative, representational, and generic apparatus of *Battlestar Galactica* struggles to contain the transgressive female hero, employing a range of strategies to define the action heroine as "macho/masculine, as mothers or as Others; sometimes even as all three at different points within the narrative" (Tasker 1998, 69). What follows is a detailed analysis of Starbuck within this context, in relation to her status as masculinized heroine, as heterosexual mother figure, and as monstrous Other, concluding with an attempt to understand the peculiar ending to Starbuck's narrative trajectory by which she simply disappears into thin air.

Starbuck as Figurative Male

Starbuck exemplifies the apparent gender neutrality on board Battlestar *Galactica*, consistent with the gender ambiguity that circulates in the images of many action heroines. Her character might be productively understood as a tomboy, considered by Yvonne Tasker (1998, 68) in relation to female characters in *Twister*, *Speed*, and *Bad Girls*; a boyish "Final Girl" according to the archetype Carol J. Clover (1992) identifies in horror cinema; and/or a self-conscious combination of male and female qualities that Barbara Creed (1987, 65) sees in the science fiction heroine of the *Alien* franchise. Such gender play is evident not only in Starbuck's depiction as "muscular," her "male proletarian guise" (Tasker 1998, 81), but also in the sense that Katie Sackhoff literally assumes the identity of a male character, played by Dirk Benedict in the original *Battlestar Galactica*. The rebooted Starbuck reproduces, at an extradiegetic level, the "gender thefts" O'Day (2004) sees as a theme of action adventure films (203) in a transgendering act of appropriation, permanently assuming a role previously held by a male. As Carla Kungl (2008) details, the decision to cast Starbuck as a woman was criticized by fans of the original series and the actor playing the original part, who attacked the casting decision as a money-making ploy, a sop to political correctness, and a negative consequence of four decades of feminism (200–201). The form and ferocity of such criticisms indicates the significant investment in gender boundaries that the move challenged. Tasker (1998) may well be referring to the reimagined fighter pilot when she writes of the cross-dressing heroine as a figure who "reinforces the ambiguous gender identity of the female action hero, or rather points to the instability of a gendered system and the production of an alternative space through that instability" (68–69). It is, arguably, this threatening ambiguity and alternativity to which early fans and critics of the show were responding and which produced the hysterically cisgendered claims Kungl relates Dirk Benedict as expressing.

The gender dynamics of *Battlestar Galactica* have notable precedents in science fiction literature, film, and television. Life onboard *Galactica* is comparable to the "wish-fulfilling, utopian, seemingly feminist" world of *Alien* considered by Judith Newton (1990, 84), expressing the same stunning egalitarianism observed by Constance Penley (1990) in which each role in the film script was reportedly written for actors of either gender (124–25). Subsequently, the military forces of *Aliens*, *Starship Troopers*, *Farscape*, and *Space: Above and Beyond* reproduce a gender-blind organization of rank, living conditions, and field-related duties. The short-lived *Space* series, Moody (2002) relates, "extrapolate[s] a military service in which both sexes serve without apparent segregation, sexism (or racism)" (55), albeit at the absence of a civilian politics that might contextualize this depiction of the future in a more ideologically meaningful way. *Battlestar Galactica* is also largely removed from the social and domestic, being almost entirely set on a fleet of military craft traveling through deep space. The elision of the domestic, as Newton (1990) also observes in *Alien*, means that a major site of inequality is ignored and a gender-neutral utopia maintained. Moreover, the hypermilitarized culture of *Battlestar Galactica* might also be more critically considered a hypermasculine, rather than gender neutral, one. Being male is the norm to which female characters conform, evident in the practice of calling superior officers of either gender "sir." As in *SAAB*, "gender integration into the military" involves "becoming an honorary male" (Moody 2002, 71). Characters who reflect common tropes of femininity—femme fatale cylon Number Six, the oversexual Ellen, the needy mother Kali—are disruptive and problematic within the male culture of the Battlestar, ruled over by gravel-voiced Admiral Adama. The cold dark surfaces and grey fatigues of the ship construct a hard-edged, utilitarian, tough-bodied aesthetic in which Starbuck, first seen jogging through the ship's corridors, is entirely at home. Visually, as Kungl (2008) observes, Starbuck's short hair and muscular body give her a notably masculine appearance (203). Starbuck engages in traditional male activities: she drinks shots, smokes cigars, taunts superior officers about the infidelity of their wives, fights inside and outside the boxing ring, flies, shoots, and even finds time to enjoy the occasional zipless frack. Her Caprica home, seen briefly in "Valley of Darkness" (2:2), is a domestic disaster, messy, graphitized, disconnected from utilities for nonpayment of bills. But she does have a fully functional pickup truck in the garage. Like the postapocalyptic Sarah Connor, Starbuck is a combination of signs signifying both masculinity and toughness, defining her as "'one of the boys'" (Inness 1999, 128), a representation that problematically realigns maleness and active heroism. In this respect, the hotshot pilot reflects the figurative masculinity Clover (1992) sees in the slasher trope of the Final Girl victim-hero, a figure who arguably "has very little to do with femaleness and very much to do with phallocentrism" (53). Along similar lines, Sarah Conly (2008) provocatively asks if Starbuck has "simply become a man in a female body" (230).

At the same time, Elizabeth Hills (1999) critiques the kind of "binaristic logic" inherent in such perspectives, drawn as they are from psychoanalytic frameworks and theoretical models that deny the possibility of female agency and dismiss potentially transgressive and transformative characters as "pseudo males." Hills's reading of the *Alien* heroine is of a character challenging those very limiting normative gender distinctions and divisions, dismantling traditional notions of the body through experimental connection with machines, objects, and environmental features to push the limitations of the body under patriarchy. Although Hills never mentions the author, her celebration of the feminist potential in this boundary-unsettling melding of body and technology resonates strongly with Donna J. Haraway's (1991) seminal cyborg manifesto. This cyberfeminist polemic argues for the liberating potential of contradictions, partiality, irony, and blasphemy, symbolized by the cyborg, "a cybernetic organism, a hybrid of machine and organism, a creature of social reality as well as a creature of fiction" (149). The same fusion of human and technology can be seen in Starbuck's relationship with her viper, with the blackbird stealth ship, and most dramatically, in the cylon craft through which she escapes an inhospitable planet after crashing in "You Can't Go Home Again" (1:5). Kungl (2008) rightfully considers this an exemplary Starbuck episode, depicting "a tough girl pilot who is not saved by even tougher men" (205). Moreover, Starbuck's very physical integration into the sticky, wet machine of the cylon raider, the means of her triumphant escape from the planet, celebrates the blurring of boundaries between male and female, organic and inorganic, cyborg and human, while underlining the queer hybridity of the action heroine herself.

Starbuck as Lover, as Mother

Battlestar Galactica, unlike *Alien*, is not devoid of heterosexual relationships, and in this respect its egalitarianism is potentially disturbed. Indicative of the extent to which, as Richard Dyer (1997) observes, normative heterosexual practices appear rooted in power imbalances, whenever heterosexual couples within *Battlestar Galactica* feature in domestic arrangements, the tensions of sustaining such gender-neutral relationships become apparent. In many ways, it is this aspect of popular culture representation, requiring that women in heterosexual relationships take a subordinate position to their male partners, rather than sexuality itself, that undermines the power of tough women in such scenarios. Starbuck can be seen as resisting this tendency. The suspicion that she contributed to the death of her lover, Lee's brother, and Adama's son by passing him as a pilot when he was not ready to fly, hangs over the character as indicative of the disastrous potential of allowing romantic feelings to compromise her toughness. As Conly (2008) observes, the pilot is never willing to sacrifice her goals or principles to keep a man happy (234). Following her first night with Sam, Starbuck is clearly more concerned with the mission than with his emotional needs. His character frequently assumes the traditional feminine role in their relationship, desiring of romantic as well as physical intimacy, while in season four Sam comes increasingly to resemble a female cylon hybrid. If the dynamic of Starbuck and Sam's relationship is foregrounded by a pyramid ball game where she kicks his ass, Starbuck's more egalitarian relationship with Lee is evident in the boxing match of "Unfinished Business" (3:9), where the two end up equally matched and exhausted, falling against each other in balanced unity. Renny Christopher (2004) makes a comparable assessment of *Farscape*'s Sunn and Crichton, claiming the gender-neutral military background of the Peacekeepers affords a reinvention, rather than simple inversion, of gender roles (273–74).

There is no use of the f word in *Battlestar Galactica* (Kirkland 2008a, 337). The suggestion is that within the show's (masculine) gender-neutral universe, the battle between the sexes has either ended or never needed to take place.

This serves to divest Starbuck's character of the explicit radical potential that would accompany her more substantial diegetic situation within discourses of Western identity politics. Nevertheless, there are episodes clearly engaging with issues of gender, particularly in the context of war. Scenes in "Flesh and Bone" (1:8), where Starbuck tortures a cylon prisoner, are comparable to the military thrillers discussed by Moody (2002), reflecting similar debates around women's suitability for combat. Given the series's contemporaneity with the Iraq War, premiering just months before *60 Minutes* broadcast pictures of army private Lynndie England participating in the abuse of prisoners in Abu Ghraib, the episode has chilling political resonance. "The Farm" (2:5), as Kungl (2008) notes, is also of particular interest. Here, Starbuck is incapacitated in a sinister hospital, attended by a lone doctor who argues that, as a woman, her primary concern should be to repopulate the near-extinct human race. The pilot's resistance to this suggestion is dismissively pathologized by the doctor who, observing marks of childhood abuse on her body, notes that this response is common among victims of such trauma. There is something of the female Gothic in these scenes of a bedridden woman kept drugged, isolated, and uncertain as to the trustworthiness of those caring for her. This uncertainty remains until the crucial point-of-view shot where Starbuck spots a known cylon in the office outside her room, revealing the hospital's true nature as an enemy facility. The logical conclusion of the cylon doctor's suggestions are revealed in the horrific image of a ward full of women connected to machines, reduced to baby-making units. If Starbuck's integration into the body of the crashed cylon vessel represents an example of the cyborg as radical hybrid, this constitutes the cyborg as monstrous slave of a military-industrial pharmaceutical complex, something also considered alongside politically positive manifestations of the figure in Haraway's (1991) necessarily contradictory essay. Starbuck is significantly weakened in this episode, killing her captor, escaping the prison, but requiring the assistance of Sam and Helo's assault team to defeat the cylon army as she cowers on the hospital steps.

A similarly problematic aspect of Starbuck's story is her ongoing relationship with Leoben. When living under occupation on New Caprica, Starbuck is kept hostage by the cylon and forced to adopt the role of domesticated housewife. Like the show's depiction of institutional pressure for women to reproduce, this scenario constitutes a critique of "compulsory heterosexuality." This term, coined by Adrienne Rich (1993), refers to ways in which women are coerced into conforming to patriarchy-serving patterns of coupledom and marriage and concurrent forms of sexual orientation. Socializing agents, including health professionals, economic structures, and the culture industries all conspire to define heterosexuality as the natural, inevitable choice for women. The claustrophobic and prison-like nature of monogamous domestic heterosexuality is reflected in the stark, fake home Leoben constructs in the New Caprica detention center in an attempt to force Starbuck to become his loving partner. This is a role Starbuck steadfastly resists, stabbing her captor with a steak knife before wiping her bloodied hand on the carpet and sitting down to enjoy her dinner. As an act she has apparently performed many times before the start of season three, this constitutes the closest Starbuck gets to a *Thelma & Louise*–style expression of feminist rage (Kirkland 2008b, 141).

If Starbuck's containment within and resistance to such medical and domestic structures critique the cult of motherhood and compulsory heterosexuality, subsequent developments appear less radical in their politics. The introduction of a young girl, said to be Starbuck's daughter, represents a shift in the pilot's attitude towards her captor. Traumatized at having suddenly discovered herself a mother, guilty after the child is injured while in her neglectful care, and consequently grateful to Leoben for arranging her medical attention, Starbuck moves tentatively into the arms of her tormentor. This furthers the narrative's critique of the nuclear family, suggesting the ways in which maternity is imposed on women as a means of maintaining patriarchal order, while less positively implying that even a hardbodied heroine's heart can be melted at the prospect of motherhood. As the exodus of New Caprica begins, Starbuck is knocked unconscious by Leoben, rendering her in a similarly helpless state as her child, a damsel in distress rescued by Lee. Upon regaining consciousness, Starbuck initiates a return to her former domestic prison to rescue the girl, the action heroine's power returning in the form of maternal instinct to protect the child she believes to be her own. In this respect Starbuck assumes, however briefly, the "heroic maternal figure" Jill Good (2007) identifies in the *Alien* series's Ripley, and which Waites (2008) sees as compromising Connor and Kiddo (205). These narratives show maternity validating and making plausible the heroine's activity. While Good (2007) argues the hybridity of hero and mother represents a potential challenge to traditional "feminine" positions, in the example of *Kill Bill*, maternity functions to restore patriarchal roles, transforming Kiddo "from a ruthless assassin to a responsible mum" (75). The story of Starbuck's shift from serial executioner of abusive spouse, to complicit mother, to heroic maternal figure is brought to a close when, upon returning to Galactica, the pilot realizes that she has been deliberately misled and that the child belongs to another New Caprica colonist.

Starbuck as Other

Sarah Crosby (2004) writes of the brutal cull of strong women in American television, occurring in the spring of 2001, as the heroines of *Dark Angel*, *Buffy the Vampire Slayer*, and *Xena Warrior Princess* all committed sacrificial suicide at the conclusion of their respective seasons. Crosby interprets their deaths in the context of an American republican ideology that affords, even encourages, female heroism in the name of individualism and self-assertion but that cannot allow the challenge to patriarchy inherent in allowing women to enjoy political power, which is the ultimate conclusion of comparable male-centered hero narratives. Instead, the tough female is, at the end of her story, transformed into a sacrificial heroine in the name of patriarchal authority. This "rubber band effect"—whereby screen women are permitted freedom to act heroically, aggressively, self-assertively, only to be suddenly reined back in at a major point in their character arc—is what Crosby calls "the snap."

Starbuck undergoes two such snaps. The first related to her death near the end of season three in "Maelstrom" (3:17), although, indicative of her deviation from previous female action characters, her demise sits uneasily with Crosby's model of the processes heroines must undergo in order to facilitate the reaffirmation of patriarchy inherent in their sacrifice. Unlike Xena, Starbuck feels no guilt associated with her heroism. There is no sense that Starbuck, like Buffy, wishes to become a "normal girl." Unlike Max, Starbuck has not had the opportunity to reject any alternative to patriarchy, given that no such alternative exists in the world of *Battlestar Galactica*, although this simultaneously precludes the kind of feminist transcendence that Crosby suggests might allow such narratives to be optimistically interpreted. Starbuck's death is part of her heroic journey, her calling, signaled by visual connections between a circular spiraling image with which Starbuck seems preoccupied, a religious symbol, and the pattern of a cloud storm over a nearby planet. The fact that Starbuck's destiny involves suicidal flight into the eye of the storm reproduces the affinity between her gift and death that Crosby sees as part of Buffy's road to self-sacrifice. Starbuck's death might carry aspects of the patriarchal capitulation Crosby identifies, as it involves embracing the role which Leoben attributes to her in more ways than one. A dream sequence opening the episode shows the unusually scantily dressed pilot attempting to obliterate the circular symbol from her apartment wall, only to end up writhing in the arms of her erstwhile captor surrounded in thick white paint. More troubling than the pilot's acceptance of her destiny as asserted by the cylon is the suggestion that Starbuck harbors erotic desires for the man who imprisoned and abused her on New Caprica. Subsequently, Starbuck flies into the storm, and to her death.

And yet Starbuck is not dead. Like many women heroes, Starbuck returns, but unlike Buffy or Xena, Starbuck does not seem to suffer in her death, and her resurrection is not a painful experience. She simply reappears at the end of season 3, surprising Lee in the cockpit of his viper, assuring him that she knows the way to Earth. Throughout season four, Starbuck remains a profoundly ambiguous character, her exact nature questioned by all around her and never satisfactorily resolved. The show has always indicated that Starbuck is unique, important, holding a special destiny often denied to female heroes, evident in her mother's caustic assertions and Leoben's mystical claims, but also in Cain's glowing praise and Adama's evident respect for the pilot. Following her return from the dead, that specialness seems now to compromise Starbuck's humanity, with constant speculation concerning her status as a ghost, as an angel, as a cylon, as a harbinger of death, suggestive of the ambiguous hybridity that characterizes the action heroine's liminal status. As her sanity is questioned, Starbuck's abject status is symbolized by the castoff latrine ship that she is given to captain in her search for Earth, and the rebelling crew members who increasingly distrust her judgment. The discovery on the ruined planet Earth of what appears to be Starbuck's own body in a crashed viper ship raises more questions than it answers. "If that's me lying there, then what am I?," Starbuck demands of a dumbfounded Leoben, the only person in the universe who seems capable of giving a response. The show does not. As the climax approaches, Starbuck is increasingly compromised as a transgressive action heroine. Flashbacks suggest a pathology to her success, the pilot's proficient skills stemming from a single mother's relentless demands. All is forgiven, as Leoben, along with many other cylon models, form an alliance with the human fleet. In a final capitulation to the demands of the Oedipal narrative, in "Someone to Watch Over Me" (4:19) Starbuck befriends a piano player, the ghost of her absent father, and together they compose a song combining Starbuck's childhood memories, notes drawn by a cylon child, and the melody that activated four of the Final Five at the end of season three. These notes become instrumental in helping Starbuck find the correct jump coordinates to the new Earth. As a consequence, the pilot's destiny is ultimately managed by the combined efforts of a manipulative stalker, an abusive mother, and a deserter father, all of whom, it transpires, know Starbuck better than she knows herself. Moreover, saving humanity is not achieved by Starbuck's mobilizing the abilities for which she has been known throughout the series: skills as a pilot, a tactician, a shooter, or even a pyramid ball player. Instead, in an admittedly dramatic sequence, Starbuck finds Earth by pressing buttons on a keyboard.

Then, as the colonists descend on the planet in the series conclusion, Starbuck's second snap occurs. Admittedly, she is saved the punishment, humiliation, and death, which would seem to be the common narrative conclusions available to active women in film and television. She is not forced to relinquish her arms, to settle down in domestic bliss with Lee, as would be another possible outcome according to the logic of compulsory heterosexuality. Neither is she permitted social or political leadership, something the republican ideology would deny a woman, this role being naturally reserved for the admiral's son. Instead, indicative of the continued failure of popular narrative culture and the dominant ideologies with which it accords to imagine a satisfactory conclusion for tough, active women, without any fuss, violence, heroism, or redemption, Starbuck simply vanishes.

References

Christopher, Renny. 2004. "Little Miss Tough Chick of the Universe: *Farscape*'s Inverted Sexual Dynamics." In *Action Chicks: New Images of Tough Women in Popular Culture*, edited by Sherrie A. Inness, 257–81. Basingstoke, UK: Palgrave Macmillan.

Clover, Carol J. 1992. *Men, Women and Chain Saws: Gender in the Modern Horror Film*. London: BFI.

Conly, Sarah. 2008. "Is Starbuck a Woman?" In *Battlestar Galactica and Philosophy: Knowledge Here Begins Out There*, edited by Jason T. Eberl, 230–40. Oxford: Blackwell.

Coon, David Roger. 2005. "Two Steps Forward, One Step Back: The Selling of *Charlie's Angels* and *Alias*." *Journal of Popular Film & Television* 33 (1): 2–11.

Creed, Barbara. 1987. "From Here to Modernity: Feminism and Postmodernism." *Screen* 28 (2): 47–68.

Crosby, Sara. 2004. "The Cruellest Season: Female Heroes Snapped into Sacrificial Heroines." In *Action Chicks: New Images of Tough Women in Popular Culture*, edited by Sherrie A. Inness, 153–78. Basingstoke, UK: Palgrave Macmillan.

Daugherty, Anne Millard. 2002. "Just a Girl: Buffy as Icon." In *Reading the Vampire Slayer: An Unofficial Critical Companion to Buffy and* Angel, edited by Roz Kaveney, 148–65. London: Tauris Parke Paperbacks.

Dyer, Richard. 1997. "Heterosexuality." In *Lesbian and Gay Studies: A Critical Introduction*, edited by Andy Medhurst and Sally R. Munt, 261–73. London: Cassell.

Good, Jill. 2007. "Maternal Instinct: Representations of Maternal Action Heroines." In *Crash Cinema: Representation in Film*, edited by Mark Goodall, Jill Good, and Will Godfrey, 68–76. Newcastle, UK: Cambridge Scholars.

Gray, Jonathan. 2010. *Show Sold Separately: Promos, Spoilers, and Other Media Paratexts*. London: New York University Press.

Haraway, Donna J. 1991. *Simians, Cyborgs, and Women: The Reinvention of Nature*. London: Free Association Books.

Hills, Elizabeth. 1999. "From 'Figurative Males' to Action Heroines: Further Thoughts on Active Women in the Cinema." *Screen* 40 (1): 38–50.

Inness, Sherrie A. 1999. *Tough Girls: Women Warriors and Wonder Women in Popular Culture*. Philadelphia: University of Pennsylvania Press.

Kirkland, Ewan. 2008a. "A Dangerous Place for Women." In *Battlestar Galactica and Philosophy: Mission Accomplished or Mission Frakked Up?*, edited by Josef Steiff and Tristan D. Tamplin, 337–48. Chicago: Open Court.

Kirkland, Ewan. 2008b. "Starbuck and the Gender Dynamics of *Battlestar Galactica*." In *Finding Battlestar Galactica: An Unauthorised Guide*, edited by Lynette Porter, David Lavery, and Hillary Robson, 131–44. Naperville, IL: Sourcebooks.

Kungl, Carla. 2008. "'Long Live Stardoe!' Can a Female Starbuck Survive?" In *Cylons in America: Critical Studies in* Battlestar Galactica, edited by Tiffany Potter and C. W. Marshall, 198–209. London: Continuum.

Magoulick, Mary. 2006. "Frustrating Female Heroism: Mixed Messages in *Xena, Nikita*, and *Buffy*." *Journal of Popular Culture* 39 (5): 729–55.

Moody, Nickianne. 2002. "Displacements of Gender and Race in *Space: Above and Beyond*." In *Aliens R Us: The Other in Science Fiction Cinema*, edited by Ziauddin Sardar and Sean Cubitt, 51–73. London: Pluto Press.

Mulvey, Laura. 1975. "Visual Pleasure and Narrative Cinema" 16 (3): 6–18.

Newton, Judith. 1990. "Feminism and Anxiety in *Alien*." In *Alien Zone: Cultural Theory and Contemporary Science Fiction Cinema*, edited by Annette Kuhn, 82–87. London: Verso.

O'Day, Marc. 2004. "Beauty in Motion: Gender, Spectacle and Action Babe Cinema." In *Action and Adventure Cinema*, edited by Yvonne Tasker, 201–18. London: Routledge.

Penley, Constance. 1990. "Time Travel, Primal Scene and the Critical Dystopia." In *Alien Zone: Cultural Theory and Contemporary Science Fiction Cinema*, edited by Annette Kuhn, 116–27. London: Verso.

Rich, Adrienne. 1993. "Compulsory Heterosexuality and Lesbian Existence." In *The Lesbian and Gay Studies Reader*, edited by Henry Abelove, Michèle Aina Barale, and David M. Halperin, 227–54. London: Routledge.

Tasker, Yvonne. 1998. *Working Girls: Gender and Sexuality in Popular Cinema*. London: Routledge.

Waites, Kate. 2008. "Babes in Boots: Hollywood's Oxymoronic Warrior Women." In *Chick Flicks: Contemporary Women at the Movies*, edited by Suzanne Ferriss and Mallory Young, 204–20. London: Routledge.

Willis, Sharon. 1997. *High Contrast: Race and Gender in Contemporary Hollywood Film*. London: Duke University Press.

Episode Guide

"Miniseries." *Battlestar Galactica*. Syfy Channel. New York City, December 8, 2003.

"Bastille Day" (1:3). *Battlestar Galactica*. Syfy Channel. New York City, November 1, 2004.

"You Can't Go Home Again" (1:5). *Battlestar Galactica*. Syfy Channel. New York City, November 15, 2004.

"Flesh and Bone" (1:8). *Battlestar Galactica*. Syfy Channel. New York City, December 6, 2004.

"Colonial Day" (1:11). *Battlestar Galactica*. Syfy Channel. New York City, January 10, 2005.

"Valley of Darkness" (2:2). *Battlestar Galactica*. Syfy Channel. New York City, July 22, 2005.

"Resistance" (2:4). *Battlestar Galactica*. Syfy Channel. New York City, August 5, 2005.

"The Farm" (2:5). *Battlestar Galactica*. Syfy Channel. New York City, August 12, 2005.

"Sacrifice" (2:16). *Battlestar Galactica*. Syfy Channel. New York City, February 10, 2006.

"Unfinished Business" (3:9). *Battlestar Galactica*. Syfy Channel. New York City, December 1, 2006.

"Maelstrom" (3:17). *Battlestar Galactica*. Syfy Channel. New York City, March 4, 2007.

"Someone to Watch Over Me" (4:19). *Battlestar Galactica*. Syfy Channel. New York City, February 27, 2009.

PART II

Expanding the Horizons of the Woman Fantastic

From SuperOther to SuperMother:
The Journey toward Liberty

—Nicola Mann

C onservative cultural theorist Charles Murray (1984) dominated 1980s understandings of African American women with his infamous critique of the American welfare system, *Losing Ground*. Murray's book argued that liberal social welfare programs like Aid for Dependent Children (AFDC), aimed specifically at inner-city blacks, encouraged the rise of what he called a "culture of poverty" (60). He argued that by making it economically feasible for single mothers to remain unmarried, welfare increased out-of-wedlock childbirth, thereby escalating the decline of inner-city communities through unemployment. According to Murray's formulation, instead of empowering people, welfare created a dangerous dependency on government aid, a process that destroyed people's initiative, preventing them from acquiring the productive skills needed to succeed in America's market economy. Consequently, the sociologist proposed denying single mothers child support payments from nonresident fathers since we live "in an age where contraceptives and abortion are freely available" (Work and Responsibility Act 1994).

Murray's policy prescriptions found a rapt audience in the Reagan administration's conservative government. Reagan's oft-repeated 1984 anecdote about an irresponsible, breeding "welfare queen" who takes public funds to support a lavish lifestyle encapsulated the sentiment of the administration. Mobilized by associated appeals to the reputed unfairness of social policies such as quotas, affirmative action, and special treatment extended to African Americans and other communities of color, Murray and Reagan were instrumental in influencing efforts to reform and eventually eradicate the welfare state (Gray 1995, 17). A slew of subsequent sociological and political scholarship continued in this destructive vein, alternatively identifying solo mothers as "unwanted by everyone around them" (Kaplan 1997, 18), as a seeping "contagious" infection" (Anderson 1991, 391), or as "cancerous" individuals who "[breed] criminals faster than society can jail them" (Glasner 2000, 9). While various academic, political, and journalistic commentators contributed to the denunciation of single mothers during the 1980s, however, there was perhaps no greater critic than popular culture.

Heated debates over solo mothers found their way into the American visual imagination through sensationalized network television, daily newspapers, and weekly magazine reports. These include fictionalized representations such as the *Saturday Night Live* comic character Cabrini-Green Harlem-Watts-Jackson[1] and documentary treatments as in CBS's 1986 news series *The Vanishing Family—Crisis in Black America*. While many visual culture outputs from the 1980s promoted destructive representations of single mothers, a revisionist characterization found its way into the pages of *Give Me Liberty: An American Dream* (1990). Set in the near future, the four-issue comic book miniseries follows superhero Martha Washington from her birth to a single mother in Chicago's Cabrini-Green public housing project to her death as a notorious and highly respected superhero. Produced by the American comic book creator and *Sin City* (2005) director Frank Miller and the British comic book artist Dave Gibbons, *Give Me Liberty* chronicles Washington's attempts to thwart the corrupt economic policies of President Erwin Rexall in a series of bloody, hard-fought adventures. Overcoming seemingly insurmountable odds, she defeats Rexall. As an African American woman, Washington not only re-scripts the familiar trope of the white male superhero but also offers an alternate vision of the children of urban single mothers. Washington excels in physical strength, leadership skills, and intelligence, endowments that contest political scientist James Q. Wilson's (2003) assertion that "the children of single moms are more likely than those of two-parent families to be abused, to drop out of or be expelled from school, to become juvenile delinquents, to take drugs, and to commit adult crimes" (8). In a contemporary nod to Patrick Henry's call to the people at the beginning of the American Revolution—"give me liberty or give me death"—the comic series reimagines young, African American women as empowered individuals capable of deciding their own futures. In reference to her eighteenth-century political namesake, Martha Washington becomes a First Lady for the twenty-first century.

In order to chart Washington's journey towards "superness," this chapter follows a chronological trajectory. Frank Miller (Miller and Gibbons 2009) characterizes the sequential nature of Washington's story in the following terms: "She journeyed from housing-project prisoner to drugged-out victim of an insanity ward, from soldier to explorer to savior of the world, to mother of a new generation worthy of your name" (Introduction). Gibbons exploits the inherently dialectical nature of *Give Me Liberty* by inserting dates between panels—2002, 2003, and 2007—a technique intended to chart a movement in time and focus. The inclusion of dates also has implications for the believability of the narrative. As comic book aficionado Will Eisner (1985) notes, "A comic becomes 'real' when time and timing is factored into the creation" (138). Taking this narrative cause and effect arc as a guiding philosophy, this chapter documents the chain of events that led Washington to achieve *Liberty*. Washington's challenging start to life is made unmistakably clear in the opening few pages of the first installment of the *Give Me Liberty* series, *Homes and Gardens* (Miller and Gibbons 1990). Dominated by frenetic scenes of domestic, gang, and police brutality, the comic locates Cabrini-Green as a stage for oppressive environmental obstacles. Black smoke billows from broken windows while canary yellow graffiti tags stating simply "NO" punctuate exterior walls. To reinforce the familiar trope of inner-city pathology, Gibbons and Miller cast Washington as the child of a single mother. A blood-splattered sequence of five small panels documents her father's death at the hands of violent armed police while protesting poor living conditions in Cabrini-Green, just one year after her birth. Over a series of three lower-tier panels, Washington's narrative voice explains that "Dad died in a **protest** against the **green**. Dad said the green's a **prison** for people who haven't done anything **wrong**. They call it **social welfare** but dad calls it a **prison**. It's got **barbed wire** like a prison. And they **shoot** you if you try and get **out**. Nobody ever gets out. Not even when they're dead" (Miller and Gibbons 1990, Vol 1., emphasis in original). Washington's emphasis on certain words (protest, green, prison, wrong, social welfare, barbed wire, shoot, out) functions as a kind of staccato heartbeat. This breathless, almost strangulated indictment of her home—compounded by the inclusion of a tombstone in the final panel of the page—effectively sentences Washington to a life of pain in the "prison" of Cabrini-Green.

The opening theme of environmental trauma reaches a crescendo as we find a seven-year-old Washington pursued by a crazed pedophile and running for her life through muddy labyrinthine alleyways, past syringes, crowds of drug-addled homeless people, and puddles of lime green vomit. Alternating between tiny close-up fragments of Washington's wide-eyed face and narrow elongated panels showing the attacker closing in on our terrified hero, Gibbons's compressed "breakdowns"—defined as the "blocking out of the visual perspective and time of action for each panel" (Witek 1989, 21–22)—enhance the rising tempo of terror and evoke the feeling of mental and physical confinement. This is an out-of-kilter city space, full of secret hiding places, characterized by a netherworld of jaunty perspectives, skulking shadows, and monstrous inhabitants of the night. When Washington manages to hide from her enemy in a disused locker-room, Gibbons gilds the scene in a sickly sea-foam green, petrifying public housing with the omniscient specter of death. The green color bleeds into her body like an infection, an artistic strategy which implies that her living environment has consumed her—she *is* Cabrini *Green*. This frenetic opening section serves to establish the environmental obstacles that Washington and real public housing residents must contend with on a daily basis.

In its almost celebratory emphasis on nihilistic despair, the comic also illustrates the vice-like hold of late-twentieth-century mass-media representations of single mothers from public housing. Projected into our living rooms, televisual manifestations of single motherhood came to define, clarify, and solidify a social boundary—who belongs and who does not. A useful example of this border control can be found in the form of CBS's 1986 documentary *The Vanishing Family—Crisis in Black America*. Presented by media analyst Bill Moyers, the show reported on the social changes caused by the disappearance of two-parent black families in Newark, New Jersey's inner city public housing neighborhoods. Following a muted introductory sequence featuring the crumbling exteriors of project buildings, the camera cut to the ominous question, "What happens to families when mothers are children, fathers don't count, and the street is the strongest school?" As the text fades out, we find Moyers seated opposite seventeen-year-old public housing resident and welfare recipient Clarinda Henderson, a solo mother for two years, who justifies her single status with the defiant, "I wouldn't want no man holding me down." With these final words, the credits roll against a darkened lingering image of Henderson, a visual effect that situates the black female body as the central protagonist in this drama.

In his seminal investigation of black televisual representation in the 1980s, *Watching Race*, Herman Gray (1995) argues that such racialized imagery was central to "the consolidation of a conservative cultural and political hegemonic block." Network television positioned Reagan's discourse at the forefront of national political and public debate, "staging" a version of "blackness" that maintained, promoted, and circulated conservative agendas (14). One of these primary agendas was to focus debates on the eradication of the liberal welfare establishment via a "them" and "us" divide. In 1991, while appearing as a guest on ABC's *This Week*, Murray suggested that single mothers unthinkingly "waste" public money on frivolous expenses and that the only fair solution "for us" would be to "get rid of the whole welfare system, period, lock, stock and barrel" (14). As Gray argues, Murray's references to "waste" and to "us" play against historic and racialized discourses about welfare at the same time they join law-abiding taxpayers to an unmarked but normative, idealized racial, and class subject—hardworking whites. Furthermore, in asserting that such cuts are the only solution "for us"—*This Week's* white interviewer and the white middle-class viewers sitting at home—Murray defines the racial and class fault lines that run through his rhetoric: just as the single mother threatens to drain the public's purse by siphoning off valuable resources from the state, she also simultaneously ensures its moral and social survival because, as sociologist Patricia Hill Collins (2000) notes, "Those individuals who stand at the margins of society clarify its boundaries. African-American women, by not belonging, emphasize the significance of belonging" (7). When coupled with intense televisual scrutiny, this model of inner-city pathology ensured that, in their educational, moral, and cultural deviation from accepted societal norms, African American single mothers became the ultimate "super-other."

Give Me Liberty manipulates the reader's view of public housing, focusing on Washington's journey towards the "fantastic" in order to define and undermine the societal parameters solidified by late-twentieth-century media outlets. Gibbons achieves this via shifts in the reader's physical vantage point, a technique termed *aspect-to-aspect* transition (McCloud 1993, 72). Following the frenzied opening, several panels chart the movement of a police helicopter approaching a building clearly recognizable as the massive high-rise Cabrini-Green Extension North. The comic book equivalent of a filmic zoom, the shifting viewpoints of the panels resemble camera cuts in cinema and television. The reader views the helicopter and the building to which it is headed from below, then from above, and then again from below. Moving at a frantic pace, these bewildering jumps in point of view serve partly to heighten concern about public housing as a scene of crime surveillance, but perhaps more importantly, to place the reader at an impersonal distance; we see buildings not as the residents see their homes (from the inside) but from a peripheral bird's-eye view. Spiraling between detachment and fear, these shots reinforce the distanced way that mass-circulation newspapers, magazines, and popular television shows tend to view public housing and residents, including single mothers—from a distance and rarely in dialogue. The reader's elevated vantage point serves to maintain our distance above, beyond, and superior to public housing residents, a position that promotes the agency of the onlooker over the looked-at. Compounding this visual attack, Gibbons avoids dialogue balloons altogether in favor of a sound effect drawn directly inside the panels amongst shrapnel-like falling snow. The pervasive "WHUP, WHUP, WHUP" of the helicopter's blades pulse in the background, an effect that renders the helicopter, and as a consequence, those positioned outside, the only valid speakers in this narrative. The onomatopoetic refrain performs a linguistic and ideological function common to outside designations of public housing—it is content to attack (or "WHUP") from a distance.

In the following sequence, Gibbons and Miller take the narrative one step further by shifting the reader's perspective *inside* Cabrini-Green, thereby provoking a dialogue with the object of intense political scrutiny and constant media bombardment. The shots of the helicopter give way to a view of one of the building's windows, which, in turn, becomes an interior shot of Washington, looking out defiantly. Facing the viewer at an intimate eye-level perspective, this symbolic final page of the first installment of Washington's life history indicates a vital power shift to a personal point of view. Furthermore, in contrast to earlier references to Washington, which Miller forms in a detached second- and third-person singular form, a strategy in keeping with her objectified positioning within the panel frame—"*She*'s black. Grew up poor. Would've ended up a junkie or a hooker . . . *you*'ll never make the history books. *You* won't even score a footnote"—the writer litters this panel with the repeated use of first-person pronouns. This technique helps to focus the verbal text on Washington and her control rather than on the outside designations. Here, too, Washington has shed the green epidermis of earlier panels and has regained her natural skin color. Moving from the urban night, through the window, and into the interior of public housing, the visual strategies combine to signal a narrative bridge from a peripheral to a personal point of view for the remaining three issues of Washington's life story.

Washington's eye-level perspective and "I" voice also implicates the audience in an important shift. For cinema scholar Angela Ndalianis (2003), "The notion of the 'passive spectator' as voyeur collapses when media experiences immerse the viewer in spectacles that are aimed at perceptually removing the presence of the frame" (358–59). By looking us directly in the eye, Washington's private reader-character identification reminds us that we are not just bystanders in this story—this superhero is part of *our* world. This begs the obvious question: if Washington looks at "us," then who are "we"? For many years, comic books were considered simple power fantasies for adolescents seeking an easy escape on a lazy Saturday afternoon. Traditionally filled with juvenile humor, cosmic japeries, and big-breasted babes, the adventures of Superman, Batman, and others allowed one to escape into a fictional world characterized by spectacular but unsophisticated battles between good and evil. More recently, however, several comic book series have sought to amalgamate this absurdist legacy with a political edge, combining historical and fictional narrative. Indeed, while more than a faint whiff of ludicrousness clings to this Martha's life story, an effect manifest through Gibbons's gigantic fortresses and flying motorbikes, there is a contemporary political reality that underscores Washington's tale. This verisimilitude becomes evident in both the comic's architecture and characterization. For example, *Give Me Liberty*'s frequent inclusion of "Cabrini Green" signs serves to equate the environmental turbulence within its opening pages to a real-world location. Moreover, Washington operates on a sophisticated level of political consciousness, dealing with unglamorous real-world issues like poverty, social repression, and government corruption. This claim to literal truth is evident first in the attitudes of the creators themselves:

> When we started with Martha, we were actually much more kind of serious, we wanted to do something grim and gritty, and grim and political, but we actually both realized that we were more interested in doing something that had a bit of satirical edge to it and something that was, in many ways, absurd, because that can be more effective in skewering things than, you know, being dead on and very serious about it. . . . I think that many of the concerns that we had and that we extrapolated in "Martha" have actually come to pass. Again, because it's comics and because it's a work of fiction, it's kind of heightened, but I'm really pleased that we ended up with a real resonance between Martha's fictional world and our real world. (Manning 2010)

As the opening issue of the *Give Me Liberty* saga makes clear, there were few places more politically resonant than at Cabrini-Green during the 1980s. Regarding the current turn toward ideological importance in comic book narratives, cultural theorist Scott Bukatman (2003) states that "the traumatic body of the superhero now signifies a traumatized *reality*" (125). Thus, when Washington looks into our eyes, she is not just asking us to look beyond our "but it's *just* a comic" prejudice; she also asks that we look past one-note, hysterical representations of the lives of single mothers—that we step inside her world to see an alternate version of this reality in the remaining three issues of the saga.

Miller throws the reader straight into the heart of this "traumatic reality" in the second issue of the series, *Martha Washington Goes to War* (1994). Under the helm of the corrupt and power-hungry President Howard Johnson Nissen—modeled on a bizarre combination of Richard Nixon and Ronald Reagan—the government has extrapolated Cabrini-Green into a roofed-in facility where nobody goes in or out, while budget cuts force authorities to shut down prisons and mental institutions, bringing hideous poverty and violence to city streets. Driven by a desire to thwart Nissen's tyrannical control, a now fifteen-year-old Washington signs up for a fictitious military group, the PAX Peace Force. The organization offers Washington a place to fight to defend the rights of her fellow public housing residents and to rescue the United States from the brink of destruction.

Gibbons documents the pinnacle of Washington's achievements in the form of a spectacular physical fight with Nissen's henchman, Lieutenant Moretti, across a double-page spread of blood-curdling panels (see Figure 2.1). The large number of frames, their close proximity to one another, and their shifting visual perspective seem designed to compress time—like a slow-motion action replay—ensuring that the viewer witnesses the full extent of what will become a memorable victory for Washington. To heighten the magnitude of the event, Gibbons delays Washington's physical domination of Moretti until final frame of the spread. After wrenching a knife out of her opponent's hand and breaking his wrist in the process, Washington straddles Moretti, who lies screaming on the floor. Save for the "KRAKK" of the lieutenant's injury, Gibbons strips the panel of all accessories, a technique designed to focus attention on the narrative importance of her triumph. Indeed, this final panel is notable for its lack of framing border. While a requisite rectangular black line filled with visceral, close-up action shots confine all of the previous fight sequences, the last frame floats in the blank white space between borders. McCloud (1993) refers to this white space as the "gutter" and identifies it as one of the most important narrative tools in comic architecture (66). The use of the gutter in this instance holds importance for the broader ideological aims of the *Give Me Liberty* series and this chapter as a whole. Trapped within the darkened pixels of *The Vanishing Family* documentary, television portrayed Clarinda Henderson in a way that presented her as the cause of her own situation. Through selected questioning, editing choices, even down to the sultry, moody lighting, *The Vanishing Family* cast Henderson as a shifty, apathetic foil to Moyers's white male authority figure. By emerging into the pure white space of the gutter and revealing the questionable morals of her male colleagues along the way, however, Washington re-scripts such narrow framing devices, breaking out of the shackles of pathology regularly attached to single mother families from Cabrini-Green.

When coupled with Washington's defeat of her main adversary, the absence of a frame—and the related narrative quantum leap towards "openness"— suggests a new way of seeing and appreciating female comic book characters. Washington quite literally wrestles the elder statesman's stronghold on the heroic out of his hands—not before she takes the chance to kick him in the balls, however! Refusing to wait in subordination for the help of Clark Kent's or Peter Parker's alter egos, Washington subverts and challenges comic book gender role norms and the typical boy-rescues-girl adventure story. Nor does she assume the vapid, tousled-haired role of female "superheroes" like

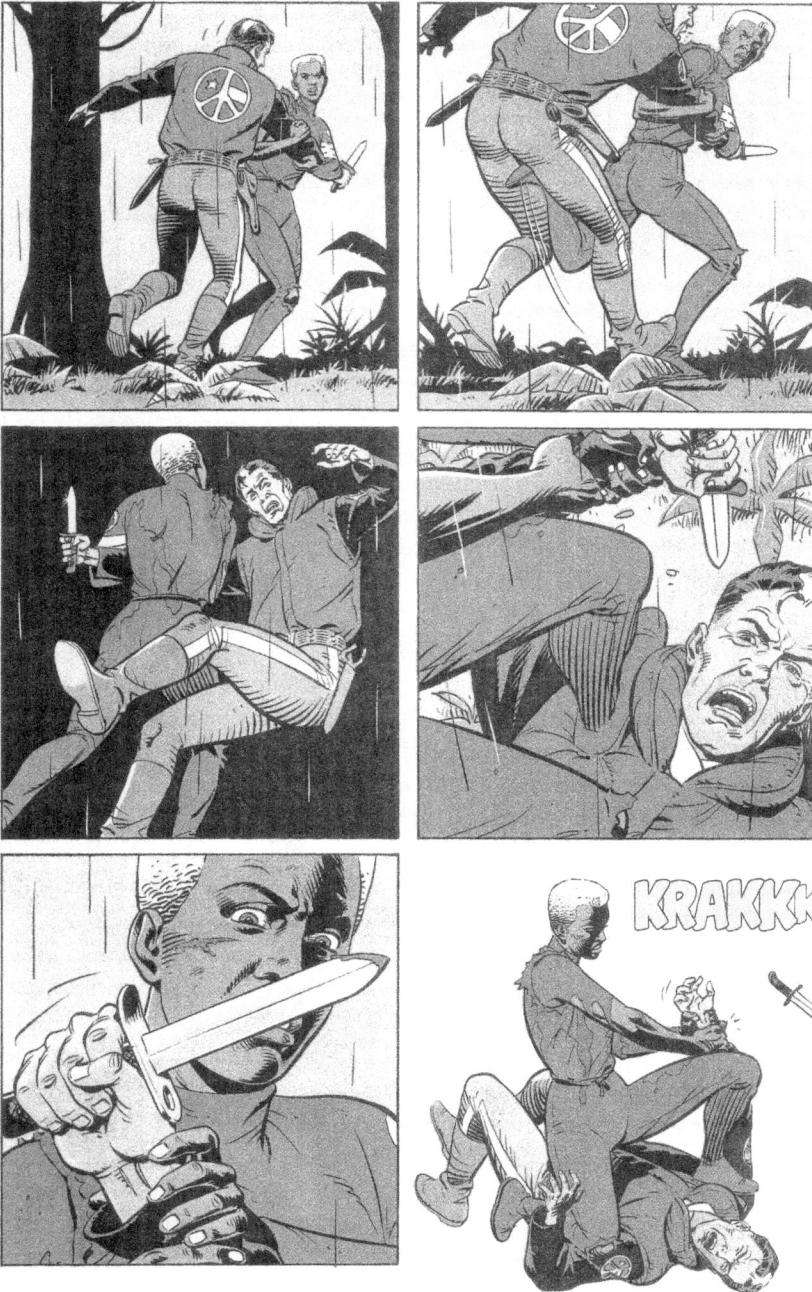

Figure 2.1: Washington fights Lieutenant Moretti (Miller and Gibbons, *Give Me Liberty: Travel and Entertainment*, vol. 2, Milwaukie, OR: Dark Horse Comics, 1991).

Catwoman (Halle Berry) or Barb Wire (Pamela Anderson). Replete with a shaved head, the costume- and makeup-free Washington adopts behaviors and a physical appearance traditionally ascribed to men in comic books, so much so that she is often mistaken for a man and called "sir." As Gibbons (2009) acknowledges, "Martha is an alternate-world version of the traditional patriarchal comic book hero, of whom the undisputed daddy is Captain America, created in 1941 by Joe Salmon and Jack Kirby" (234). Just as Washington shirks the traditional appearance of a female comic character, in her journey into the pure white space of the gutter, Washington attains the kind of unrestricted mobility that Gary Engle (1992), in his analysis of Superman's flying abilities, terms "part of America's dreamwork" (337). While Superman slinks through the air, Washington now too floats into the airy space of the gutter once reserved for only brawny, white male, all-American superheroes. By comparing Martha to Captain America—like Superman, a nationalistic and patriotic superhero—Gibbons defines Washington's American citizenship. No longer situated as a homogenous "super-other," Washington now assumes a multidimensional existence that allows her to both maintain a position within a long line of respected US superheroes and remain a product of Chicago's public housing.

In a later adventure titled *Insubordination* (1995), Gibbons pays homage to (and subverts) this comic book legacy, pitting Washington and the archetypal red, white, and blue "superman" and "super-soldier" Captain Kurtz in a fight against Aryan Thrust, a terrorist group intent on destroying Philadelphia. Following a bloody battle with their adversaries, the comic artist pictures a battered and listless Captain Kurtz clutching the city's Liberty Bell with Washington, bruised but undaunted, to his rear. The iconographic implications embedded in this image are clear—the patriarchal comic book hero must relinquish the super-soldier mantle and the responsibility to defend the nation's liberty to a new wave of hero: a female public housing resident. In dodging bullets, evading mortar shells, or taking on army tanks by herself, the aggressive, physically potent, and intelligent Washington eliminates the cultural divisiveness present in television shows like *The Vanishing Family*, showing how women can be as tough as, if not tougher than, their white, male opponents.

In her metamorphosis into the ultimate comic book hero, Washington rescripts not only stereotypes about female superheroes, but also what it means to be a resident of the real Cabrini-Green. Over the years, many female public housing residents traversed traditional power dynamics, refusing to remain within the restricted frame of societal definitions of who they are, emerging victors in protests against their own Lieutenant Moretti. During the 1980s, inept management, including inefficient and inadequate maintenance and services, forced many to build their own political structure by becoming community leaders. Commonly referred to as Queen Bees, real-life superheroes commanded resident management corporations, which serviced facilities such as laundromats, security, and day-care centers. Women's political struggles over the resources controlled by the city and the local housing authority expanded the definition of public housing residents beyond the requisite single mother characterization. In their research on community activism, Sara Evans and Harry Boyte (1981) offer historical evidence that public housing "can serve as the arenas where people can distinguish themselves from elite [societal] definitions of who they are, [and] gain the skills and mutual regard necessary to act as a force for change" (56). A telecourse aired by PBS Adult Learning Services between 1994 and 2000 titled Low Income Women's Resistance sought to combat the denigrating rhetoric attached to Chicago's Wentworth Gardens housing project. The accompanying study guide describes the documentary in the following terms: "Women and Social Action goes beyond social theories and popular politics, offering a first-hand look into how women are influencing society on a grassroots level. Personal stories from over seventy women and men reveal the complexities of our lives and highlight the commitment, vision, humor, and compassion that result in effective social action" (Thompson 1997). This documentary inverts, contradicts, and in some fashion presents an alternative to commonly held homogenous ways of seeing female public housing residents.

While many female public housing residents attempt to counter restrictive representations of social marginalization in the "real" world, Washington makes a similar claim in *Give Me Liberty*, breaching the edges of panels, elongating their boundaries with her fists, energy blasts, and chants. A useful example of this desire for spatial possession occurs in a double-page spread placed immediately after Washington's historic fight with Moretti. In a section of Miller's story, titled *Martha Washington Saves the World* (1997), Gibbons features an undeniably phallic-looking rocket blasting off into outer space leaving a broad patina of white crayon in its wake. The effect illustrates—in the bluntest terms—the comic equivalent of a "cum" shot and the ultimate catharsis of victory. Compositionally positioned across two upwardly vectored tiers, the act of the moving rocket not only becomes a visual quip on patriarchic limitations, but also mirrors Washington's unique journey in life. Indeed, Washington's physical ascension into space symbolizes her lifelong desire to escape a series of ground-level restrictions. From the "prison" of Cabrini-Green, to the cocoon of a school locker room, to the clutches of archenemy Moretti, until the point where she jets off in a spaceship in *Saves the World*, Washington's life consists of one big Venus flytrap. Snaking from the early life netherworld of tiny, claustrophobic panels to her eventual destiny in double-page spreads of cosmic scenery, Washington's bodily movement in life and space reverses all spatial constraints. Washington's rocket-like propulsion, power, and movement through and above city space is an act of exploration, self-possession, and a freedom and liberation from the constraints of patriarchal dictators who attempt to constrain her movement.

Mobility has always been a key feature of the comic book genre—after all, it is the very nature of the superhero and her "superness" to animate the spaces they inhabit. However, Washington's elastic movement through space in *Saves the World* is particularly unique. In addition to repeating the firing rocket motif, Gibbons employs a number of compositional techniques and symbols in support of Washington's physical and mental ascension from powerlessness to power. One such approach is the use of motions lines, or as many comic book aficionados term them, "zip ribbons" (McCloud 1993, 111), which imply the high-speed environmental effects of Martha's body on her surrounding environment. While her victims—propelled backwards and upwards by her sheer strength—fly out of the panel foreground with their backs to the reader, Washington's defiant frontal stance and accompanying bold, blurred streaks of color convey a sense of spatial ownership and virtuosic perspectival limitlessness. The zip-ribbons, which emanate from her gun, cloaking the scene in pulsating tones like extraordinary kaleidoscopic entities, become rainbow-like "declarations of intent" (Arnall 2000) implying the gestural arc of Washington's bodily performance and ambitions: she is here, but she also affects there, and thus she is pure energy.

Seeing Washington explode from one jagged panel to the next, trailing lightning bolts through the dividing line of the gutter, it is occasionally easy to forget that she is but a mere mortal. Gibbons and Miller remind the reader of her vulnerability in the final installment of the saga, *Martha Washington Dies* (2007). In this brief seventeen-page finale, we find a now one-hundred-year-old Washington in her final moments of life, among the aged rubble of what used to be her Cabrini-Green home, surrounded by her children and friends. As if to imply her impending death, a new third-person narrative voice appears atop the scene to reiterate Washington's life journey: "Martha Washington has done many things in her century. She's been many things. A soldier, a warrior, an explorer of the wildest depths of the universe, a wife and mother and a leader and a teacher." Devoid of a final drawn-out bloody battle, *Dies* amounts to a moving farewell complete with the only last words she could possibly have uttered: "Give Me Liberty" (see Figure 2.2).

Washington's children feel a sense of responsibility to preserve their mother's legacy. After she draws her final breath, they take up their guns, heading

Figure 2.2: Washington's death (Miller and Gibbons, *Martha Washington Dies*, Milwaukie, OR: Dark Horse Comics, 2007).

out of the frame as a narrative voice explains, "Ganne has gone back to the source of all things. But the war goes on. And we are ready. The end." Breaking free of the concrete visual frame around her, Washington's presence in the liminal gutter space between "now" and the "future," along with the implied presence of a "diegetic horizon" (Barthes 1977, 65) beyond (or outside) of the comic frame, pulls the image forward in time and space, hinting at the broader implication of her fight for future generations. The familiar icon of the immobile, closed panel no longer contains time but instead hemorrhages and escapes into the surrounding atmosphere like an echo, as if to imply the fight will go on. (McCloud 1993, 103). Washington's death, then, signals not the end, but merely a stage in a broader political and social fight for female residents from public housing.

In late 2009, Dark Horse Comics released its own tribute to Washington and the mentors she inspired in the form of a one-hundred-dollar, six-hundred-page, oversized hardcover volume containing her complete life story. *The Life and Times of Martha Washington in the Twenty-First Century* stands as an epic tribute to Washington's life and work and to the strength of residents from Chicago's public housing. This homage was primarily at the request of Gibbons, who as his sentimental conclusion to the *Life and Times* tome reveals, developed a unique attachment to the comic character over her lifetime:

> I feel I should offer some words of farewell to Martha, imaginary though she
> is, although it doesn't feel that way. She's been part of my life for almost twenty
> years, through good times and bad. It's as if she were an old friend whom I would
> meet from time to time, the years dissolving when I did, always optimistic, always
> brave, always decent and honorable. In fact, over the years Martha has attained a
> kind of reality for me. Not all fictional characters you deal with do, but I think I
> speak for myself and Frank when I say that we really do have a sense of knowing
> Martha as a real person. I'll miss her. (Miller and Gibbons 2009, 549)

In an online interview for *ComicBookMovie*, Gibbons (2000) revealed that he and Miller planned to explore the character on the big screen with *Sin City* (2005) star Rosario Dawson in the role of Washington. "Frank and I have been in love with Martha since we first created her and I'd like to think that maybe movie-goers would be as well," he said.

Miller enhances this real world identification by separating Washington from most traditional crime-fighting action heroes such as Batman, Catwoman, or Wonder Woman. In place of unrealistic superpowers, she possesses natural superendowments such as speed and fighting ability and the logical faculties to which we can all aspire. In other words, she is an everyday Super Woman. In the absence of the requisite superhero adornment—the mask— Washington comes to personify every public housing resident in every American city who secretly feeds the hope that one day, from the inner depths of their personality, there can emerge a superhero capable of making the same life altering decisions as the superhero from Cabrini-Green. This process of real world self-identification is central to Miller and Gibbons's ambitions for the *Give Me Liberty* series. As Gibbons (Miller and Gibbons 2009) describes in the conclusion of *The Life and Times of Martha Washington in the*

Figure 2.3: The "gutter" functions as an essential communication tool (McCloud, *Understanding Comics: The Invisible Art*, 1993, 198).

Twenty-First Century, "I think Martha's legacy is that she's been an inspiration to the people in the story, that she's always been straightforward and honorable, and brave, and a hero in the *true* sense. She's just a decent, decent person, someone who I'd love to have as a friend, who I'd probably follow anywhere, and I think throughout her life she had an integrity that would be an example to anybody." The comic panels inspire real world female agency, while at the same time functioning as vital spatial fields on a pathway to a variegated way of seeing single mothers from public housing (see Figure 2.3). As comic book scholar Joseph Witek (1989) observes, "Reading a comic book always entails a degree of Peeping Tomism, as we peer through the 'windows' of the panel borders at a world beyond our own" (72). The gutter functions as an essential component in the readers' participation, opening up an arena of subjective universality, asking the readers to "join in a silent dance of the seen and the unseen, the visible and the invisible" (McCloud 1993, 92).

McCloud explains: "Several times on every page the reader is released—like a trapeze artist—into the open air of imagination. Then caught by the outstretched arms of the ever-present next panel. Caught quickly so as not to let the reader fall into confusion and boredom. But is it possible that closure can be so managed in some cases—that the reader might learn to fly?" (ibid., 90). Dave Gibbons's ambiguous realities, peculiar temporal jumps, and absurd perspectives require that the reader occupy a key role as animator of the piece, actively stitching together the narrative frames via the topology of images, absences, and excess (Dittmer 2010, 230). The readers travel back and forth, back and forth between the metaplanar surface of the comic page and their own imaginations, animating a three-dimensional space of inquiry and the possibility of multiple narrative approaches. *Give Me Liberty* holds out the possibility of introducing what geographer Jason Dittmer (ibid.) calls a new "optical unconscious," "one that holds open opportunities for more plural, flexible narratives connected with public housing residents to emerge from a singular montage" (223).

Readers experience Washington's rocket-like propulsion, thrust, and movement through and above city space as an act of exploration, self-possession, and a freedom and liberation from the constraints of those who attempt to constrict her agency. Her individual journey toward political awakening, earned respectability, and personal empowerment reanimates single mothers in the American visual imagination, placing the reader firmly in the driving seat on this narrative pathway to a new way of seeing; like Washington, we must all become explorers.

Notes

1. Television, in particular, magnified demonized imaginings of single mothers to ridiculous proportions, none more so than the *Saturday Night Live (SNL)* comic character, Cabrini-Green Harlem-Watts-Jackson (played by Danitra Vance), who appeared in the show's 1985–1986 season. As the sole African American female performer on the show at the time, Vance's character encompassed a hypercaricatured cross section of urban single motherhood. Cabrini-Green (Chicago), Harlem (New York), Watts (Los Angeles), and Jackson (Mississippi) geographically locates each US city's most notorious public housing projects—famous for high rates of unemployment, endemic crime, welfare dependency, and single parent households. Taken together, within the context of Vance's quad-barreled character name, they encapsulate the pervasive national spread of the single mother "infection." In other words, not only is Cabrini-Green-Harlem-Watts-Jackson a resident of public housing, but she is, in addition, a single mother, a dynamic that works to conflate environmental notoriety and solo motherhood into a single dystopian mantra. The attendant image to this rhetoric is Murray's "culture of poverty" thesis, which focuses on women's reproductive practices as the driving force behind inner-city pathology. In her racial, educational, marital, and environmental deficiency, *SNL*'s dangerously "humorous" characterization of a slothful "baby-factory" mother came to represent the ultimate "(m)other."

References

Anderson, Elijah. 1991. "Neighborhood Effects on Teenage Pregnancy." In *The Urban Underclass*, edited by Christopher Jencks and Paul E. Peterson 203–32. Washington, DC: Brookings Institution.

Arnall, Dick. 2000. "Taking a Line for a Walk: The Animated Itinerary of Jonathan Hodgson." *Animate!* http://www.animateonline.org/editorial/2002/08/taking-a-line-for-a-walk.html (accessed July 3, 2010).

Barthes, Roland. 1977. "The Third Meaning." In his *Image-Music-Text*, 52–68. New York: Hill and Wang.

Bukatman, Scott. 2003. "The Boys in the Hoods: A Song of the Urban Superhero." In his *Matters of Gravity: Special Effects and Superman in the Twentieth Century*. Durham, NC: Duke University Press.

Collins, Patricia Hill. 2000. "Mammies, Matriarchs, and Other Controlling Images." In her *Black Feminist Thought: Knowledge, Consciousness, and the Politics of Empowerment*, 69–97. London: Routledge.

Dittmer, Jason. 2010. March. "Comic Book Visualities: A Methodological Manifesto on Geography, Montage, and Narration." *Transactions of the Institute of British Geographers* 35 (2): 222–36.

Eisner, Will. 1985. *Comics and Sequential Art*. Taramac, FL: Poorhouse.

Engle, Gary. 1992. "What Makes Superman So Darned American?" In *Popular Culture: An Introductory Text*, edited by Jack Nachbar and Kevin Lause, 331–43. Bowling Green, OH: Bowling Green State University Popular Press.

Evans, Sarah, and Harry Boyte. 1981. *Free Spaces: The Sources of Democratic Change in America*. Chicago: University of Chicago Press.

Glasner, Barry. 2000. *The Culture of Fear: Why Americans Are Afraid of the Wrong Things*. New York: Basic Books.

Gray, Herman. 1995. *Watching Race: Television and the Struggle for Blackness*. Minneapolis: University of Minnesota Press.

Kaplan, E. B. 1997. *Not Our Kind of Girl: Unraveling the Myths of Black Teenage Motherhood*. Berkeley: University of California Press.

Manning, Shaun. 2010. "Gibbons Discusses 'Martha Washington.'" *Comic Book Resources*, March 23. http://www.comicbookresources.com/?page=article&id=25341 (accessed November 10, 2010).

McCloud, Scott. 1993. *Understanding Comics: The Invisible Art*. Northampton, MA: Kitchen Sink Press.

Miller, Frank, and Dave Gibbons. 1990. Vol. 1: *Give Me Liberty: Homes and Gardens*. Vol. 2: *Give Me Liberty: Travel and Entertainment*. Vol. 3: *Give Me Liberty: Health and Welfare*. Vol. 4: *Give Me Liberty: Death and Taxes*. Milwaukie, OR: Dark Horse Comics.

———. 1995. *Insubordination*. In *Happy Birthday, Martha Washington* (A Three-Part Series). Milwaukie, OR: Dark Horse Comics.

———. 2007. *Martha Washington Dies*. Milwaukie, OR: Dark Horse Comics.

———. 2009. *The Life and Times of Martha Washington in the Twenty-First Century*, edited by Diana Schutz. Milwaukie, OR: Dark Horse Books.

Moyers, Bill. 1986. *The Vanishing Family—Crisis in Black America*, Columbia Broadcasting System Special Report.

Murray, Charles. 1984. *Losing Ground: American Social Policy, 1950–1980*. New York: Basic Books.

Ndalianis, Angela. 2003. "Architecture of the Senses: Neo-Baroque Entertainment Spectacles." In *Rethinking Media Change: The Aesthetics of Transition*, edited by Henry Jenkins
and David Thorburn, 355–73. Cambridge, MA: MIT Press.

"Rormachine." 2010. "Miller Wants Rosario Dawson for "Martha Washington," *Comic-
BookMovie*. http://www.comicbookmovie.com/fansites/notyetamovie/news/?a=8893
(accessed December 12, 2010).

Thompson, Martha E. 1997. *Women and Social Action: Teleclass Study Guide*. Dubuque, IA:
Kendall/Hunt.

Welfare Reform Proposals, Including H.R. 4605, the Work and Responsibility Act of 1994.
Hearings before the Committee on Ways and Means and its Subcommittee on Human
Resources of the House of Representatives, 103rd Cong., 2nd Sess., July 14, 26, 27, 28, and
29; Aug. 9 and 16, 1994.

Wilson, James Q. 2003. *The Marriage Problem: How Our Culture Has Weakened Families*.
New York: HarperCollins.

Witek, Joseph. 1989. *Comic Books as History: The Narrative Art of Jack Jackson, Art Spiegelman, and Harvey Pekar*. Jackson: University Press of Mississippi.

"Don't Underestimate Her Ability to Talk, It's Her Superpower": Epistemic Negotiation and the Power of Community in Carrie Vaughn's *Kitty Norville* Series

—Rhonda Nicol

Astroll through the sci-fi/fantasy section of any bookstore provides ample evidence that first, urban fantasy (UF) is currently a strong presence in today's marketplace, and second, UF is dominated by women. Many, if not most, of the most popular UF series are written by women, and the overwhelming majority of the protagonists of these series are also women. As writer Daniel Abraham (2010) points out, a result of this is that UF "is a genre sitting on top of a great big huge cultural discomfort about women and power," and it is perhaps inevitable that the figure of the "angry chick in leather," as writer Lilith Saintcrow (2008) has dubbed the typical UF protagonist, has been scrutinized closely and her potential gender-paradigm-subverting potential hotly debated by both fans and writers in the UF community.

Although there is a growing body of scholarship devoted to the study of "kick-ass heroines" in popular culture,[1] discussions about the feminist potential (or lack thereof) of the UF heroine in particular are still confined largely to the fans and writers within the genre community itself. Joanne Hollows and Rachel Moseley (2006) note that feminist critiques of popular culture all too often assume that "feminism, or the feminist, can tell us about popular culture, but [do] not examine what popular culture can tell us about feminism" (1) and suggest that it might be provocative and enlightening to start with the assumption that we can learn from popular culture rather than dictate to it. My analysis of the *Kitty Norville* series is therefore framed within the context of these vibrant and engaging arguments from within the UF community. It is my intention here to build a bridge between fan/writer discourses and academic discourse in order to explore what the UF community can tell us about the state of feminism in popular culture, especially as it relates to questions of women and power.

Saintcrow (2008) argues that UF "is pretty much the only genre today exploring not only the ethics of power and consent, but also serious questions of violence and gender relations from a primarily female point of view" and postulates that part of the wide appeal of UF is that "female UF protagonists are almost without exception extraordinarily tough, and . . . *violence is acceptable for them to use*. This a huge revolution in the type of stories our culture tells itself" (emphasis added). Saintcrow (ibid.) singles out for particular accolades the early novels in the *Anita Blake* series, claiming that the series "blew the doors and the lid right off one of the most persistent myths of our time—that women don't get angry." She sees Anita's in-your-face attitude, one inherited by legions of UF heroines, as a powerful cultural bellwether. Saintcrow's argument is compelling, but the first Anita Blake novel, *Guilty Pleasures*, was published in 1993, and the success of the series has spawned a whole host of imitators; at this point in the popular culture landscape, the figure of the "kick-ass heroine" in UF is in danger of becoming a cliché, a caricature rather than an archetype.

UF is not alone in presenting (and endlessly replicating) a certain breed of "kick-ass" female protagonist, and many media studies scholars have identified the "action chick" character type, which has appeared with increasing frequency in film and television. Jeffrey A. Brown (2004) notes that the female action hero "represents a potentially transgressive figure capable of expanding the popular perception of women's roles and abilities," but the character type "runs the risk of reinscribing strict gender binaries and of being nothing more than sexist window-dressing" (47). Caroline Heldman (2012) concurs, noting that in action films, a figure she calls "the fighting fuck toy" is ubiquitous, part of a herd of characters that Heldman describes as "hyper-sexualized female protagonists who are able to 'kick ass' (and kill) with the best of them. The FFT appears empowered, but her very existence serves the pleasure of the heterosexual male viewer. In short, the FFT takes female agency, weds it to normalized male violence, and appropriates it for the male gaze." I suggest that UF is in danger of replicating the same type of character; the revolution that Anita Blake started can all too easily be repackaged to maintain and perpetuate sexist paradigms. One need only to survey a collection of UF novels and note the highly sexualized (and highly improbable, as Jim C. Hines effectively demonstrates[2]) poses of the cover models to see how the genre, despite being wildly popular with women readers, seems to be marketed to appeal to the heterosexual male gaze.

Are UF's kick-ass protagonists simply other iterations of Heldman's "fighting fuck toy" paradigm? I suggest that the very success of the kick-ass UF heroine has presented writers currently working in UF with a classic double bind: either choosing to have a kick-ass, aggressive, sexualized heroine or one whose performance of gender might be read as more conservative or "traditional" leaves one either way open to criticism. If the female hero is established as "tough" simply through her willingness and ability to be physically aggressive, then she might be rejected as a mere cliché. If the female hero does not conform to the by-now established kick-ass norm, then the author is open to accusations of creating a protagonist who undermines the genre's counterhegemonic impulses, which is also problematic. Saintcrow's point that UF protagonists have legitimated female anger is indeed a powerful one, but if the power or agency of the typical UF protagonist is measured by her ability to wield weapons and mete out physical punishment, that is a strength with limited transgressive potential, and as critics such as Brown and Heldman have pointed out, one readily co-opted. At this point in UF's evolution, we need to consider how questions of strength might be considered in the context of power, as something more than simply ability to dominate.

Carrie Vaughn, author of the *Kitty Norville* series, which features a radio DJ who becomes a werewolf and parlays her experiences with the supernatural world into a hit syndicated call-in radio show, concurs with Abraham and Saintcrow that UF is, as a genre, concerned with issues of women, violence, and power. However, although she acknowledges that "this genre is admired for its strong women characters," she wonders if "the genre is also guilty of undermining some of those strengths" (Vaughn 2009b). She has a number of objections to some of the ways that the "kick-ass heroine" trope has been deployed in UF, singling out for particular critique those series wherein an ostensibly "powerful, confident" protagonist is in actuality "a woman who uses aggression and violence to mask a variety of dysfunctions, insecurities, and stereotypical low self-esteem issues" (2000a). Vaughn has been outspoken in her mission to create a UF heroine who complicates the simple binary of kick-ass goddess or weak girly-girl. She argues that

> sometimes I'm afraid that violence and kicking ass have become synonymous
> with "strong woman character." Like if a character doesn't wear leather pants and
> carry a Glock she can't possibly be a strong woman. A powerful woman. But I
> don't think this is true. A character doesn't have to be violent and confrontational
> to be a strong woman character. There seems to be a point where she crosses
> the line and becomes simply pissed off and unpleasant, and frankly, I don't need
> to spend 400 pages reading about someone who's perpetually pissed off and
> unpleasant. Instead of being strong, she takes on a victim mentality, feeling like
> the whole world is out to get her and the only way she can respond is by kicking
> ass. (2008a)

At one point in the series, Vaughn (2010) pokes fun at this clichéd version of the kick-ass heroine: Kitty has a caller who clearly serves to represent the type of UF protagonist that Vaughn derides (ibid., 22–25). The joke here is that the caller might very well be Anita Blake herself; the caller says that her many boyfriends "deserve someone better, someone who isn't always getting into trouble, who doesn't have my temper. Someone *prettier*" (ibid., 24). Kitty urges the woman to seek counseling, and when the caller hangs up in a huff, Kitty tells her listeners, "We're all in this together, and life is a little easier when we act like it" (ibid., 25).

Kitty's emphasis on cooperation and community makes her a different kind of heroine from Anita Blake and her ilk. Jennifer K. Stuller (2010) argues that there is value in, and space for, a female hero who embodies traditionally feminine traits of nurturing and caring. She does acknowledge the cultural conflation of the emotional and the female that Tan points out and observes, "The assumption that love is inherent in women, but not in men, is a sticky, even sexist concept, and the idea that a female superhero's greatest gift is her nurturing temperament of her ability to love selflessly certainly had the potential to reinforce stereotypical feminine ideals" (88). However, she asserts that the emphasis on "redemption, collaboration, and compassion" in a number of representations of powerful female heroes suggests the possibility of "a new form of heroism for popular culture" (ibid.). Significantly, Stuller claims that "collaboration with friends, family, or community is common to the female hero—not because she is incapable of succeeding on her own, but because she is more successful when she recognizes, encourages, and utilizes the talents of others" (ibid., 92). I argue that the *Kitty Norville* series attempts to address this process of cultural devaluing that Tan identifies by building a bridge between the kick-ass heroine trope and other, more traditionally feminine gender tropes, especially those of compassion and cooperation, in order to advance UF's continued potential as a space for exploring and complicating scripts of gender and genre. Vaughn's series insists that Kitty's interpersonal skills and adeptness at community building are as valuable as her physical power, thus making Kitty an example of the new breed of heroine that Stuller identifies. Thus far, the series arc as a whole (twelve books as of this writing) chronicles Kitty's ascent from a young, submissive werewolf in what amounts to an abusive relationship with her pack Alpha into a confident woman, married to a fellow werewolf (and her former human lawyer), Ben, with whom she serves as the Alpha pair of Denver's werewolf pack and as a leader in the public sphere who serves as an example for other supernaturals.

Although Kitty may be a different kind of heroine from many other UF protagonists, she is typical in that along her journey, she finds herself devalued and dismissed by others, often because she is a young and attractive woman. She is often stymied by patriarchal systems of power and oppression and is often fighting against paternalism and sexism, which are manifested in both overt and benevolent ways. Kitty is repeatedly underestimated and treated as a naïve dupe who can't really be all that powerful because she's a woman. When Darren, a werewolf working at the behest of a vampire named Nasser to take over the Denver pack, tries to undermine Kitty's leadership, he tells her, "You've had to work hard to be an alpha. Because you're not, really. You certainly weren't born an alpha. You were happier when you had someone taking care of you, weren't you?" (Vaughn 2013b, 220–21). Kitty notes that Darren's strategy is to "wear me down with impenetrable, paternalistic kindness. He was only trying to help, really. The more I argued, the more I'd prove his point" (ibid., 222). Later in the series, Kumarbis, the vampire who sired Roman, the main adversary through most of the series, seeks Kitty's help to assassinate his son, but Kumarbis's "kindly patriarch" performance and his insistence upon treating her as the "rebellious teenager" frustrates and irritates her: "He wouldn't listen to me, he'd only pay attention to the role he'd constructed for me in his own dusty brain" (Vaughn 2013c, 246, 198).

Kitty's strategy for resisting paternalistic oppression and navigating her own path to power is to create a support network, sharing power rather than hoarding it. Throughout the series, Kitty utilizes what Sharon Ross calls "epistemic negotiation" to navigate the supernatural world and to emerge as a leader of the Denver supernatural community. In her analysis of Xena and Buffy, Ross (2004) argues that the two heroines are examples of female heroes who "privilege epistemic negotiation as a productive means to being heroic. The strategies involved favor communal action, interdependency, and emotional knowing" (233) and claims that Xena and Buffy "break through patterns of heroic toughness that prioritize individualism, isolationism, and emotional withdrawal" over "harmony and community" (248). Kitty also uses the strategies of epistemic negotiation that Ross elucidates; her entire ideological stance is based on the idea that power and authority should be negotiated through cooperation and support of shared interests rather than imposed by force.

For Kitty, her wolf aspect is the first and most critical figure with whom she attempts to negotiate a pact of mutual cooperation. Interestingly, by referring to her wolf form as Wolf and locating it as Other, Kitty is effectively making a distinction between her human self and the Wolf; Wolf is always "she," not "I." The two are not, as far as Kitty is concerned, parts of a seamless whole entity but companions who need to cooperate in order to survive. When the series begins, Kitty is losing the battle to stay human: "Maintaining enthusiasm for the human life had been difficult. Useless, even. I slept through the day, worked nights, and thought more and more about those times I ran in the forest as a wolf, with the rest of the pack surrounding me" (Vaughn 2005, 10). Kitty can only become an active participant in the supernatural community once she achieves a rapprochement between her human and Wolf aspects.

Kitty's wolf form is linked very intimately to her existence as a woman in a patriarchal culture, one where threat of sexual violence is pervasive; her transformation into a werewolf occurs in the wake of a sexual assault. She had escaped the clutches of a date rapist and fled to what she thought was the relatively safety of an isolated mountain area, where she was found and set upon by Zan, one of the lowest-ranked, weakest, and most emotionally unstable werewolves in the Denver pack (ibid., 181–84). Once she is turned, she comes under the authority of Denver-area pack Alphas named Meg and Carl, and with Carl she quickly developed an abusive sexual relationship. She recalls, "Those early weeks, my first time meeting the pack, surrounded by wolves, I'd only wanted to know what I had to do to keep from getting hurt, from making them angry. I'd been the most submissive one in the room, to keep Carl happy, to make sure he protected me" (ibid. 2008b, 132). Because she unconsciously associates being a werewolf with being a victim of sexual violence, she initially replicates the pattern of sexual abuse and domination that began with her rape. For Kitty, being raped and being turned into a werewolf are paired violations that underscore the extent to which her werewolf nature is, at least, something that is forced upon her and was introduced within a context of disempowerment, so her struggle to live with her new Wolf aspect symbolically figures as a way to reestablish ownership over her own body, which has been violated and transformed against her will. It is also representative of her struggle to achieve personal and social power in a society where young women are routinely degraded and abused.

Although Kitty begins her werewolf life as a submissive pack member, she quickly begins to chafe under Meg and Carl's yoke, and an early—and critically important—act of defiance comes when she impulsively turns her gig as a late-night DJ at a local Denver radio station into a call-in show about the supernatural. The show becomes a point of pride for Kitty and a source of tension with Carl: "Carl didn't like the show because he didn't have any control over it. It was all mine. I was supposed to be all his" (Vaughn 2005, 25). The radio show that comes to be known as *The Midnight Hour* gives her a new sense of purpose and a renewed dedication to maintain her humanity.

Kitty's ethos is predicated upon a definition of "human" that is rooted in actions rather than states of being. When a vampire calls her very first show and asks her for advice on reconciling his supposedly damned state with his

Catholic faith, both a career in talk radio and a philosophy for leadership are launched. Kitty tells him, "I think in some ways every single person, human, vampire, whatever, has a choice to make: to be full of rage about what happens to you or to reconcile with it, to strive for the most honorable existence you can despite the odds" (ibid, 8). In the early days of her call-in radio show, Kitty responds to a werewolf caller who wonders why all supernaturals don't just do as they please: "The thing I keep hearing from all the people I talk to is that despite what they are and what they can do, they still want to be a part of human society. Society has benefits, even for them. So they take part in the social contract. They agree to live by human rules. Which means they don't go around 'wreaking havoc.' And that's why, ultimately, I think we can all find a way to live together" (ibid., 33). For Kitty, whether or not a supernatural starts out human and is transformed (werewolves, vampires) or was never actually human to begin with, to live as part of any kind of community with humans is effectively to be human oneself. Kitty defines "human" in the context of the social contract, and the human subject position as Kitty defines it confers both privileges and responsibilities.

One of those responsibilities is, as Kitty sees it, not to abuse power. As she grows more assertive and confident, she starts to stand up for others who are being oppressed and victimized, eventually confronting Carl and Meg and, with the help of mate Ben and a few other allies, killing or otherwise dispatching them; she and Ben replace Meg and Carl as Alphas of the Denver-area werewolf pack. In the confrontation, although Kitty shoots Meg with a silver bullet to stop her from torturing Ben (ibid. 2008b, 302), she leaves Carl's punishment to the pack, telling him that she can't accept his offer to leave Denver (and its pack) to her and Ben, saying, "I'm sorry, Carl. That's not for me to decide" (ibid., 304). This early decision to let the pack mete out justice sets the tone for her and Ben's stewardship of the pack. Kitty continually strives for consensus among pack members and resists displays of dominance and subordination whenever possible, noting that Meg and Carl's claims to a leadership style based on "natural" wolf behavior were based upon a flawed premise:

> Some research into wolf behavior—wild wolves, not the lycanthropic variety— suggests that the alphas of a pack aren't necessarily the strongest, biggest, and toughest wolves, contrary to conventional belief. Instead, the leaders were sometimes the wolves best able to keep peace. They were the most diplomatic, the ones most able to negotiate compromise and organize the pack into the most efficient unit for hunting prey and raising young. The alphas were the ones who were best able to keep more members of the pack alive. (ibid., 212)

She operates under the belief that neither her Wolf nor her human aspects need to be "animals" in the pejorative sense of the word, and she and Ben strive to avoid terrorizing their pack in order to ensure their cooperation. As Kitty tells her listeners, "I try to resolve conflicts by talking. I've built my career on it. Actually, I try to avoid conflicts entirely by talking. Usually it even works" (ibid. 2012, 319).

Additionally, Kitty sees dissemination of information as essential to empowering individuals as well as enabling collective action. In the series, those who seek to limit knowledge are immediately suspect. Roman is essentially the embodiment of a patriarchal impulse toward mastery and subjugation, and the guerilla war in the supernatural world that develops over the course of the series is ultimately a war of values. Kitty believes in true equality and democracy, and she considers her ability to share information foremost among her weapons. Kitty's sign-on for the show, "I'm Kitty Norville and you're listening to *The Midnight Hour*, the show that isn't afraid of the dark or the creatures who live there" (Vaughn 2005, 30), effectively encapsulates Kitty's worldview. When still a subordinate member of the pack living under Carl and Meg's rule, she recognizes that her life as a werewolf as it has been presented to her leaves little opportunity for forging bonds of compassion and mutual cooperation: "Anger and fear. That was what this whole life was about, anger vying with fear, and whichever won out determined whether you led or followed" (ibid., 60). Her strategy for combating fear is rooted in a belief that knowledge shared can forge alliances, and her radio show quickly becomes a public forum for exploring the mysteries of the supernatural world. As the show becomes more popular and Kitty herself more notorious, she remarks that "some people accused me of being a sensationalist, of fishing for controversy. Really, I loved drawing back the curtain, dragging this stuff into the open, kicking and screaming sometimes, and shining a bright light on it. I thought of it as dispelling ignorance. Ignorance bred fear, and I didn't like to be afraid" (ibid. 2009c, 219). Kitty's journey from powerlessness to power is marked by her increasing dedication to an ethics not only of mutual cooperation but also of sharing of information between supernatural creatures and mundane humans.

If knowledge is the antidote to fear, then the questions of what kinds of knowledge are valued and who is allowed to have such knowledge become significant. Alessandra Tanesini (2011) points out that in the Western philosophical tradition, epistemology "has inherited a tradition that privileged propositional knowledge (so-called 'knowledge that') over practical knowledge (so-called 'knowledge how') and knowledge by acquaintance of people and places. Such privileging is still in place" (886). The series resists this privileging and implicitly argues that "knowledge how" is an equally important type of knowledge, and that knowing is a constantly evolving and changing process rather than a static body. Kitty regularly uses her radio show to build knowledge via the collective. When Kitty and her pack are being pursued by some sort of demonic-seeming entity, for example, Kitty turns to her listeners, presenting the information they have about their attacker and "looking for information from the group mind" (Vaughn 2009c, 245). Although the usual mishmash of cranks and crackpots call in, eventually one of the more helpful callers tells her it's an ifrit, a mischievous fire spirit, and the knowledge gained enables Kitty and her allies to trap it. In a later novel, Kitty once again appeals to the wisdom of the collective by posting a book of shadows left to her by Zora, a witch ally who was killed in a skirmish with Roman, on the Internet to see if it would call additional allies forward: "Could be, the thing would do exactly what we wanted, and attract the attention of people who could help. Not just warn the world that Roman was out there, but raise an army to stand against him" (ibid. 2013c, 239).

In taking a public stand against Roman, Kitty becomes a de facto moral leader of the supernatural community, and she grows into her role in part by observing and learning from other leaders, choosing what and what not to emulate. One of her most influential mentors is Alette, a vampire who stands as Master of Washington, DC. Vaughn notes that vampires can serve as "walking repositories of 'living' history," calling them "historical aliens" (ibid. 2013a) In the context of the series, the vampires' status as "historical aliens" affords them both a good deal of propositional as well as practical knowledge, and how Alette gathers and uses knowledge serves as a model for Kitty.

When Kitty is called upon to testify before a Senate committee hearing on the supernatural, she is intercepted and escorted to Alette's home upon her arrival in DC. Although initially fearful, Kitty is immediately intrigued by Alette's surprising home: "This vampire held court in a room with windows—covered with heavy brocade drapes, but windows nonetheless. . . . All the lamps were lit, but softly, so the room had a warm, honey-like glow. Scattered among the other decorations were pictures, small portraits, a few black-and-white photographs. I wondered who they all were" (ibid. 2006, 39). The space itself affirms Alette as a different kind of vampire, one who seeks to integrate herself into the human world. Although Alette is initially a bit disrespectful of Kitty's autonomy, asking that Kitty report her doings like an errant teenager, she is motivated by a sincere desire to protect Kitty, and Kitty's observation of the "genuine, seemingly uncoerced loyalty Alette inspired in her people" makes her somewhat more inclined to see Alette's high-handedness as well-intentioned, if intrusive (ibid., 90). Meddlesome she may be, but Kitty comes to appreciate Alette's strong sense of altruism and her desire to help others, to use her immense personal and social power to protect the disenfranchised. Alette tells Kitty, "I happen to believe that immortality ought to make one more sensitive to the plight of the downtrodden, and more apt to work toward the betterment of humanity. Not less. We have the luxury of taking the long view" (ibid., 188). Alette's willingness to come to Kitty's aid and help other supernaturals convinces Kitty that Alette is a genuine kindred spirit and a valuable mentor.

Kitty discovers an additional layer to Alette's ongoing interest in humanity when Alette reveals to Kitty that the human members of her household staff are actually her descendants: "They're my children, do you understand? My children's children. I've looked after my family all these years. I've provided for them, watched over them, watched them grow and prosper. That's all I wanted for them, to prosper" (ibid., 275). Kitty realizes that for all the humans she'd met who'd be willing to do Alette's bidding, "that loyalty came from ties of blood. . . . I thought of all those portraits in the dining room, the photographs in the hall, in the parlor, all of them were her children. She kept pictures of her family throughout the house, like any doting mother" (ibid., 276). Alette exercises tremendous power and influence in DC, but she uses it for the good of her community, which extends from human kin to humanity in general, rather than to accrue power so that she can subjugate others. Her way is alien to many other vampires, who can't see the point of acquiring power without using it to subjugate those weaker and less influential than themselves. When Leo, Alette's vampire companion (whom she herself sired), eventually tries to stage a coup, he tells Alette and Kitty he did so because "you are the worst waste of resources I have ever encountered. You command an empire, Alette. And what do you use it for? *Nesting.* You are an immortal goddess, and you can't seem to do anything but play the part of a stupid woman" (ibid., 285).

Leo's dismissal of Alette as a "stupid woman" reinforces the extent to which traits such as willingness to cooperate and to care for others are often attributed to female characters and derided by male characters in the series. Although this division is not absolute, female characters are more often inclined to cooperate with one another, and most of the characters who wish to dominate and enslave others are male. Even allies such as Rick, Master vampire of Denver, and Cormac, Ben's bounty hunter cousin turned wary ally, are independent and not particularly investing in building community and fostering interpersonal relationships until their association with Kitty makes them see the value in it. In the war against Roman and his minions, though, many of Kitty's male allies come to see that her ability to talk, to bring people together through conversation and sharing information, is one of their most effective weapons against the enemy. Kitty notes, "This was my gift, my super-power: making people feel like they could talk about anything. Making them open up and reveal their secrets" (Vaughn 2010, 66).

When a vampire of Kitty's acquaintance tells her she's truly become a leader among supernaturals, Kitty thinks, "People listened to me—I based my whole career on that. I'd worked for that. Now I had to face up to the consequences of that: People listened to me. What was I going to do with that power?" (ibid., 276). Unsurprisingly, Kitty uses her power to encourage others to forge bonds of friendship and understanding. When called upon to give the keynote speech at a symposium for supernatural studies, Kitty acknowledges the growing discord that public acknowledgment of the existence of supernatural has fostered and urges people to move toward mutual acceptance and cooperation:

> As always, I turn to conversation as a solution. I ask you to stay in touch with each other. Talk to each other, tell each other your problems, get help. Isolation is dangerous, because when we're isolated our enemies take advantage of us, make us afraid, and use that fear. They will divide us and label us. Together, though— together we're a fortress. Communication—the basic act of talking—has always been my most powerful weapon, and I believe it can save us. (ibid. 2012, 320–21)

Sophia McDougall (2013) observes, "In narrative terms, agency is far more important than 'strength,'" and Kitty's agency is tied to her ability to communicate. Over the course of the series, Kitty goes from being a cowed, emotionally and physically abused woman to a strong, confident leader, and she does so by building a network of strong allies and recruiting others to her aid by virtue of their respect not for her physical strength (although she is capable of physical violence when necessary) but her willingness and ability to lead in a moral sense. She leads by example and by negotiation, not by brute strength. Thus, she not only achieves agency for herself but encourages others to find their own agency by giving them a public forum in which to discuss their lives, thus affirming their right to exist and to be heard.

This assertion of female agency, the resistance to being silenced, is particularly relevant to consider in light of UF's treatment in academic discourse. Candy Tan (2008) notes that "there's much casual contempt for literature that deals with the emotional and the female," citing this dismissiveness as "a logical extension from a culture that devalues female experiences in general," and when Alexander C. Irvine, author of the "Urban Fantasy" chapter in *The Cambridge Companion to Fantasy Literature* (2012), complains that the term itself "is now diffused in a fog of contradiction (and, it must be added, marketing noise; the writers of 'paranormal romance' have all but co-opted the term for the broad American readership)" (200), it sends a clear message to the scholarly community that the apparent commercial dominance of female writers in UF might easily be dismissed, relegated to an aside. Although he does briefly mention Emma Bull and Elizabeth Hand in his analysis of the genre, he devotes the majority of his critical attention to the works of male writers, particularly Jeff VanderMeer and China Miéville, effectively dismissing the evolution of the genre into something femalecentric as mere "marketing noise" and not worthy of serious consideration. This relative lack of serious critical engagement with UF in the current academic discourses on fantasy needs to be remedied in order to resist that kind of silencing of alternative discourses that Kitty herself identifies.

Notes

1. See esp. Jennifer K. Stuller's *Ink-Stained Amazons and Cinematic Warriors* (2010) and *Action Chicks: New Images of Tough Women in Popular Culture* (2004), edited by Sherrie A. Inness.

2. See the "Striking a Pose (Women and Fantasy Covers)" blog entry on the Hines's personal website (http://www.jimchines.com/2012/01/striking-a-pose/).

References

Abraham, Daniel. 2010. "MLN on UF: Why Jayne Heller Won't Get Raped." Lizard Brain, October 10. http://www.danielabraham.com/2010/10/29/mln-on-uf-why-jayne-heller-wont-get-raped (accessed October 30, 2013).

Brown, Jeffrey A. 2004. "Gender, Sexuality, and Toughness: The Bad Girls of Action Film and Comic Books." In *Action Chicks: New Images of Tough Women in Popular Culture*, edited by Sherrie A. Inness, 47–74. New York: Palgrave Macmillan.

Heldman, Caroline. 2012. "*The Hunger Games*, Hollywood, and Fighting Fuck Toys." Ms. Magazine Blog, April 6. http://msmagazine.com/blog/2012/04/06/the-hunger-games-hollywood-and-fighting-fuck-toys/ (accessed September 15, 2013).

Hollows, Joanne, and Rachel Moseley. 2006. "Popularity Contests: The Meaning of Popular Feminism." In *Feminism in Popular Culture*, edited by Joanne Hollows and Rachel Moseley, 1. Oxford: Berg.

McDougall, Sophia. 2013. "I Hate Strong Female Characters." *New Statesmen*, August 15. http://www.newstatesman.com/culture/2013/08/i-hate-strong-female-characters (accessed September 15, 2013).

Ross, Sharon. 2004. "'Tough Enough': Female Friendship and Heroism in *Xena* and *Buffy*." In *Action Chicks: New Images of Tough Women in Popular Culture*, edited by Sherrie A. Inness, 231–56. New York: Palgrave Macmillan.

Saintcrow, Lilith. "Angry Chicks in Leather." 2008. Pat's Fantasy Hotlist, December 16. http://fantasyhotlist.blogspot.com/2008/12/ad-lib-column-lilith-saintcrow.html (accessed October 30, 2013).

Stuller, Jennifer K. 2010. *Ink-Stained Amazons and Cinematic Warriors: Superwomen in Modern Mythology*. New York: I.B. Tauris.

Tan, Candy. 2008. "How We Know Vampire Romances Have Finally Hit the Big Time." Smart Bitches Trashy Books, May 12. http://smartbitchestrashybooks.com/blog/how-we-know-vampire-romances-have-finally-hit-the-big-time (accessed October 30, 2013).

Tanesini, Alessandra. 2011. "Feminist Epistemology." In *The Routledge Companion to Epistemology*, edited by Sven Bernecker and Duncan Pritchard, 885–95. New York: Routledge.

Vaughn, Carrie. 2005. *Kitty and the Midnight Hour*. New York: Grand Central Publishing.

———. 2006. *Kitty Goes to Washington*. New York: Grand Central Publishing.

———. 2008a. "Kick Ass Heroines." RR@H Novel Thoughts and Book Talk, February 15. http://rrahnovelthoughts.com/2008/02/15/carrie-vaughn-guest-blogging (accessed January 12, 2014).

———. 2008b. *Kitty and the Silver Bullet*. New York: Grand Central Publishing.

———. 2009a. "Carrie's Analysis of Urban Fantasy Part II: When Things Go Wrong." Filling the Well, January 6. http://carriev.wordpress.com/2009/01/06/carries-analysis-of-urban-fantasy-part-ii-when-things-go-wrong (accessed October 30, 2013).

———. 2009b. "Carrie's Analysis of Urban Fantasy Part III: Deconstructing Urban Fantasy." Filling the Well, January 7. http://carriev.wordpress.com/2009/01/07/carries-analysis-of-urban-fantasy-part-iii-deconstructing-urban-fantasy (accessed October 30, 2013).

———. 2009c. *Kitty Raises Hell*. New York: Grand Central Publishing.

———. 2010. *Kitty's House of Horrors*. 2010. New York: Grand Central Publishing.

———. 2012. *Kitty Steals the Show*. New York: Tor.

———. 2013a. "How I Learned to Stop Grumbling and Love Vampires." Tor/Forge Blog, April 1. http://torforgeblog.com/2013/04/01/how-i-learned-to-stop-grumbling-and-love-vampires/ (accessed January 31 2014).

———. 2013b. *Kitty Rocks the House*. New York: Tor.

———. 2013c. *Kitty in the Underworld*. New York: Tor.

Placing Parker: Negotiating the Hegemonic Binary in *Leverage*

—Elyce Rae Helford

Within the white patriarchal capitalist realm of contemporary American television culture, there exists space for negotiation in both the production and reception of texts. Speculative programming (fantasy, science fiction, horror, etc.) may offer particularly engaging opportunities for thought experiments related to gender and sexuality through emphasis on the suspension or alteration of physical and biological laws. Moreover, even negotiated depictions and interpretive challenges to the status quo of presumed gender absolutes and heterosexism are governed by the culture, language, and technologies through which such oppositions in encoding or decoding may take place. Nonetheless, as the concept of cultural hegemony makes plain, dominant ideologies are always in flux, requiring constant justification. In an era in which gender and sexual norms are undergoing significant and visible negotiation and reinterpretation (media attention to gay marriage laws and rising awareness of trans rights, for just two salient examples), popular culture offers a compelling locus for study of tensions over meaning and power and a shifting status quo.

In particular, this chapter is invested in contemporary media culture's challenges to what Mimi Martinucci (2010) discusses as the "hegemonic binary": "the coalescence of gender, sex, and sexuality into exactly two fundamentally distinct natural kinds: women and men," where the paradigmatic man is anatomically male, masculine in gender, and woman-oriented in sexuality, and the paradigmatic woman is anatomically female, feminine in gender, and man-oriented in sexuality (76). This essentialist position is based on the traditional doctrine of natural kinds, which divides the human world into two privileged, distinct, non-overlapping categories (ibid., 75–76). Of course, not all individuals fit their respective categories perfectly. The doctrine of natural kinds assumes that failure to exemplify definitive features of the hegemonic binary illustrates defectiveness in the individual. Texts that permit or encourage an understanding of gender as socially constructed provide feminist challenges to such essentialist absolutes. Yet if sex and sexuality are also socially constructed, the feminist challenge must be matched with a queer one.

To explore the mobilization of the fantastic as it offers queer feminist interpretive opportunities within contemporary popular cultural negotiations of the hegemonic binary of natural kinds, this chapter provides a case study of the character Parker in TNT/Electric Entertainment's *Leverage* (2008–2012). The character, as portrayed by Beth Riesgraf, offers superficial adherence to contemporary norms of feminine image and behavior, including her young, white, thin, blonde appearance, graceful stunt acrobatics, and apparent heteronormativity. A close reading of the character's placement within the series, however, illustrates the potential for reading her as a fantastic female who challenges the feminine and heterosexual norms she at first seems to exemplify so well. The presentation of Parker's personal history and her super-heroic (or super antiheroic) thieving abilities challenges gender absolutes. Simultaneously, her romantic relationship with the series's African American computer hacker character, Hardison, encourages a more fluid understanding of sex and sexuality. Taken together, Parker's diverse and contradictory psychological, physical, and relational traits, explored over the five-year run of the series, demonstrate hegemonic negotiation of the theory of natural kinds that continues to dominate popular culture. In this way, she emerges as an important exemplification of today's "woman fantastic."

For the uninitiated, *Leverage* is best described as an action-drama series about five vigilantes who help the disempowered and disenfranchised by "pick[ing] up where the law leaves off," as their leader, "Mastermind" Nathan "Nate" Ford (Timothy Hutton) repeatedly declares in defense of their illegal actions. Nate is joined by a team of outlaws, including "Grifter" Sophie Devereaux (Gina Bellman), "Hitter" Eliot Spencer (Christian Kane), "Hacker" Alec Hardison (Aldis Hodge), and "Thief" Parker (Beth Riesgraf). Together, they labor to right wrongs done by the greedy and the heartless, from corporate executives and corrupt politicians to Mafia bosses and sweatshop owners. Each episode has a happy ending, making the program less gritty realism than wish-fulfillment fantasy. Furthermore, outright fantastical elements, including impossibly high-tech gadgetry and equally implausible confidence trickery, are played with an often heavy-handed wink and nod, as in the frequent audible beeps, clicks, and whirs that no computer or cell phone ever makes and the science-fictional security laser grids that Parker nimbly cartwheels across in many episodes. Equally fanciful are the titles of con jobs frequently bandied about by the team, from the horror-inspired "The Mummy's Tiara" to the fairy tale-inflected "Wicked Step-sister." Through such details, the series toys with the fantastic à la James Bond or the *Mission: Impossible* franchise rather than overtly science fiction or paranormal programming.

Intertextual references help to place the series more fully within the realm of the fantastic for the viewer. The wiki tvtropes.org goes so far as to identify the series as "so full of Shout Outs" and homages, "it's practically Reference Overdosed" ("*Leverage*: Shout Outs"). Members of the team take on obvious pseudonyms offering allusions to speculative film and television, for example. In "The Inside Job" (2010, 3.3) Sophie and Hardison use the names Emily Peel and Jonathan Steed as part of the scam, in obvious homage to *The Avengers* (1961–1969). One of the most through and complex reference schemes appears in "The First Contact Job" (Garcia 2012, 5.3). Eliot takes on the name "Willie Riker," an allusion to the character Will Riker, first officer of the Starship Enterprise on *Star Trek: The Next Generation* (1987–1994), a figure of which the villain has on his own desk. Extratextually, we can also note that Jonathan Frakes, who portrayed Riker, directed the episode. More generally, during a press conference scene, one reporter wears the costume of the eleventh incarnation of Doctor Who; Parker and Hardison play characters modeled on the main characters from *Men in Black* (1997); and Parker quotes several lines from *E.T.: The Extraterrestrial* (1982). Throughout the series, primarily through the geeky fanboy tendencies of Hardison, references are made to many popular texts and franchises, from *Star Wars* and *Ghostbusters* to *World of Warcraft*.

If, through such evidence, we read *Leverage* as an action-drama that uses elements of the fantastic to enhance its adventurous appeal while lightening its tone, we may then ask whether such elements contribute to challenging the hegemonic binary. Into this context we may bring a close consideration of Parker, the series's strongest female and least gender-normative character. She features only a single, gender-neutral name and matches a fetishistic love of cash with an addiction to daredevil stunts, particularly to leaping from tall buildings wearing only a cord and a harness. Adding gender-significant depth, Parker is not only athletic and acrobatic as well as devoted to her work as a thief, but she also has difficulty managing interpersonal relationships, particularly romantic ones—even as part of a con. By contrast, the young blonde's gymnastic skills show off a thin, supple body. She thus offers the "both/and" of negotiated hegemony, with an emphasis on the social construction of gender, particularly of femininity as a learned performance. When gathering information at a cocktail party in Serbia, for example, her flirtation skills go from poor to dangerous as she cannot stop herself from acting on outrage. She stabs a callous hitman in the chest with a fork, without fear but threatening the con. Such inability to display submissive femininity becomes a recurring theme in the series, with Parker needing to go so far as to mutter "Don't stab, don't stab, don't stab" on the way to meet a mark in "The Girls' Night Out Job" (Downey and Kao 2011, 4.13). "The Runway Job" (Kim 2010, 2.10) reaches even greater excess as Parker manages to pass herself off as a runway model before making a clumsy spectacle of falling from the catwalk to draw attention away from Eliot, who is secretly removing data from a designer's computer. As she rises, she adjusts her neck with a loud crack, showing her toughness even when sprawled among the paparazzi in a strapless gown.

The primary explanation given in the series for Parker's display of non-traditionally gendered behavior is her background as an abused orphan in the foster system. A flashback, shown in the pilot episode, "The Nigerian Job" (Rogers and Downey 2008, 1.1), reveals an abusive foster father who slaps her foster mother offscreen and then takes young Parker's stuffed rabbit, telling her she must either do what he tells her . . . or become a better thief. After a cut, we see the child, sometime later, walking away from the house. The bunny is clutched tightly in her arms as the home blows up behind her. Showing both (feminine) affection for her stuffed animal and (feminist) rejection of patriarchal authority, she takes the (masculine) advice to improve her thieving skills to heart. In third season episode, "The Boost Job" (Kim 2010, 3.8), we learn that a twelve-year-old Parker was part of a car theft ring before spending time in juvenile detention when abandoned by the older boy who taught her the trade. Only a few episodes earlier, in "The Inside Job" (Thorne 2010), we discovered that soon after escaping detention, she was extensively trained by one of the world's greatest thieves, Archie Leech (Richard Chamberlain)—a name chosen for Cary Grant fans. Leech, we learn, did not adopt her. He kept her separate from his law-abiding image and family but taught her thieving skills, exemplified by spectacularly stunt-performed and absurdly unnecessary tumbles and flips through fantastical laser grid mazes.

Given her background, it is unsurprising that Parker often simply does not understand how to behave in social situations. She publicly and audibly sniffs others' hair, for example, and is unfamiliar with concepts such as "midlife crisis." She also believes in Santa Claus and time machines. Significantly, Parker's eccentric behavior is directly inflected by gender and sexual norms. In "The Runway Job" (Kim 2010), when the three men on the team all agree that a temporary grifter replacement for Sophie is "hot," Parker joins in, echoing their declaration in the same tone. The men fall silent and stare at her, but she doesn't understand why. In dismay, she tries "Warm?" and then "Cold?" as they shake their heads and walk away. And in "The Inside Job," she naively asks Eliot what "sexting" is. His response is to refuse to discuss the subject with her. In such examples, we see the theory of natural kinds at work: patriarchal leader Nate, womanizer Eliot, and even nerd Hardison show Parker she is performing heterosexual femininity incorrectly. We as viewers must choose whether to laugh at or with her as she innocently challenges the hegemonic binary.

Most difficult for Parker, as the above examples suggest, is understanding how to manage sexual attraction and interpersonal intimacy. As she grows increasingly drawn to Hardison—as a sibling-like friend and eventually a lover—we do not see her fall prey to traditional gender roles. Hardison is shown to be far more emotionally sensitive than Parker or the other two male team members, with only mother figure Sophie displaying equal need for warmth and connectedness. Thus, for example, it is Hardison, not Parker, who cries when the team is able to give a corporate criminal's mansion to a military family dispossessed from their small, Katrina-hit Mississippi home in "The Snow Job" (Kim 2009, 1.9). Hardison even tears up when talking about battling robots who "bleed out" oil. By contrast, Parker is fearless, calling Hardison a "big baby" in the series's second episode, "The Homecoming Job" (Rogers 2008, 1.2), when he complains about having to rappel from a window with an untested harness (ibid.). Late in season four, during a controlled drop down a building's stairwell in "The Radio Job" (Downey and Guyot 2012, 4.17), we see Parker's perspective allied with hypermasculine Eliot's against a terrified Hardison. As the three look over the edge of the railing, the following exchange takes place:

PARKER (TO ELIOT): It might be easier if he's asleep.
ELIOT (TO PARKER): Want me to put him to sleep?
HARDISON: Hey! I'm standing right here, okay? . . .
PARKER: Relax! We're gonna lower you really slowly, but if you bump into anything, the walls, the windows, anything, you will set off the alarms.
HARDISON: Yeah, yeah, yeah, I get it. It's like the game Operation, except I'm the tweezers. Look, whatever you do, do not drop me. Come on, I'm tired. I've had it. Being pushed off of damn buildings and stuff and windows . . .
(Eliot and Parker together push Hardison off the ledge.)
HARDISON: Wh-o-o-oa! Really? It's not funny. It's not funny. I see you laughing. I see you laughing. I'm a person! A human being! I got feelings, and I don't feel none of this. I'm tired of being pushed off of stuff. We all havin' a serious conversation when this is over with. This is . . . s-squishy. Oh. Peed my pants. All right.

Hardison has no masculine authority in the situation, nor is there sympathy for his feelings of insecurity and vulnerability. The dangerous and dehumanizing experience is met with laughter from both Eliot and Parker.

Despite this example, Parker is more out of touch with her emotions rather than truly callous, exemplified in "The Double Blind Job" (Glenn and Reader 2010, 3.5), as she becomes jealous of a client who is friendly with Hardison. When Sophie mentions the client's name, Parker absently crushes a beer bottle in her hand (to comic, not bloody effect, fitting with the series's general tone). Sophie counsels her, telling her she is jealous and that she should share how she feels with Hardison. She has to be taught both femininity and heteronormativity from a female character who exemplifies both. Parker stops denying her feelings and makes an attempt to communicate with Hardison but comes up short. Sitting at the counter with Hardison in the bar where they meet clients, she looks down at a bowl of pretzels and says, "So the thing is, I think that maybe I might be having feelings. Like weird, weird feelings for . . . pretzels." Hardison understands her inability to speak what she feels, and his expression shows quiet affection and patience, unlike any other character in the series. He replies, "Pretzels? Okay. Well, they're right here . . . when you want them."

To complicate gender and sexual interactions between the two further, we find Hardison seems to have limited, if any, sexual experience, while Parker is surprisingly comfortable with her sexuality. She is willing to kiss Hardison passionately to protect their identities when the con calls for it, for example, as shown in "The Jailhouse Job" (Rogers 2010, 3.1). When caught by security, Parker pretends to be Hardison's private secretary and lover. After they are safe, Hardison exclaims, "I like it when we pretend to kiss." Parker takes the moment in stride, replying, "Pretend?" We also see Parker strip down in front of Eliot and Hardison several times, displaying an ease in her body and no fear of sexual vulnerability. Hardison again plays the innocent suitor when he photographs Parker as part of the con in "The 15-Minute Job" (Schaer 2011, 4.3). Parker shows utter ineptitude when trying to look sexy, but she takes off all of her clothes without being asked. Sophie expresses shock while Hardison turns away and then wonders, aloud, why he isn't taking the opportunity to ogle.

Imbalances that may be connected with gender roles balance when mutual affection of a more familial sort, including willingness to help one another in a crisis, reveal that any disparities are superficial. If a theory of natural kinds claims men are supposed to protect women or women nurture men without taking power, the relationship between Parker and Hardison challenges such essentialist formulations. When Parker panics at having to wear weighted boots in one episode because they keep her from the lightness and agility that has helped her escape any threat, Hardison calms her, humming a soothing melody his Nana (a nickname for his foster mother) used to sing. He softly says, "I got you, girl," so she knows she is not alone in her moment of fright (Veach and Kirsch 2011, "The Queen's Gambit Job," 4.10). In an earlier season and a not-dissimilar panic on Hardison's part in "The Grave Danger Job" (Kirsch 2011, 4.7), he suffers extreme claustrophobia after being buried alive in a coffin by drug dealers. Although hesitant to take the phone when he calls from within the coffin, begging for help, Sophie must assure Parker that she is the one Hardison needs. She is familiar with being in tight spaces, such as the Hollywood-sized air ducts she often climbs through on cons. Parker reluctantly takes responsibility for Hardison as best she can, helping him to slow his breathing while the team seeks him out. She declares, "Hardison, you have to make it through this because . . . because you're my friend, and I need you. Do you hear me, Alec? I need you!"

Gender complexity need not lead to portrayal of equally complex notions of sexual orientation. Like Parker's thin, youthful blondeness that might signal a sexist status quo, Parker's attraction to Hardison and not, for example, to Sophie, can be read as illustrating an unquestioned heteronormativity that is echoed in all the characters in the series. The team never helps an openly homosexual or trans character, for example. In fact, in five seasons, there are only a handful of references to any sort of queerness in *Leverage*, and these are mostly in the form of heterosexist or transphobic jokes. In "The 12-Step Job," Eliot and Hardison need access to Nate when he is locked in a rehabilitation center, so Eliot flirts with the receptionist and claims he is Nate's brother. Hardison, racially unconvincing as a blood relative and annoyed by Eliot's selfishness and machismo, pretends he is Eliot's lover in stereotyped, effeminate fashion. With a focus on pornographic double standards, "The First David Job" (Rogers 2009, 1.12) shows Parker embracing and kissing Hardison to distract security guards. With all of the team using ear-bud communicators, Eliot can hear this and salaciously inquires whether Parker was making out with Hardison or Sophie.

Clearly, *Leverage* offers more opportunities to question gender norms than those of sexual orientation. To find a true challenge to the hegemonic binary, however, we must see in Parker's attractions some evidence of resistance to heteronormativity. This is best accomplished by exploring the construction of heterosexuality in the series. As Adrienne Rich (1993) declared in "Compulsory Heterosexuality and Lesbian Existence," "To take the step of questioning heterosexuality as a 'preference' or 'choice' for women—and to do the intellectual and emotional work that follows," is no easy matter, but it can bring "a freeing-up of thinking, the exploration of new paths, the shattering of another great silence" (216). Such efforts have been accomplished in multiple directions by queer theory and feminist sexuality studies. Thus, we might begin to read *Leverage* as a contemporary site of Rich's feminist labor to find "new paths," via Nicole LaMarre's (2011) declaration that "when it comes to sexual identity, nothing is as 'straight' as it seems. . . . Recent research suggests that, although people may identify as one orientation or another, their sexual practices, desires, and fantasies have a fluidity that challenges the notion of fixed sexual identities" (253). I posit that the representation of Parker's heterosexuality aligns with such conclusions, with particular attention to issues of kinship and miscegenation taboos. To explicate and illustrate this argument, we must turn to the work of Judith Butler.

In "Is Kinship Always Already Heterosexual?," Butler discusses turn-of-the-millennium debates in France over kinship and marriage in the context of anti-immigrant racism. She sees in the discourse a return to the structuralism of Claude Lévi-Strauss. In this constellation, the incest taboo works in conjunction with the miscegenation taboo as parts of a "racialist project to reproduce culture" (Butler 2002). Butler asks, "When Lévi-Strauss makes the argument that the incest taboo is the basis of culture and that it mandates exogamy, or marriage outside the clan, is 'the clan' being read in terms of race . . . ?" (ibid.). If so, a double-bind is established:

> Marriage must take place outside the clan. There must be exogamy. But there must also be a limit to exogamy; that is, marriage must be outside the clan but not outside a certain racial self-understanding or racial commonality. So the incest taboo mandates exogamy, but the taboo against miscegenation limits the exogamy that the incest taboo mandates. Cornered, then, between a compulsory heterosexuality and a prohibited miscegenation, something called culture, saturated with the anxiety and identity of dominant European whiteness, reproduces itself in and as universality itself. (ibid., 33)

Butler's formulation of "culture" in this equation brings readings of nation and race into considerations of the hegemonic binary, rejecting the discourse of natural kinds, or rather exposing its arbitrariness and basis in cultural dynamics of race and power.

Applying such focus to *Leverage*, we might interpret Parker's attraction to Hardison as a challenge to both incest and miscegenation taboos. Though they do not marry by the conclusion of the series, they declare themselves a couple and seem to cohabit—though explicit sex scenes are never shown. Vital to an understanding of their relationship is the fact that Parker considers the team her family. "The Inside Job" concludes with former father figure Archie expressing regret that he did not take Parker home and make her part of his "real" family but then recognizing, "You went out and made your own." Individuals within the group of five bicker and even part company for a time at several points in the series, but they always return and protect and care for one another. Moreover, the final season contains many references to a family-like bond between the members of the group as the program builds to climax. Sophie calls Parker "baby bird" and enthuses that she has learned how to fly in "The Broken Wing Job" (Veach and Kirsch 2012, 5.8). And Nate and Sophie leave the crew to marry in the last episode, suggesting a reversal of grown children leaving home. Eliot promises them he will watch out for Harrison and Parker until the day he dies, suggestive of an older brother role in "The Long Goodbye Job" (Rogers and Downey 2012, 5.15).

Within this context, Parker's romantic union with Hardison challenges the incest taboo. We know they share similar backgrounds within the foster care system, where family was temporary and not always benevolent—or, particularly for Parker, even benign. Through their years together, they come to value the Leverage team as members of a more permanent family. In addition, Parker is arguably the most stereotypically white member of the team, while Hardison is the only black character. (Parker's pale skin, long, straight blonde hair, and blue eyes differ significantly from Sophie's brown eyes, dark wavy hair, and tan skin. This difference is accentuated by Sophie's ability as a grifter to play women of diverse backgrounds, from a Russian escort to a biracial executive from India.) The contrast between Parker and Hardison, not just in terms of personality and gender performance but also in terms of race, openly defies miscegenation taboos. The relevance of this reading is enhanced in the episode "The Van Gogh Job" (Downey 2011, 4.4), about an ill-fated World War II–era relationship between Dorothy, a privileged young white woman, and an articulate young black man named Charlie. The two fall in love at the small town's roller skating rink and decide to escape her racist, domineering father by hopping a train to France. The plan fails, leaving the lovers separated for life. By the time Charlie (Danny Glover) returns to town as an old man, Dorothy has died. The miscegenation taboo at the heart of the episode is brought into present-day relevance by the fact that the cast reenacts Charlie's story in flashback, with Parker playing the young woman and Hardison playing young Charlie. The episode is unique for having no mark and also less focus on the recovery of a hidden Van Gogh painting than the story of Charlie and Dorothy. In the closing moment of the episode, we see its importance for Parker and Hardison when Charlie says to Parker, "There's one thing I want to tell you. Don't waste time." Parker responds by turning to look at Hardison in the doorway and smiling. The episode ends as the two walk out of Charlie's room, hand in hand.

That breaking the miscegenation taboo still resonates culturally is evident in that there are no sexually intimate scenes—even kissing—once Parker and

Hardison are clearly a couple. By contrast, Nate and Sophie's relationship deepens, depicted by several kissing scenes as well as the pair waking up in bed together. Clearly, the pairing of Parker and Hardison illustrates a complex negotiation of taboos within a media culture structured around natural kinds and the hegemonic binary.

Ultimately, it would be easy to dismiss the character of Parker and the escapist fantasy program in which she is situated. Her presentation as a tough-but-cute young white woman within a white, male-dominated team superficially supports familiar notions illustrated by television's many fantasy girls—and more *Charlie's Angels* than even *Buffy the Vampire Slayer*. And her choice of the team's sole black character for her "boyfriend" (as she calls him in the final season) can easily be downplayed in terms of racial difference by their shared outsider status, foster child backgrounds, and the fact that playboy-type Eliot is the only other man available within the central cast of characters. Nonetheless, a more nuanced exploration shows, in case study fashion, that popular culture's reliance on essentialist gender and sex absolutes is not, itself, absolute. Even within texts that seem at first to offer limited potential for feminist and queer interpretation, we may find complexities and contradictions that signal ongoing struggles over the meaning and power of the woman fantastic.

References

Berg, Amy and Chris Downy, writers. February 3, 2009. "The 12-Step Job." *Leverage* 1.10, directed by Rod Hardy. Paramount Home Video.

Butler, Judith. 2002. "Is Kinship Always Already Heterosexual?" *differences: A Journal of Feminist Cultural Studies* 15 (1): 14–44.

Downey, Chris, writer. July 17, 2011. "The Van Gogh Job." *Leverage* 4.4, directed by John Rogers. Paramount Home Video.

Downey, Chris, and Paul Guyot, writers. January 8, 2012. "The Radio Job." *Leverage* 4.17, directed by Dean Devlin. Paramount Home Video.

Downey, Chris, and Jenn Kao, writers. December 11, 2011. "The Girls' Night Out Job." *Leverage* 4.13, directed by Marc Roskin. Paramount Home Video.

Garcia, Aaron Denius, writer. August 5, 2012. "The First Contact Job." *Leverage* 5.3, directed by Jonathan Frakes. Paramount Home Video.

Glenn, Melissa, and Jessica Reader, writers. July 11, 2010. "The Double Blind Job." *Leverage* 3.5, directed by Marc Roskin. Paramount Home Video.

Kim, Albert, writer. January 27, 2009. "The Snow Job." *Leverage* 1.9, directed by Tony Bill. Paramount Home Video.

———. January 13, 2010. "The Runway Job." *Leverage* 2.10, directed by Marc Roskin. Paramount Home Video.

———. August 1, 2010. "The Boost Job." *Leverage* 3.8, directed by Marc Roskin. Paramount Home Video.

Kirsch, Rebecca, writer. August 14, 2011. "The Grave Danger Job." *Leverage* 4.7, directed by John Harrison. Paramount Home Video.

LaMarre, Nicole. (2006) 2011. "Sexual Narratives of 'Straight' Women." In *Introducing the New Sexuality Studies*, edited by Steven Seidman, Nancy Fischer, and Chet Meeks, 253–259. New York: Routledge. Citations refer to the second edition.

"*Leverage*: Shout Outs." April 16, 2014. TV Tropes. *tvtropes.org*.

Martinucci, Mimi. 2010. *Feminism Is Queer: The Intimate Connection between Queer and Feminist Theory*. London: Zed Books.

Rich, Adrienne. "Compulsory Heterosexuality and Lesbian Existence." In *Adrienne Rich's Poetry and Prose*, edited by Barbara Charlesworth Gelpi and Albert Gelpi, 203–24. New York: Norton: 1993.

Rogers, John, writer. December 9, 2008. "The Homecoming Job." *Leverage* 1.2, directed by Dean Devlin Paramount Home Video.

———. February 17, 2009. "The First David Job." *Leverage* 1.12, directed by Dean Devlin. Paramount Home Video.

———. June 20, 2010. "The Jailhouse Job." *Leverage*. 3.1, directed by Dean Devlin. Paramount Home Video.

Rogers, John, and Chris Downey, writers. December 7, 2008. "The Nigerian Job." *Leverage* 1.1, directed by Dean Devlin. Paramount Home Video. DVD.

———. December 25, 2012. "The Long Goodbye Job." *Leverage* 5.15, directed by Dean Devlin. Paramount Home Video.

Schaer, Josh, writer. July 10, 2011. "The 15-Minute Job." *Leverage* 4.3, directed by Marc Roskin. Paramount Home Video.

Thorne, Geoffrey, writer. June 27, 2010. "The Inside Job." *Leverage* 3.3, directed by John Rogers. Paramount Home Video.

Veach, M. Scott, and Rebecca Kirach, writers. August 28, 2011. "The Queen's Gambit Job." *Leverage* 4.10, directed by Jonathan Frakes. Paramount Home Video.

———. September 9, 2012. "The Broken Wing Job." *Leverage* 5.8, directed by John Harrison. Paramount Home Video.

Hillary Orbits an Alternative Universe Earth: Interpreting the USA Network's *Political Animals* as Science Fiction

—Marleen S. Barr

Many of Mrs. Clinton's supporters couldn't understand why she didn't divorce her Monica Lewinsky–tainted husband after they left the White House. In this make-believe iteration [depicted in *Political Animals*], the betrayed wife doesn't stand by her man; she kicks him out. Moments after her concession speech, she leaves the hotel suite, pausing at the door to say to her husband, "Oh, and Bud, I want a divorce." (Stanley, 2012)

I n the six-episode miniseries *Political Animals* (2012), Sigourney Weaver portrays Elaine Barrish Hammond, a fictitious version of Hillary Rodham Clinton.[1] Elaine is a former First Lady, governor of Illinois, failed presidential candidate, successful secretary of state—and potential new presidential candidate. This essay asks "what if" questions in regard to how fiction applies to the miniseries. What if the series is viewed as science fiction rather than realistic fiction? My question interests Weaver, who specifically states that she was not invested in playing an imitative version of Hillary. Her performance differs from Julianne Moore channeling Sarah Palin in *Game Change* (2012), for example: "I wouldn't have been interested in that kind of quasi-realism," Weaver said. Rather, what drew her to her first major television role was "exploring the dynamic of a powerful woman in charge at work but in over her head personally" (Chozick 2012).

With Pamela Sargent's (1999) "Hillary Orbits Venus" in mind—an alternative future story in which Hillary becomes an astronaut—I explore how *Political Animals* presents Weaver cast in a science fiction media scenario of the ilk of *Avatar* and the *Alien* films. "'I'm a Rorschach test,' Clinton herself once said, referring to the way people tend to project their own hopes and anxieties onto to her" (Morrison 2008, xiii). When I watch *Political Animals*, I project my baby boomer generational anxieties and my feminist hopes about

Hillary's connections and responses to Bill on to her in terms of science fiction. To my mind, *Political Animals*, as a power fantasy for women, recasts Hillary as an alternative history superhero. I am not alone in this perspective; Alessandra Stanley (2012) also classifies *Political Animals* in terms of alternative history: "This half-comic, half-serious soap opera á clef could be awful, but instead it is surprisingly fun: a fictional look at Mrs. Clinton that blends what-if alternative history with wish fulfillment fantasy: if only she would." The show's feminist viewers can experience a "what if" wish fulfillment Hillary who divorces Bill and fervently desires to run for president without him.

To me, the real Hillary, on the cusp of her second run for president at the time of this writing, is fantastic in the sense of "terrific." Questions about women's relationship to power and family that form the crux of Weaver portraying Hillary relate to the generic fantastic. I discuss this relationship in four sections: Fiction/Current Media/Reality, which positions *Political Animals* in the context of popular media's routine blurring of the distinction between fiction and reality; Space Opera/Soap Opera, which analyzes how Hillary's soap opera life has been equated with science fiction and how Elaine epitomizes a fantastic improved feminist version of it; *Political Animals*/Science Fiction, which exemplifies interpreting the show as a science fiction narrative; and Elaine Barrish/Marleen Barr(ish), which contains opinion, preposterous proposition, and imaginative political scenario.

Fiction/Current Media/Reality

Equating *Political Animals* with science fiction is congruent with the media's current penchant for blurring the demarcation between fiction and reality. Rush Limbaugh and Fox News, for example, routinely alter reality to fit conservative agendas; these conservative views are in a different universe vis-à-vis the reality-based community. *Girls* (2012–) makes the exaggerated glamor fantasy depicted in *Sex and the City* (1998–2004) real. *The Newsroom* (2012–) is a fictitious drama that portrays real recent events in what is, from the viewers' perspective, a time travel premise. Like *Mad Men*, *The Newsroom* enables viewers to see the reality of "the way it was." The *Mad Men* (2007–2015) protagonists experience a more historically accurate flower child era, Vietnam War, and Kennedy assassination; *The Newsroom* protagonists experience an historically accurate Gabby Giffords shooting, Anthony Weiner scandal, and Casey Anthony trial. In *The Newsroom*, Jane Fonda plays Leona Lansing, a female version of her cable news media mogul former husband Ted Turner. Even though viewers have to be aware of Fonda's sojourn as Turner's wife to understand the joke, Leona is a plausible female television executive image.[2] I say "image" because just as no woman has been elected president of the United States, no woman has achieved media power that equals Turner's. In this respect, Fonda's Leona Lansing, a female version of Ted Turner, is also fantastic.

Unlike these shows, *Veep* (2012–) is unabashedly fictitious. In light of the fact that Geraldine Ferraro did not become vice president, there is no real counterpart to Julia Louis-Dreyfus's vice president, Selina Meyer. Not so for Weaver's Elaine Barrish Hammond. Elaine's presidential aspirations were thwarted by a younger, less experienced male candidate—President Paul Garcetti. Ditto for Hillary. Elaine resembles Hillary in her political trajectory, with only personal differences. Elaine ends her marriage to philandering former president Donald "Bud" Hammond. She has two twenty-eight-year-old sons: the perfect offspring Chelsea-clone Douglas, her chief-of-staff, and his flawed twin T.J., a gay renegade and recovering addict. While Dorothy Rodham was never emphasized in relation to Hillary's public life, Elaine's mother Margaret Barrish (Ellen Burstyn) is prominently featured. Elaine, in addition to having an omnipresent mother, is influenced by her friend and mentor, the first openly gay Supreme Court justice, Diane Nash (Vanessa Redgrave). With no connection to Bill's infamous reference to what the definition of *is* is, Elaine is and is not Hillary. She even uses Hillary's exact words as she accepts a cabinet post: "When the president asks you to serve, you serve" (Stanley 2012). Elaine emerges as an alternative history science fiction protagonist.

The publicity staff of *Political Animals* uses the show's website to create alternative history science fiction via a fictitious newspaper called *The Washington Globe*. Reporter protagonists—the Maureen Dowd counterpart Susan Berg and her young, unscrupulous rival Georgia Gibbons—write copy about the Hammond family in *The Globe*. (Susan is a strong woman who at first opposes Elaine but eventually becomes her ally. Like Elaine, Susan has an influential mother, a former doctor.) *The Globe* features political cartoons that spoof Elaine and Bud and articles about the era of the Hammond presidency and the Garcetti White House. *The Globe*'s relation to Elaine's Washington functions analogously to the *Daily Planet*'s relation to Superman's Metropolis. The comparison is fitting: Elaine is Superwoman.

Space Opera/Soap Opera

While Elaine might emanate from an alternative universe Earth, Hillary does not come from Krypton. Nonetheless, she is imbued with a science fiction aura. The science fiction tenets that I attribute to Elaine-as-Hillary have not sprung from the head of the show's creator, Greg Berlanti, sans precedent. Dowd (2008a) describes her superheroic powers: "Hillary has created a regal force field that can be breached only with permission." And Dowd's *New York Times* columnist colleague Gail Collins (2008) wonders if Hillary is secretly an extraterrestrial: "What if she [Hillary] has a secret life as a French undercover agent or a space alien?" In a similar vein, Charlie Jane Anders (2008), writing on the *io9* blog, proclaims that "Sarah Palin = *Star Wars*, Hillary Clinton = *Star Trek*" and "Sarah Palin is Yoda, Hillary Clinton is Deanna Troi." Anders states that "Sarah Palin uses Jedi mind tricks, Hillary Clinton makes a deal with the Borg. In other words: Hillary Clinton = science fiction.

While Anders offers a relatively benign, humorous comparison, Hillary and science fiction are sometimes juxtaposed to communicate an excessively deprecating message. The *Gawker*'s Richard Blakeley creates the "Hillerator" image, relating her to the violent cyborg played by Arnold Schwarzenegger in the original film *The Terminator*. The Hillerator is not a pretty picture; Blakeley portrays Hillary as threatening and monstrous. Ian Spiegelman (2008), in a *Gawker* post titled "Maureen Dowd Calls Hillary Clinton Sci-Fi Monster," couples Blakeley's "Hillerator" with Dowd's textual photon torpedo aimed at Hillary. Dowd (2008b) writes, "It's impossible to imagine The Terminator, as a former aide calls her [Hillary], giving up. Unless every circuit is out, she'll regenerate enough to claw her way out of the grave, crawl through the Rezko Memorial Lawn and up Obama's wall, hurl her torso into the house and brutally haunt his dreams." This morphing, rapacious, relentless Hillary is no angel in the house.

Creator Berlanti does not kill the angel in the former White House. He instead presents Elaine as a Superwoman who saves the United States and as a Supermom who diligently attends to her family's trials and tribulations. The premise that Elaine is both her sons' Supermom and America's Superwoman is apparent in the following incredible scenarios from the miniseries:

1. When three journalists are taken hostage in Iran, Elaine authors a plan to save the hostages while adeptly juggling the crisis with the fact that it causes the party celebrating Douglas's engagement to Ann Ogami to be disrupted.
2. When President Garcetti refuses to rescue a Chinese submarine crew trapped off the West Coast, Elaine convinces him to change his mind. Garcetti learns that if the United States undertakes a rescue mission, the Chinese will destroy the submarine. A catastrophic radiation release will ensue. Garcetti, influenced by Elaine, nullifies the Chinese threat by making it public and organizes a successful rescue mission.

3. When Air Force One crashes and Garcetti is killed, Elaine averts a potential constitutional crisis by convincing Vice President Fred Collier, rather than taking the oath of office, to invoke the Twenty-fifth Amendment to become acting president. She accomplishes her political objective while dealing with Douglas and Ann's decision to elope.

Perhaps Berlanti purposefully tries to nullify the Hillerator image by having Elaine function as Superwoman in both heroically plausible and maternal ways. Elaine, no Elainerator, is an alternative universe Hillary who improves upon the original. The real Hillary was not an independent single career woman starting her professional life alone in the manner of 1960s television's protofeminist protagonists in *That Girl* and *The Mary Tyler Moore Show*. Ann Marie (Marlo Thomas) and Mary Richards (Mary Tyler Moore) had no Bill counterpart to act as a launching pad for their careers. Nonetheless, links to these TV predecessors are evident as *Political Animals* presents its airbrushed, privileged, white feminist wish-fulfillment version of Hillary. We can ask, "What do feminists want in relation to Hillary?" Perhaps they wish that Hillary acted more like an Anne Marie or Mary Richards clone. Unable to grant this wish, *Political Animals* attends to its implications as it presents a version of Hillary who jettisons Bill later in life. Elaine is then free to run for president under the auspices of her own independent orbit. The character rectifies the faults Wendy Wasserstein (1998) points out in her analysis of Hillary that

> women like Hillary Rodham suddenly had the same career opportunities as the men they were supposed to wed. Marriage would be for love or companionship, but would no longer be a substitute for individual destiny. If anyone's life would have been transformed by the burgeoning women's movement, it should have been hers. . . . Sadly, however, her current popularity seems a bridge to the past rather than the future. . . . The wife of the presidential candidate who told a CBS interviewer in 1992 that "I'm not some little woman standing by my man like Tammy Wynette" is now being applauded for doing precisely that. The First Lady who dared to take on health care reform has now been diminished to a popular soap opera heroine. Maintaining the dignity of her marriage, difficult as that may be, is now seen as her greatest professional triumph.

Wasserstein concludes that "Hillary Rodham Clinton was hardly a feminist icon. She has always sent confusing signals. . . . She has flip-flopped on so many issues of image that her behavior can justifiably be called erratic. . . . Personally, I wish the talented Hillary Rodham Clinton would stand up and sign in please. We women of her generation had hoped she would break new ground. Yet what seemed initially so positive is becoming a very unsavory parable." Wasserstein, a woman who never married and earned prominence on her own, is correct. Hillary, who launched her political career by attaching herself to Bill, is no feminist icon. But her analysis is, of course, out of date. In 2001, the "talented" Hillary did "stand up and sign in" when she embarked upon her US Senate space odyssey. In 2009, she became secretary of state. When Hillary signed in as a politician in her own right, her marriage license made her signature possible. Her connection to Bill can never be erased. However, rewriting Hillary's life as a science fiction scenario positions her current popularity as a bridge to the future rather than the past. An alternative reality Hillary who eventually does divorce Bill imbues the Tammy Wynette comment with an extrapolated means to speak truth to patriarchal power. Elaine—who ultimately enjoys her own solo political orbit as a single woman—is at once a science fiction hero and a soap opera heroine. *Political Animals* enables genre fiction to function as a political platform for a new, improved, more iconically feminist Hillary.

There is, of course, more than one way to look at Hillary. Susan Morrison (2008) describes these differing perspectives in the introduction to *Thirty Ways of Looking at Hillary: Reflections by Women Writers*: "Women say they want to like her but are disturbed by the antifeminist message inherent in the idea of the first woman president getting to the White House on her husband's coattails. Then there are women, like the late playwright Wendy Wasserstein, who are queasy over the way Clinton's popularity spiked only after she was perceived as a victim (xiv)." Science fiction alleviates feminists' nausea—and soap opera makes the coattail-snipping, marriage-contract-ripping (and castrating?) Elaine more palatable for a television audience. Elaine Barrish, no longer Elaine Barrish Hammond, is finally an independent woman—and always a devoted mom.

Political Animals/Science Fiction

Morrison (2008) inadvertently describes one way of looking at Hillary in terms of science fiction: "In an episode of 'The Simpsons' . . . Bart gets a glimpse thirty years into the future and sees that his sister Lisa has been elected president" (ix). The show doesn't make a lot of fuss over the notion of a woman commander-in-chief. (In fact, in an aside we learn that Lisa is the first *straight* woman president.) But it's impossible not to notice that President Simpson looks a lot like Hillary Clinton: "Her spiky hairdo has been smooshed down into a power-helmet; she wears monochrome pants suits and a string of pearls" (ibid.). And it's impossible not to notice that the power-helmet-haired, monochrome-pants-suit-attired President Lisa/Hillary looks a lot like a female science fiction protagonist. (The pearls are thrown in for good soap opera acceptability measure.) With apologies for beginning this section by commenting on Elaine's appearance, her clothes are without question from another planet. No Earth woman would dress like Elaine. She wears jumpsuits that feature an alien cummerbund-like waist accessory. And her skirts have waists so high they seem to defy gravity.[3] These outfits are out of this world, more appropriate for George Jetson's hypothetical female boss than for a hypothetical Hillary. Pantsuits are real; not so for styles and accessories that are located in a universe far, far away from professional female sartorial credibility.

In addition to aliens, real animals figure in the relationship between *Political Animals* and science fiction, namely elephants, the symbol of the Republican Party. When Elaine stands in front of elephants at the National Zoo accompanied by Susan, she explains to the reporter that "they are a matriarchal society. When the males reach mating age, the females kick them out of the herd" (*Political Animals* 2012a). Some women who populate separatist feminist science fiction texts—such as Pamela Sargent's *The Shore of Women* (1986) and Sheri S. Tepper's (1988) *The Gate to Women's Country*—act in kind. Elaine would do well to follow their example. The men in *Political Animals* do not behave properly. Margaret Barrish left her husband because he was a heroin addict. T.J. steals Margaret's property in order to obtain money to buy drugs. Douglas, ignoring Elaine's best political interests and the fact that he is her chief of staff, has sex with Susan. And as for former president Bud Hammond, he acts like Bill. "You should leave me. I'll cheat again. I'll lie again," Bud admits to Elaine (ibid. 2012b). Surrounded by this morass of male malfeasance, strong women—in the manner of feminist science fiction protagonists—survive by bonding with each other. Elaine relies upon her mother, her female Supreme Court justice mentor, and her new confidant, Susan. And Margaret forges a close relationship with her new granddaughter-in-law, Ann. In this world of female solidarity, the normality of a female president of France can be taken as a given.

Moreover, Elaine verbalizes power fantasies for women. When she speaks, she incarnates female power—and speaks truth to male power. She informs Bud that what he does best is to "make shit up." And her following announcement of her candidacy for president would do separatist utopian denizens proud: "I am sick of the men. Self-involved male ego soaks up all of the oxygen in this town. It makes me puke. I'm running for president" (ibid.). Elaine's directness is music to the ears of those who share Wasserstein's (1998) opinion. Elaine says the magic words that feminist Hillary supporters long to hear: "Yes, Bud. I am going to run for President—without you" (ibid.). These words are not congruent with the reality Hillary inhabits; they communicate a "when it changed" moment that real American feminists have not yet experienced. When Elaine declares her power and divorces Bud, she imbues the Republican elephant political party symbol with new feminist meaning. As she looks at the real elephants in the zoo, it is as if her female gaze re-sees the Republican elephant designation in a new kick-ass (in which "ass" refers to the Democratic donkey symbol) light. Elaine enables the usually solidly Republican elephant also to signify a juxtaposition of politics and matriarchy. This re-vision dilutes the Republican elephant's standard symbolic potency.

It seems that Elaine has inherited her directness from her mother. When Elaine tells her mother that she is considering running for president again, her mother responds, "You can be Queen Shit of the United States of Elaineland" (ibid. 2012c). Margaret, a woman who also divorced her husband, gives this advice to her divorced daughter: "You'd be miserable if you don't go for it. So go for it. Besides, you'd look shitty in all black" (ibid.). Margaret alludes to femininity—fashion sense—when she advises Elaine to try to become the most powerful person on earth.

"Black" here refers to the color of Supreme Court justices' robes. President Garcetti, in order to prevent Elaine from running against him, wants to appoint her to the Supreme Court. Judge Diane Nash, a cross between Sandra Day O'Conner and a lesbian version of Ruth Bader Ginsburg, mistakenly advises Elaine to take the president's offer. Their conversation enables viewers to see how powerful women might speak to each other. Diane adheres to the patriarchal status quo and advises what she feels is best for Elaine. Diane is a realist who describes the gulf between women's ambitions and women's reality:

> DIANE: Ambition looks better on men.
> ELAINE: I don't care what it looks like.
> DIANE: I'm offering you a chance to tell Presidents what they can and can't do. (ibid.)

As the conversation continues, Elaine is superheroically sure of herself. She insists upon doing what she, not her mentor, thinks is best. She forges a new generational path, sticks to her guns in a manner that nonetheless respects the female solidarity she shares with Diane:

> ELAINE: Diane, I don't want to be on the Supreme Court. I want to run for President again. Paul Garcetti did not have you for a teacher. He did not learn to be rigorous. I have to run again.
> DIANE: You better win, Elaine. (ibid.)

Diane plays Yoda to Elaine's Jedi knight. Elaine seems to wield a phallic light saber of feminist defiance and force of self will in front of Diane. Diane, conceding to Elaine's fervent desire, acquiesces: "May the feminist political force be with you," Diane seems to say.

Elaine's alternative world has characteristics of postseparatist feminist science fiction as well. In *Political Animals*, all the women are not good and all the men are not bad. Susan has the most to fear from her younger colleague Georgette; her male boss is supportive of her. Unlike Bill, who did not benefit from a strong father figure, Bud recalls his happy experiences on his "grandpa Hammond's farm"—the place where, as a ten-year-old, he first contemplated running for president. In the manner of Bill supporting Hillary's political ambitions, Bud tells Elaine that she is "the woman leader of the moment." "Say you are going to run," he insists (ibid. 2012d). But it is Elaine who is the more powerful of the two. She runs the show. When Bud wants to be sent to Iraq to save the hostages, he has sex with Elaine in order to carry out his agenda. Bud wants to be a superhero, too. Elaine responds to his hostage rescue mission by observing that he "wants to save the world" (ibid.).

In the alternative world *Political Animals* depicts, saving the world is ultimately a woman's job. Elaine is the superhero, not Bud; he is a man who cries. During the Chinese submarine crisis, Elaine very directly dictates her action plan to President Garcetti: "I am running against you. You will save those men and then I will run against you. . . . I want you at your fighting weight when I thrash you. . . . You are not setting off a bomb along our coast" (ibid.). When Elaine stands up to the president, she literally becomes a superhero who saves twenty-two million people from a new Cuban missile crisis.

She cannot, however, save the president from becoming an Air Force One crash fatality. In the end, President Garcetti becomes an extraneous *Star Trek* "red shirt" in relation to Elaine as the ship-of-state's captain. However, the president positioned as deceased red shirt signals that becoming president cannot be the most important aspect of a true superhero's world. Viewers never know whether or not Elaine becomes president. Family is the most important thing in her life. Even though she divorces Bud, she does not jettison him out of her familial orbit. Elaine, no feminist separatist planet inhabitant, is not alien to femininity. She loves her children—and Bud, too.

In the final episode of *Political Animals*, Elaine again speaks with Susan, her former antagonist and present ally, at the National Zoo in front of the elephants. Elaine's recasting of the Republican elephant symbol as real matriarchal elephants signifies a new viable woman-centered political party system that embraces female ambition and solidarity—the feminist and the feminine.

Elaine's view of the real elephants as newly representing revised Republican ideologies positions them as the most important "political animals" in the alternative reality/soap opera/political zoo she inhabits.

Elephants, of course, are not feminist political party symbols. Perhaps this fact explains why Hillary's life is what critic Stanley (2012) describes as being "juicier" than Elaine's life: "Mrs. Clinton's life, with all its political triumphs and private torments, turned out to be juicier than any script a movie or a television studio could conjure. And the writers, at least, don't want that to end. 'Can you keep a secret?' Elaine asks a Secret Service agent at her side. 'I'm going to run for president again, and this time I'm going to win.'" We can only hope that, in the very near future, the political prediction Elaine Barrish fervently articulates will describe Hillary's political reality. President Hillary Clinton inhabiting an Oval Office "room of her own" in the White House is on the cusp of transcending feminist fantasy.

Elaine Barrish/Marleen Barr(ish)

Bill is the elephant in that hoped-for room. As chief executive, Elaine would be called "President Barrish." I would like Hillary to become "President Rodham." I am not advocating divorce—and neither is Sargent.[4] I merely hope that if Hillary is elected, she reclaims her own name.

In further, blatantly Barr(ish) terms, I agree with what Wasserstein wrote in 1998. I do not think that women should attain success via attaching themselves to men's coattails. As a member of Hillary's generation, I very purposefully forged my feminist science fiction scholar career as a single woman. I did not get married until I was a forty-six and a recent Pilgrim Award winner. I wish that the first woman president of the United States would not have male coattails attached to her inauguration attire. (Male coattails, after all, are a fashion no-no for women—with the exception of Marlene Dietrich.) I wish that the next President Clinton would be another brilliant female Clinton: Chelsea. Chelsea Clinton did not take her husband's name. Alternately, taking political experience into account, I would like the chance to vote for President Elizabeth Warren.

But enough already with reality. I vote for throwing New York City Mayor Bill de Blasio's daughter Chiara into a time machine, bringing her back from the future in an older incarnation, and nominating her for president—immediately, if not sooner. Her father was propelled to victory via the coattails of his two charismatic young adult offspring. Chiara is the most charming, engaging, and honest person currently in the political spotlight.[5] She is nineteen.

The possibility of President Chiara de Blasio seems positioned to become future political reality.

In the end, what might the future hold for Hillary? Sargent (1999) describes one science-fictional possibility: "As the ship's engines reached peak acceleration and settled into a steady background drone, mission specialist Hillary Rodham sat back in her chair and thought about how her life might have been different. It was a common human tendency, she thought, to reflect on one's life aboard trains, planes, buses, and even during an interplanetary voyage aboard the Sacajawea, now bound for Venus." Hillary can direct her talents toward becoming a completely effective feminist role model; she can forge an independent career as an astronaut. Spacesuits do not have coattails. Hillary can aspire to orbit Venus. But she won't.

Sargent's (ibid.) story also addresses Hillary's reality:

> There had been detours along the road that had taken her to Houston and the
> Johnson Space Center and to Cape Canaveral, but Hillary had kept her goal in
> sight, determined to be among the corps of men and women who would reach
> for the stars. Her marriage had been one such detour—or so it had seemed for
> a while. She had promised herself never to completely surrender her own name
> and identity, to lose her life to her husband's career, yet she had come perilously
> close to doing that.

Hillary has kept her goal in sight; she has never completely "surrender[ed] her own name and identity." Hillary, after all, insists on being called, "Hillary Rodham Clinton," not Hillary Clinton. Hillary Rodham Clinton, although not a perfect feminist icon, is a damn good one nonetheless. She is currently the best hope for a woman successfully to symbolically reach for the stars, to ascend to the exalted political firmament called the United States presidency. And Hillary can open her 2016 candidacy by echoing Elaine's words: "I'm going to run for president again, and this time I'm going to win" (*Political Animals* 2012e).

Once upon a time, one of the many female captains of Star Fleet might time travel to 2016 America, ignore the Prime Directive, and "make it so." Just in case this scenario does not come to pass, President Hillary Rodham Clinton is exceedingly realistically plausible. This definition of what *is* is applies to her presidential candidacy: the political force is with her. Hillary can add her own feminist definition to the iconic feminist science fiction words "for a while" (Sargent 1999; Russ 1972). Having no need for the USS Enterprise, she very well may fly as commander-in-chief aboard Air Force One.

Full speed ahead Hillary, no need for a warp factor.

Notes

1. Since Hillary Rodham Clinton is routinely called "Hillary"—in order to avoid confusion in regard to the many Clintons, Barrishes, and Hammonds I discuss—I will refer to people and protagonists by their first names.

2. A real family relationship also figures in *Political Animals*. Linda Powell, the daughter of former secretary of state Colin Powell, appears in the first episode as the National Security Advisor to President Garcetti.

3. Elaine's jumpsuits are pictured here: http://www2.usanetwork.com/series/politicalani mals/theshow/bw/index.html#p1-3.jpg (accessed May 15, 2014); and http://www2.usanet work.com/series/politicalanimals/theshow/bts/index.html#14.jpg (accessed May 15, 2014).

Elaine's high-waisted skirts are pictured here: http://www2.usanetwork.com/series/ politicalanimals/theshow/bts/index.html#1.jpg (accessed May 15, 2014); http://www2.usanet work.com/series/politicalanimals/theshow/bts/index.html#12.jpg (accessed May 15, 2014); and http://www2.usanetwork.com/series/politicalanimals/theshow/bts/index.html#6.jpg (accessed May 15, 2014).

4. In a manner that also contains the phrase "for a while," Sargent (1999) offers a sympathetic description of Hillary's decision not to divorce Bill: "And the most important reason for staying with him, for sometimes looking the other way even when his lapses had hurt her—she loved him. Throughout all the arguments, the demands of his work and hers, the flings with other women that he had not entirely given up even after they were married, she had continued to love him. She had stuck it out, stayed the course, and again Hillary was grateful that she had, even though it had meant postponing her own dream for a while" (1).

5. The *New York Times* describes the video in which Chiara de Blasio reveals her substance abuse: "Chiara de Blasio spoke in candid terms about a battle with depression throughout her adolescence that led to drinking and drug abuse. . . . 'If you look at this video, it speaks to a whole set of challenges that we face in our society,' the mayor-elect said. 'She speaks to it with incredible courage and clarity and, you know, with a voice that really suggests an incredible wisdom for someone who's only 19 years old.' Ms. de Blasio, in winter coat and with her father's hand on her back, spoke only a few words" (Hernández and Grynbaum, *New York Times*. December 25, 2013). Her winter coat is not tailored with her father's coattails; Bill owes his victory, in part, to Chiara.

References

Alien 3. 1992. David Fincher, director. Twentieth Century Fox. DVD.
Alien. 1979. Ridley Scott, director. Twentieth Century Fox.
Alien: Resurrection. 1997. Jean-Pierre Jeunet, director. Twentieth Century Fox.
Aliens. 1986. James Cameron, director. Twentieth Century Fox.
Avatar. 2009. James Cameron, director. Twentieth Century Fox
Chozick, Amy. "Madame Secretary's Oval Office Ambitions." *The Chronicle Herald*. July 15, 2012. Web. May 15, 2014.

Collins, Gail. 2008. *New York Times*. March 13.

Dowd, Maureen. 2008a. *New York Times*. February 3.

———. 2008b. *New York Times*. March 23.

Game Change. Jay Roach, director. HBO Films, 2012.

Girls. HBO. 2012– .

Hernández, Javier C., and Michael M. Grynbaum. 2013. "De Blasio's Daughter Reveals Substance Abuse." *New York Times*. December 24. http://www.nytimes.com/2013/12/25/nyregion/de-blasios-daughter-admits-to-substance-abuse.html (accessed May 15, 2014).

io9 blog. 2008. August 8.

Mad Men. 2007–2015. AMC.

The Mary Tyler Moore Show. 1970–1977. CBS.

Morrison, Susan. *Thirty Ways of Looking at Hillary: Reflections by Women Writers*. New York: HarperCollins, 2008.

The Newsroom. HBO, 2012– .

Political Animals. 2012a. 1.01. USA. July 15.

———. 2012b. "Second Time Around." 1.02. USA. July 22.

———. 2012c. "The Woman Problem." 1.03. USA. July 29.

———. 2012d. "Lost Boys." 1.04. USA. August 5.

———. 2012e. "Resignation Day." 1.06. USA. August 19.

Russ, Joanna. "When It Changed." In *Again, Dangerous Visions*, edited by Harlan Ellison, 253–60. New York: Doubleday, 1972.

Sargent, Pamela. 1986. *The Shore of Women*. New York: Crown.

———. 1999. "Hillary Orbits Venus." Wildside Press. *Wildside.com*. eBook.

Sex and the City. 1998–2004. HBO.

Spiegelman, Ian. 2008. "Maureen Dowd Calls Hillary Clinton Sci-Fi Monster." *Gawker* blog. March 23.

Stanley, Alessandra. 2012. "From Presidential Hopeful to Secretary of Comedy." *New York Times*. July 13. http://www.nytimes.com/2012/07/14/arts/television/hillary-rodham-clinton-inspires-political-animals-sitcom.html (accessed May 15, 2014).

Tepper, Sheri S. 1998. *The Gate to Women's Country*. New York: Foundation Books.

The Terminator. 1984. James Cameron, director. Hemdale. 1984.

That Girl. 1966–1971. ABC.

Veep. 2012– . HBO.

Wasserstein, Wendy. 1998. "Hillary Clinton's Muddled Legacy." *New York Times*. August 25. http://www.nytimes.com/1998/08/25/opinion/hillary-clinton-s-muddled-legacy.html (accessed February 19, 2016).

PART III

The Woman Fantastic in Social and Theoretical Context

Body Issues in *Wonder Woman* 90–100 (1994–1995): Good Girls, Bad Girls, Macho Men

—Joan Ormrod

What Wonder Woman needs is a strong direction, a new creative team and a Hot Babe artist. . . . Female characters do not appeal to teenage boys fixated on muscles, gore and violence. . . . 5 steps for Hot Babe formula 1) a good name including dark or night, 2) visible power that doesn't deform, 3) attitude, 4) sexy tight costume, leather lycra, rubber thigh length boots, 5) artist who can draw sexy women. The writer is the least important element in any hot Book of the moment. (Sage, 1993, 29)

T he quote above indicates why, in the early 1990s, sales of DC Comics flagship heroine Wonder Woman fell so low that the comic did not even make the top 100, for this was the era of the bad girl. Bad girls were violent, silicone-breasted, wasp-waisted, and designed to appeal to a demographic that, according to Dick Gordiano, DC Comics vice chairman, was "between 17 and 26 . . . over 90% of the time is male. His basic interest is fantasy" (McCue 1993, 101). Bad girl heroines acted upon their own morality, were sexualized and extremely aggressive. Series such as *Glory* or *Lady Death* featured the protagonists in lingerie specials posed in impossible pornographic positions with orgasmic facial expressions, licking blood from swords. Such imagery had its detractors, who declared that bad girl art was no more than a strategy to build a flamboyant portfolio. However, criticisms of the sexualized representations of bad girls were strenuously refuted by their creators. Rob Liefeld, for instance, stated, "Glory is a strong business woman and she likes to go out and have a good time . . . we're trying to make Glory more real" (1995, 29). In the face of such cynical competition, it was unsurprising that the sales figures in *Wonder Woman* fell to an all-time low in 1993.

The not entirely serious quote opening this chapter was from a letter in a comics zine, but the writer did not realize that DC, with a keen eye to the boom in darker superheroes and bad girl comics, had already begun to revamp their three flagship characters: Superman, Batman, and Wonder Woman. For Wonder Woman, fan favorites William Messner-Loebs and Mike Deodato were employed to update Diana, the Wonder Woman, from a worthy good girl into a kick-ass bad girl.

Wonder Woman #90–100 begins when Wonder Woman/Diana loses her title to Artemis, the leader of the Bana-Mighdall Amazons. The Bana-Mighdall are nomadic Amazons from Egypt who turned their backs on the gods and are mortal. Recently, the Bana-Mighdall made their home on Themyscira. Where previously they had been outcasts because they betrayed the Themysciran Amazons, Queen Hyppolita rewarded them with land and immortality when they fought alongside their sisters to defeat invading demons. In the opening of the story, Hyppolita proclaims a contest to reassign the title of Wonder Woman. Artemis, the leader of the European Amazons and passionately opposed to what she regards as the decadence of the Themyscirans, wins the contest and goes into man's world as the new Wonder Woman. Once in man's world, Artemis and Diana become enmeshed in a gang war in which both sides use metahuman mercenaries to gain the upper hand. However, Artemis's impatience and arrogance lead to her failure and death. Diana once again dons the Wonder Woman mantle in volume 2, issue #100. It is the second half of this story in which Diana and Artemis come to terms with the constraints of man's world that this chapter examines. The focus of the chapter is in the representation of male and female bodies in man's world.

The chapter compares gaze theory and a discursive analysis of the metahuman body in comics in which, I argue, gaze theory is limited by its cinematic and phallocentric scope. *Wonder Woman* of the early 1990s is used as a case study because the sexualized representation of female characters demonstrates the limitations of a gaze compared with a discursive reading. The chapter begins by summarizing the main points of the debate deriving from feminist Laura Mulvey's work, followed by an analysis of female bodies using gaze theory. However, gaze theory, as a cinematic-based model, does not work with comics form and reading practices. The remainder of the chapter then demonstrates an alternative somatic approach accounting for male and female bodies within their cultural contexts, arguing that similar discourses disempower and objectify male and female bodies, although in different ways.

Representing Women, the Gaze, and Film Theory

In this narrative, Diana's and Artemis's bodies were depicted in typical bad girl style with muscular bodies wearing scanty, fetishized clothing and striking soft-core porn poses. This might suggest an analysis using gaze theory. Gaze theory emerged as a lively debate instigated by Mulvey's ([1975] 1992) article "Visual Pleasure and Narrative Cinema," which proposes that representations of women in classical Hollywood cinema contrived to disempower them by making them objects of desire. Using psychoanalytic theory deriving from the work of Sigmund Freud and Jacques Lacan, Mulvey proposed that in Classical Hollywood, cinematic practices, and audiences' spectatorship, male/female representations formed a binary that linked male/active and female/passive. This binary derived from the pleasures invoked by the system of spectatorship in which the active male gaze inspected the passive female body: "The determining male gaze projects its fantasy onto the female figure, which is styled accordingly. In their traditional exhibitionist role women are simultaneously looked at and displayed, with their appearance coded for strong visual erotic impact so that they can be said to connote *to-be-looked-at-ness*" (162).

The entrance of the woman freezes the narrative action so the camera may linger on her body in "moments of erotic contemplation" (ibid., 163). So there are two gazes upon the woman: the extra-diegetic gaze of the male audience member that is funneled through the diegetic gaze of the male characters, principally the protagonist in the film, and the gaze of the cinematic apparatus. The representation of the female body works either through fetishization of body parts or by the exaggeration of beauty. The fetishization of breasts, legs, and lips diminishes the threat of the female so that it becomes "reassuring rather than dangerous" (ibid., 164).

Mulvey's feminist polemic was political. Its aim was to expose the cinematic strategies used to produce pleasure in the text through analysis and thereby destroy the pleasure of the image. Mulvey's work was criticized on many fronts. For instance, Steve Neale (1983) argued that the male body was just as objectified as the female body in certain genres such as the Western and the Sword and Sandals gladiator film where the hero might suffer body injury before beating his enemies. MacKinnon (1999) also noted that male pinups were just as prevalent as female. There are also many more types of gendered gaze than that suggested by Mulvey. For instance, that of the heterosexual female who yet enjoyed the contemplation of female beauty. Stacey (1995), for instance, made an empirical study of female audiences' enjoyment of female stars. To address the criticisms pointing out the concentration the male gaze did not account for female pleasure in the contemplation of the female body, Mulvey (1996) wrote a second piece and based her analysis on a passage from *Duel in the Sun* (1946), in which she suggested that women viewing the female body adopted a masculine gaze in a type of symbolic cross-dressing. I have outlined a few of the main ideas surrounding Mulvey to show how her original thesis became central to the discussion of the female form since 1975, and the arguments have not moved beyond the truism that mass media tend to objectify and disempower women. Furthermore, such debates are based upon Freudian and Lacanian models of psychoanalysis. Both models are phallocentric, conferring power on the positive aspect of the binary, the male (Cixous 1992, 146–57). This does not acknowledge the dependence of the positive element, masculinity, on the negative aspect, femininity, for its cultural construction (Butler 1991, 13–32).

Comics scholars have begun to use Mulvey's ideas to analyze the disempowerment of the strong female body in the superhero comic. Certainly it is not difficult to make a reading using gaze theory. As outlined above, bad girl comics were full of images where artists drew attention to sexy women through composition and the layout of the panels on the page. For instance, in the series under scrutiny, *Wonder Woman*, Deodato employs a number of compositional and diegetic strategies. First, compositional devices are employed to fetishize breasts, hair, costumes, and naked thighs. Artemis, for instance, is the counterpart bad girl to Diana. Her design, based upon Jim Lee's character Zealot from *Wildcats*, is tall, muscular, and Spartan in appearance, her outfit echoing that of Native Americans, a loincloth that barely covers her body. Her use of a bow and arrow reflects Native American weapons but is also a reference to her Moon Goddess huntress/pastoral connotations. Her hair is red and sinuous and curls round her ankles. The length, however, is hardly practical for a warrior; its snake-like appearance is reminiscent of an Alphonse Mucha siren as it flattens the image into the panel frame for decorative effect, especially in battle scenes. Using gaze theory as the basis, one might argue that, when she enters man's world as Wonder Woman, Artemis is the typical man-hating, castrating woman who has little sympathy for men who bully women, but still less for women who allow themselves to be beaten. In a reading using Mulvey, Artemis represents the unruly woman who must be punished and disempowered.

This can be demonstrated in Artemis's encounter with her PR company, Meta-Promotions (Messner-Loebs and Deodato Jr. 1995a, 14) (see Figure 3.1). The fetishization of the female body is produced through the use of panels and the diegetic male gaze. Artemis's body is split up into three panels. The top two panels divide her body; the top panel shows her head, the middle panel her breasts in line with PR director Danial Brassalton's gaze. Danial Brassalton explains, "You want to get your message out quickly, right?," making it clear to the reader that a significant aspect of the message is her body. In a psychoanalytic reading of this page, Artemis is an example of woman as bad thing, a castrating harpy. Using a Freudian perspective, Mulvey points

Figure 3.1: Artemis's encounter with her PR company. She is depicted as the unruly woman (Messner-Loebs and Deodato Jr. 1995a, 14).

out that a male's fears of castration by the female lead them to fetishize an element of the female body. Taking her argument from Freud's (1927) essay on fetishism, Mulvey suggests that fetishism allays fears of castration through the female breast as substitute for the penis. The elevation of the breasts to fetish objects allays male castration anxiety. Using this concept to analyze the panel, it could be argued that the concentration on her breasts diminishes the threat of castration by Artemis, whose breasts are thus "reassuring rather than dangerous" (Mulvey [1975] 1992), 164). Thus, through the symbolic breakup of her body among three panels, Artemis is disempowered.

So it is clear that the images in this comic objectify female bodies but, in the context of production and reception, why would they not? They are produced by young men who wish to make a name for themselves by producing desirable images for an audience very much like themselves. However, does such a reading explain the whole image, and is Mulvey entirely appropriate to use in the analysis of comics, given the differences between their form and readership? Mulvey's reading was based upon the cinematic apparatus, the moving image, the spectator positions, and the cinematic experience. The cinematic apparatus appeals to audiences' narcissism in their cathartic interaction with the narrative, particularly in the role of the protagonist who is the equivalent of the ideal ego. Furthermore, the narrative reproduces the conditions of the peeping Tom gazing onto a narrative that seems entirely oblivious to their voyeurism in a darkened room. However, film works through the use of 24 frames per second to produce a spatial/temporal effect and uses movement and sound to advance the action. This, argues Mulvey, is crucial to the experience of male spectator, for freezing the action enables the erotic contemplation of the female body. Indeed, she notes, "This complex interaction of looks is specific to film" (Mulvey [1975] 1992, 166). Unless the audience is experiencing the film through a DVD, which can be replayed and frozen, the female image is captured within the moment dictated by the cinematographer or the director, not the audience.

However, overlooking Mulvey's own admission of the specificity of the filmic gaze, where can connections be made between film and comics? Film and comics have often been connected through the similarities of their descriptive language. However, narrative time is structured differently in comics, as noted by McCloud (1994, 94–95). The organization of the panel within the page, the speech bubbles, comics devices, and juxtaposition between panels all attempt to direct the reader to follow the story in a specific order and hierarchy. The action of the narrative can be slowed down or quickened by the panel's size. However, although the writer and artist can attempt to control the pace and direction of readership, they cannot constrain a reader to follow this structure. A splash page, for instance, might arguably slow down the action for erotic contemplation where a reader might gain pleasure from gazing on a beautiful woman's body, but the comics reader can also go back, reread any passages where they want to remind themselves of the action, or skip pages. The repetition of panels can also add to the understanding and coherence of the narrative. This is described by Groensteen (2007, 174) as *tressage*, or the interweaving of repeating panels or themes in a comic, a concept used in a comparison between female and male bodies later in the paper.

One instance where comics and film share similarities is in their production. The comic, like the film, is not the vision of a single individual but produced through a working relationship of writer, artist, letterer, colorist, and so on. When Deodato began work on Wonder Woman, he understood little English and was allowed to render the human body with relative autonomy[1]; this produced a comic with a dislocation between narrative and image. Where Deodato presents metahuman bodies as a beautiful objects, Messner-Loebs's narrative constructs the body through consumer and Classical Greek discourse. Therefore, using gaze theory alone cannot address issues of the body in this comic. In the remainder of the chapter, I want to suggest an alternative approach to analyzing gender in comics, to make a reading of the cultural construction of the body in the bad girl comic. Drawing on Heinecken's study of warrior women in television and Turner's notion of the somatic society, my aim is to demonstrate how a subgenre as two dimensional as the bad girl comic, when stripped (so as to speak) of its sexualized focus, can provide some interesting insights into culture and history in a specific era.

Somatic Discourse and Popular Culture

Contemporary culture is replete with images of the body in the culture's popular dimension, yet paradoxically, Western culture continuously rejects the importance of the materiality of the body in constructing the self. We only acknowledge our body through its shortcomings, disease, deformity, and aberrations. The responsibility for this disregard is assumed to be Cartesian philosophy as, since the seventeenth century, it has promoted the importance of the mind over the body in identity construction. Leder (1990), for instance, suggests dualism's insistence on the self as "an immortal mind trapped inside an alien body" contributes to our lack of consideration of our bodies as contributing to our sense of being (3). The body in culture can be regarded as both "product and process" (Balsamo 1996, 3). The body is a product because of its material presence in the world that we recognize through gender, racial, and ethnic characteristics, amongst others. It is a product of culture that constructs a collective understanding of what we are by our bodies. Heinecken deliberates on this notion in her analysis of strong female characters emerging in television fantasy series of the early 1990s. In her analysis of bodies in series such as *Buffy the Vampire Slayer*, *Aeon Flux*, and *La Femme Nikita*,

Heinecken reflects upon the ways characters negotiated suffering in their heroic struggles. She concludes that suffering is expressed through the body in male heroes, whereas it is endured through mental and emotional relationships with heroines. Heinecken's notion that body discourses constructed the representations informed her methodology, which included analyses of cross-media narratives.

The material body is constructed through culture, and this impacts on how a discursive somatic analysis can be produced. Where previous body discourses emphasized the body as a site of self-discipline to control bodies' desires in the service of religion, contemporary bodies are controlled in the service of consumerism. Control and discipline is at the heart of modern bodily discourse to manipulate and reform the body shape and presentation. In the late 1980s, body culture and representations in the media began to essentialize gender characteristics. Mens' bodies became harder and hypermuscular, women's' bodies became sexualized with large breasts and small waists. Brown (2004) notes how a significant number of tough women in action movies (Angelina Jolie, Linda Hamilton, Pamela Anderson) posed for *Playboy* magazine, thus conflating the boundaries between acting and pornography (64). Action and pop stars demonstrated the plasticity of body shape through a combination of exercise and surgical intervention. Linda Hamilton, John Travolta, and Madonna, for instance, used the gym to remold their bodies for acting roles in *T2*, *Staying Alive*, and *Evita*. Angelina Jolie's and Pamela Anderson's forays into plastic surgery to enhance their natural assets are well-known and merely reflected a trend in society. Bordo (1998) notes that in 1989 there were 681,000 surgical procedures on eighteen- to thirty-five-year-olds (336).

In the remainder of the chapter, I examine one aspect of the ways metahuman bodies act as metaphors for the somatic society of the early 1990s, first analyzing female body then male body representations within consumerism that, I argue, is the controlling factor in body discourses in this comic.

Consumerism and the Female Body in Man's World

Once in man's world, Artemis and Diana become subjects of consumerism and capitalism, and this drives the narrative from that point. Sporting a short haircut, Diana changes her costume from star-spangled primary colors into fetish/bondage gear designed by Brian Bolland as described in the letter pages of *Wonder Woman*, "from bits and pieces of current fashion" (#97, 24). A pair of tight-fitting cycle shorts, a bra, a bolero jacket, and short boots

Figure 3.2: Artemis meets her PR executives. The placing of her breasts in the middle panel shows just what the Brassaltons assume are her "selling points" (Messner-Loebs and Deodato Jr. 1995a, 14).

finish off her outfit, which drew a backhanded compliment from a female correspondent in the letter column, "I *like* the biker pants. They are bound to be a relief from the high-thigh cut of her old costume, especially when kicking someone as she did on page 19 [of issue 95]" (Messner-Loebs 1995e, v.2 #97, 31). Diana also has to make money. Where she previously worked in a fast food outlet, now she becomes a businesswoman as a partner of Micah Rains's detective agency. Artemis, however, naïve in the ways of consumerism and man's world, sells her skills to a shady PR company. Here I want to return to the image first analyzed through Mulvey's work where Artemis meets her PR executives, Danial and Dickie Brassalton, but this time using an overview of the body within consumerism (see Figure 3.2). A somatic analysis examines the body within the whole page rather than part of the page (Messner-Loebs and Deodato Jr. 1995a, 14).

A top wide, shallow panel depicts the New York skyline in silhouette. The Twin Towers, bastions of consumer culture in this era, are placed at the top center of the entire page, demonstrating the importance of capitalism over everyone living within their jurisdiction. In the long panel spanning the left-hand side of the page, Artemis's whole body is shown as she gazes on the city. Her hair entwines around her legs and body like a golden snake. Artemis's body is subjected to the interdiegetic gaze of the Brassalton brothers. Where the brothers suggest she has to get her message out quickly, her message clearly is for them to sell her body. The introduction of the card into this panel is the token of her subjugation to capitalism.

Conversely, Diana's body is never subjected to this treatment in man's world. The reader is introduced to her encounter with consumerism when she saves her partner, detective Micah Rains, from torture. This scene begins in an ironic manner, with a television screen showing Artemis pledging an end to violence in man's world. Micah's blood spattering across the television screen in the next panel puts a lie to Artemis's assertion. Diana interrupts Micah's torture by two thugs. However, when one of the thugs states that she won't attack them, "That would be revenge. She don't believe in revenge" (ibid. 1995b, 18), Diana proceeds to disabuse him of this notion. Leading Micah away, Diana lays the law of how their relationship will work: "We will not be called 'The Wonder Woman Agency' or anything foolish like that. . . . Any questions?," to which Micah's response, "But I'm still in charge, right?," is belied by his body slumping against Diana's taller, stronger body and assertive manner.

These two sequences compare the disempowerment of Artemis with the more knowing approach of Diana, by now well versed in the ways of patriarchy. However, they show that whether powered or disempowered, the body is always subject to capitalism. Where Mulvey contends that women are objectified by patriarchal domination, I want now to show how the male body is just as disempowered by capitalism.

Consumerism and the Male Body

Where female bodies in the early 1990s are represented as grotesque through hypersexualization, masculine power is demonstrated through bulk and hypermusculature. In comics a new company, Image, formed by disaffected writers and artists in the early 1990s, focused on hypermasculine representations of superheroes with huge bodies and pin heads. In *Wonder Woman*, Deodato represented male antagonists in a similar manner. In this section, two examples of the spectacular display of male antagonists' bodies and their discursive constructions are discussed to show their disempowerment through capitalism, for all of these antagonists sold their bodies to achieve power or wealth.

The first examples are transformation through magic in the numerous man-mountains sent by the White Magician to battle Artemis and in the transformation of the White Magician (aka Asquith Randolph) into a demon. The second example of transformation is in the technologically constructed bodies of Moot and Geoff, two cyborgs employed by Juliana Swarza to threaten her gangland rivals (see Figure 3.5). Both types of transformation potentially disempower the body through spectacle, consumerism, and the cultural and symbolic connotations of power inferred by magical and scientific transformation.

Artemis encounters a series of hypermuscular male antagonists paid by Meta-Promotions to take a dive in battle and make her look good. Male antagonists consist of those transformed by the magic of the White Magician: The Chauvinist (Messner-Loebs and Deodato Jr. 1995b), The Exploiter (ibid. 1995d), Involute the Conqueror (ibid. 1995e), and Geoff (ibid. 1995c) (see Figures 3.3 and 3.4). They epitomize notions of performative identity, for they act with extreme aggression shown in their speech bubbles, which embolden and exaggerate their names. More significantly, all three are actors, hired to convince Artemis she can make a difference in man's world. Using Groensteen's (2007, 174) notion of *tressage*, in which panels are linked throughout the comic in a continuous or discontinuous series, the actors can be connected through their appearance and their entry into the narrative through the panel. The Chauvinist attacks a woman's refuge for battered wives, The Exploiter keeps a sweatshop full of illegal immigrants, and Involute the Conqueror destroys the

Figure 3.3: The Exploiter's body connotes phallic power over that of the much slighter Artemis (Messner-Loebs and Deodato Jr. 1995d).

rainforest. All of these individuals look alike—they dwarf Artemis with their bulk and musculature even though she is over six feet tall. Their costumes are typical of the action hero (e.g., Rambo, John McClane) outfit and consist of black or grey sweatshirts, chains, jeans, and gun belts. They are also stupid. For instance, The Chauvinist "left his card . . . and the name of his agent at the women's center" he was attacking. Diana finds Bill Baker, aka The Chauvinist, on a film set. Bill is under the illusion that he was acting a part and informs her that his and his fellow actors' musculature is enhanced by magic: "Man,

Figure 3.4: Involute the Conqueror exhibits patriarchal possession of people and the land (Messner-Loebs and Deodato Jr. 1995e).

what a deal! No sweat, no steroids, just this snooty guy in white chanting a mantra! And I'm buffed for life" (Messner-Loebs and Deodato Jr. 1995e, 15).

The male antagonists' bodies are disempowered in two ways through this use of magic. Historically, masculine musculature is developed in the preindustrial age by hard work on the land. However, according to Klein (1993), in contemporary culture musculature is effected by leisure and consumer discourses. Muscles are necessary to define masculinity but through labor and hard work. The antagonists in *Wonder Woman* develop their bodies through magic, which acts in a similar transformative manner to plastic surgery and the gym. Within contemporary culture, as noted above, the body is a consuming and consumed phenomenon that must be constructed to hail a slim, toned, healthy norm. Men can bulk out to conform to a notion of a masculine size. In this case, Deodato exaggerates this bulk in keeping with the bad girl genre but also through the influence of Jim Lee's work at Image. However, as Fussell (1994) successfully argues, the male pursuit of instant or leisure musculature weakens the symbolic aspect of masculinity as it infers narcissism. This self-love is echoed in Bill Baker/The Chauvinist's continuous reference to his acting career, his delusion that Diana enjoyed his performance, and his striking a pose to show off his physique. The panel underpins other panels on the page and The Chauvinist's body dominates the space. Because he is depicted as much taller than Diana, the top two right panels are split in Diana and The Chauvinist's conversation. Nevertheless, his head is much bigger than Diana's. The biggest panel on the page in which Bill Baker displays his body mirrors earlier panels showing antagonists attacking Artemis and Diana. That Diana cannot tell the difference between Bill and his fellow actors is shown when she asks whether he also played Involute the Conqueror, to which he replies, "No, but I read for it!" This type of repetition, which Groensteen describes as braiding, holds the narrative together. It also acts to make the antagonists indistinguishable one from the other.

Antagonists' spectacular body display is also depicted in the representation of scientifically enhanced male bodies of Moot and Geoff introduced in issue #92, page 4 (Messner-Loebs and Deodato Jr. 1994). The scene begins on page 3, when Juliana Swarza, who is trying to take over the Boston gangs, is apparently caught off guard in bed by three mercenaries, The Morgue, Backblast, and Ripsaw, hired by rival gang boss Paulie Longo. A potential rape scene is represented in the splash panel with all three characters surrounding her bed, and Juliana's pose is that of the porn actress, kneeling with her back arched to exaggerate the size of her breasts. However, Julia's proposal that her potential attackers join her belies her inferred disempowerment, for when the page is turned, her attackers are faced with two hulking cyborgs, Moot and Geoff. Moot's and Geoff's bodies take up two-thirds of the frame, and they are rendered by Deodato with a gleeful exuberance in the complexity of their construction. Their heads are the only noticeably human part of their bodies, which are metallic and weighed down by weapons. Ripsaw's lifeless hand dropping his gun also draws the eye toward Juliana, Moot, and Geoff. Color and excessively elaborate drawing of monotone cybernetic technology focus the eye on the simplicity of Juliana lit up to the left center of the image, the bed acting as a frame for her body. Moot and Geoff, like their magically enhanced brothers, exemplify the grotesque body in which "exaggeration, hyperbolism and excessiveness are all considered fundamental attributes" (Bakhtin 1984, 303). The hyperbole in these representations is symptomatic of the excess of the grotesque. But there are two other fundamental issues relating to the grotesque in these representations. The antagonists are

Figure 3.5: Juliana with Moot and Geoff, the two cyborgs she uses (Messner-Loebs and Deodato Jr. 1994, 4).

mocked for their stupidity, but they also connote the body that, lacking control, extends and transgresses its boundaries and the boundaries of the frame. However, within the discussion of the somatic body, the body formed within culture, this excess demonstrates lack of control, a lack of boundary between the body and the world.

Manipulation of the body, whether through science or magic, enables the body to be modified and packaged in a conformable shape according to the norms of society. Nowhere is this more evident than in the intersection of bodies and technology in man's world. Haraway (2000, 291–324) proposes a celebratory attitude to the cyborg as a liberating phenomenon enabling the creation of new identities unrestrained by either animal or machine categories. However, as Oehlert (2000, 112–23) suggests, media representations of cyborgs tend to be rather less optimistic about their potential. Cyborgs can be berserkers like Wolverine or programmed to obey orders like Robocop. These two types of extreme cyborg behavior are indicative in Moot and Geoff's programming and raise issues of Cartesian dualism.

Moot and Geoff, like the mercenaries transformed by magic, also connote weakness through their bodies' constructions symbolically and biologically. This is inferred from their description by Juliana: "Geoff is a biomechanical construct, stolen from Star Labs. He's programmed for ferocity and loyalty. Moot is very unstable." Moot's instability and Geoff's programming demonstrate they do not control their bodies. That their cyborg bodies are also extended and transformed using prosthetics and weaponry suggests their control is questionable, given Williams and Bendelow's (1998) argument that technology challenges "what the body is, who owns it and what it might become" (79).

Conclusion

It is a truism to propose that the superhuman body acts as a metaphor for the body within wider culture. Due to the constraints of space, this analysis was narrow in focus. However, the examples used should provide the beginning of a debate on the analysis of the superhuman body. My aim in this chapter has been to show how the bad girl genre may be exploitative and two dimensional in its rendering of female bodies, but it raises much more interesting aspects of the body within its cultural context in a particular era. Gaze theory assumes a specific spectator position, and it has difficulty in accounting for a myriad of such positions. By using a somatic discursive analysis, the body can be analyzed, as Balsamo notes, which is a product and a process. This locates the body within its cultural and historic contexts. Using an analysis based upon reading male and female metahuman bodies through a cultural lens, analogies can be made between gendered identities in society in the 1990s. This storyline shows how submission and control at the heart of Moulton Marston's original concept of Wonder Woman are reinterpreted within this era. Such discourses depict disquiet over the body's plasticity and its potential to transcend its boundaries.

Notes

1. Mike Deodato Jr., e-mail communication with the author, December 23, 2009.

References

Chung, Peter, creator. 1991–1995. *Aeon Flux*, Music Television (MTV). Television Series.

Bakhtin, Mikhail. 1984. *Rabelais and His World*. Bloomington: Indiana University Press.

Balsamo, Anne. 1996. *Technologies of the Gendered Body: Reading Cyborg Women*. Durham: Duke University Press.

Bordo, Susan. 1998. "'Material Girl': The Effacements of Postmodern Culture" In *Body and Flesh: A Philosophical Reader*, edited by Don Welton, 45–61. Oxford: Blackwell.

Brown, J. A. 2004. "Gender, Sexuality, and Toughness: The Bad Girls of Action Film and Comic Books" In *Action Chicks: New Images of Tough Women in Popular Culture*, edited by Sherrie A. Inness, 47–74. New York: Palgrave Macmillan.

Butler, Judith. 1991. "Gender Insubordination." In *Inside/Out: Lesbian Theories, Gay Theories*, edited by Diana Fuss, 13–32. London: Routledge.

Deodato Jr., Mike. 2011. Interview with Dave Wallace. October 7. *Silver Bullet Comics*, Glasshouse Graphics. http://www.glasshousegraphics.com/creators/pencilers/mikedeodato (accessed May 15, 2014.

Cameron, James, director. 1991. *Terminator 2: Judgment Day*. Tristar Pictures. Film.

Cixous, Helene. [1986] 1992. "Sorties." In *A Critical and Cultural Theory Reader*, edited by Antony Easthope and Kate McGowan, 146–57. Buckingham, UK: The Open University Press.

Eisner, Will. 2008. *Comics and Sequential Art: Principles and Practices from the Legendary Cartoonist*. New York: W. W. Norton.

Freud, Sigmund. 1924–1950. "Fetishism" [1927]. In *Miscellaneous Papers, 1888–1938*. Vol. 5 of *Collected Papers*. 198–202. London: Hogarth and Institute of Psycho-Analysis.

Fussell, Sam. 1994. "Bodybuilder Americanus." In *The Male Body: Features, Destinies, Exposures*, edited by Laurence Goldstein, 43–60. Ann Arbor: University of Michigan Press.

Groensteen, Thierry. 2007. *The System of Comics*. Jackson: University Press of Mississippi.

Haraway, Donna. 2000. "A Cyborg Manifesto: Science, Technology, and Socialist-Feminism in the Late Twentieth Century" In *Cybercultures Reader*, edited by David Bell and Barbara Kennedy, 291–324. London: Routledge.

Heinecken, Dawn. 2003. *The Warrior Women of Television: A Feminist Cultural Analysis of the Female Body in Popular Media*. New York: Peter Lang.

Jeffords, Susan. 2004. *Hard Bodies: Hollywood Masculinity in the Reagan Era*. New Brunswick, NJ: Rutgers University Press.

Klein, Alan M. 1993. *Little Big Men: Bodybuilding Subculture and Gender Construction*. Albany: State University of New York Press.

La Femme Nikita. Warner Bros. Television. Television Series.

Leder, Drew. 1990. *The Absent Body*. Chicago: University of Chicago Press.

Leifeld, Rob. 1995. "Interview." *Comics Scene* #53

MacKinnon, Kenneth. 1999. "After Mulvey: Male Erotic Objectification." In *The Body's Perilous Pleasures: Dangerous Desires and Contemporary* Culture, edited by Michele Aaron, 13–29. Edinburgh: Edinburgh University Press.

McCloud, Scott. 1994. *Understanding Comics: The Invisible Art*. New York: Harper Perennial.

McCue, Greg. S. 1993. *Dark Knights: The New Comics in Context*. London: Pluto Press.

Messner-Loebs, William, and Mike Deodato Jr., 1994. "The Contest Lost . . . !)." In *Wonder Woman* v.2 #92 (December). New York: DC Comics.

———. 1995a. "Violent Beginnings." In *Wonder Woman* v.2 #93 (January). New York: DC Comics.

———. 1995b. "Poison, Claws, and Death!" In *Wonder Woman* v.2 #95 (March). New York: DC Comics.

———. 1995c. "Joker's Holiday." In *Wonder Woman* v.2 #96 (April). New York: DC Comics.

———. 1995d. "Boom!" In *Wonder Woman* v.2 #97 (May). New York: DC Comics.

———. 1995e. "Sisters!" In *Wonder Woman* v.2 #98 (June). New York: DC Comics.

Mulvey, Laura. [1975] 1992. "Visual Pleasure and Narrative Cinema." In *A Critical and Cultural Theory Reader*, edited by Antony Easthope and Kate McGowan, 158–66. Buckingham, UK: The Open University Press.

———. 1996. "Afterthoughts on 'Visual Pleasure and Narrative Cinema' Inspired by *Duel in the Sun*." In *Feminist Film Theory, A Reader*, edited by Sue Thornham. 122–30. Edinburgh: Edinburgh University Press.

Neale, Steve. 1983. "Masculinity as Spectacle." *Screen* 24 (6): 2–17.

Oehlert, Mark. 2000. "From Captain America to Wolverine: Cyborgs in Comic Books: Alternative Images of Cybernetic Heroes and Villains." In *The Cybercultures Reader*, edited by David Bell and Barbara Kennedy, 112–23. London: Routledge.

Parker, Alan, director. 1996. *Evita*. USA. Hollywood Pictures, Cinergi. Film.

Sage, David. 1993. "A Formula for Super-femmes." *Comics International* 32 (June): 29.

Stacey, Jackie. 1995. *Star Gazing: Hollywood Cinema and Female Spectatorship*. London: Routledge.

Stallone, Sylvester, director. 1983. *Staying Alive*. Paramount Pictures. Film.

Turner, Bryan S. 1996. *The Body and Society*. London: Sage. 1996.

Vidor, King, director. 1946. *Duel in the Sun*. Selznick Studio. Film.

Whedon, Joss, creator. 1997–2003. *Buffy the Vampire Slayer*. Twentieth Century Fox. Television series.

Williams, Simon, and Gillian Bendelow. 1998. *The Lived Body: Sociological Themes, Embodied Issues*. London: Routledge.

Claiming the Throne: Multiplicity and Agency in Cinda Williams Chima's *The Seven Realms* Series

—Katherine A. Wagner and Megan McDonough

The rise of young adult literature in the early 1990s coincided with an important evolution in the fantastic woman from a relatively passive, ancillary character to an active, dominant figure. Perhaps it is no coincidence, then, that many female protagonists in the young adult fantasy genre share the components that define the modern fantastic woman. Several of these qualities, including a complexity of character and a possession of agency, often blur rigid gender and other binaries. Janice C. Crosby (2000) suggests that "the female self can be a powerful agent of change" (73). Many young adult narratives featuring a female protagonist focus on the main character's development as she learns to accept herself. Through this process of maturation she claims her agency, an act that allows her to bring change to her world and for herself. Many works of young adult fantasy illustrate how this change frequently occurs by addressing cultural issues like constructions of gender, ethnicity, and class. Fewer works, however, center on how this change and the accompanying sense of agency emerge in conjunction with a female protagonist's multifaceted identity. In her high fantasy series *The Seven Realms*—*The Demon King* (2009), *The Exiled Queen* (2010), *The Gray Wolf Throne* (2011), and *The Crimson Crown* (2012)—award-winning author Cinda Williams Chima introduces the character of Raisa *ana'*Marianna, the sixteen-year-old heiress apparent to the Fells, a realm that has for centuries been ruled by women. Certainly not the only series to depict complex female protagonists, Chima's series nevertheless exemplifies an important trend of the genre: a relationship between a multiplicity of identity and agency. By highlighting the intersectionality that can exist between gender, ethnicity, and social class, these books present a female protagonist who transitions into a fantastic woman as she embraces her multiplicity and begins claiming her agency.

For the past several decades, scholars have sought to create methodology and theories for understanding identity formation. Some scholars, such as black feminist Kimberle Crenshaw, focused on what they perceived to be an important gap in this discussion, specifically how identity can be understood through the concept of intersectionality. In "Mapping the Margins: Intersectionality, Identity Politics, and Violence against Women of Color," Crenshaw (1991) argues that "recognizing that identity politics takes place at the site where categories intersect thus seems more fruitful than challenging the possibility of talking about categories at all. Through an awareness of intersectionality, we can better acknowledge and ground the differences among us and negotiate the means by which these differences will find expression in constructing group politics" (1299). In this article, Crenshaw concentrates primarily on examining the intersections between race and gender, predominantly as it affects examinations of and responses to violence against women of color. Yet Crenshaw is the first to admit that intersectionality has larger implications. She (1991) states, "While the primary intersections that I explore here are between race and gender, the concept can and should be expanded by factoring in issues such as class, sexual orientation, age, and color" (1244–45n9). Through this admission, Crenshaw allows the definition of intersectionality to broaden into a concept applicable to larger concerns of identity politics. Ann Garry (2012) expands the definition even further when she argues, "Intersectionality applies to everyone, not simply to members of subordinated or marginalized groups" (499). Approaching intersectionality from this perspective allows for a wider base of analysis, one that includes a diversity of individuals and groups regardless of gender, ethnicity, or marginalization. As a result, we are appropriating this term for our discussion of the character Raisa because, despite her privileged royal status, she encounters and must overcome oppressive forces associated with her perceived ethnicity, gender, and social class.

Young adult literature is concerned with the interplay involved in identity formation, making intersectionality a useful tool for studying fictional characters. Ann Swinfen (1984) argues that "the fundamental purpose of serious fantasy is to comment upon the real world and to explore the moral, philosophical and other dilemmas posed by it" (231). Fantasy, particularly young adult fantasy, frequently explores the real world dilemma of grappling with the ways identities are shaped by the interactions and intersections of identity-forming categories. Chima's series offers a unique solution to this dilemma by presenting a character like Raisa who must grow to accept her multiplicity in order to fully understand herself. María Lugones (2003) proposes the concept of multiplicity as a useful way to discuss how the converging of multiple categories can create a unified rather than fragmented identity. Whereas a fragmented identity might consist of "fragments, pieces, and parts that do not fit well together," within the framework of multiplicity, "each person is multiple, nonfragmented, embodied" (127). Multiplicity encompasses the idea that identities are comprised of fused, yet distinct, components rather than unconnected, fragmented bits. Chima's *Seven Realms* series suggests that learning to appropriate an inner multiplicity and embrace a diverse identity is needed in order to assert authority and independence.

Young adult literature in general is a perfect vehicle for exploring how young adults must first contend with the complexities of identity formation before they can gain the potential to claim power and autonomy. As Roberta Seelinger Trites (2000) emphasizes, "Children's literature often affirms the child's sense of Self and her or his personal power. But in the adolescent novel, protagonists must learn about the social forces that have made them what they are" (3). Often, young adult protagonists begin to see these social forces while away from the security of their homes. Venturing out into the world, they start making decisions to which they are held accountable and, in the process, claim a life-altering sense of agency. According to Clare Bradford and her coauthors (2008) in *New World Orders in Contemporary Children's Literature*, "Agency thus resides in the making of choices and taking responsibility for them, in accepting the moral imperatives which in a properly functioning civil society should determine 'the choice we choose'" (31). For many young adult novels, claiming one's agency often requires deciding which path to pursue and which paths to abandon. For Chima's *Seven Realms* series, however, agency is no longer about adopting a singular path but rather about searching for the intersections where paths converge. Raisa is confronted by the challenges of ethnicity, class, education, and civil and military issues, as well as the struggles of being a woman who is both strong and sensitive. Eventually she discovers, though, that to deny one aspect of herself is to deny the essence of who she is. Only through Raisa's acceptance of her multiplicity is she able to fully claim her agency.

At the beginning of *The Seven Realms* series, Raisa is a young woman perceived primarily by her ethnicity because she is the product of a strategic marriage between the two primary ethnic groups of the Fells: the Spirit clans and the Valefolk. The indigenous Spirit clans are comprised of several tribes, including the mountain-based Demonai warrior clan. The dark and violent characterization of the Spirit clans, the Demonai in particular, is reinforced not only through the perceptions of characters in the narrative, but also through Chima's word choice. Even the name Demonai, with connotations of demons, stands in stark contrast to the suggestions of peaceful valleys raised by the name the Valefolk. The Valefolk are the valley-dwelling lighter-skinned peoples who colonized the land centuries before. Many of the characters throughout the narrative show a bias toward the Valefolk and consider their urbanized way of life to be more civilized. Even though both of these ethnic groups are fantastical constructions, it is difficult to avoid not reading them within the framework of American history and culture. As a result, we would be remiss if we ignored the potential problems caused by these representations. Perry Nodelman (1988, 234) maintains that many readers find it difficult to identify and engage with certain texts and characters without inserting their own experiences and culturally constructed points of view. For many American readers, *The Seven Realms* series might be viewed from a cultural framework in which the Demonai/Valefolk are substituted (consciously or subconsciously) by the indigenous Native American peoples/colonizing Europeans. While some might read these books as demonstrating an identity preference for the Valefolk, or at the very least preventing the ability to remain impartial, we believe that the reality of this issue is more complex.

It is not just the readers who imbue a text with personal interpretation and experience; it is also the authors themselves. Chima, in an e-mail interview with the authors of this article, acknowledged, "I am bristling with biases . . . we all are." For authors writing books with multiple identities or even with multiplicity, it can be challenging to perfectly and equally represent these different perspectives. Chima herself seems aware of the factors that can shape biases and says,

> I never craft [a] story with an agenda in mind—that almost always gets between the reader and the story. However, I agree with Joyce when he says that all fiction is autobiographical fantasy. I would go further—I think much of the history handed down to us is autobiographical fantasy as well—it reflects the biases of the historian. The story of Hanalea and the Demon King is a fictional example of the "great lie" that is so often repeated through generations. (Cinda Williams Chima, e-mail to authors, May 12, 2014)

The story of Hanalea, an ancient ruler of the queendom, and her lover, the Demon King, has been exaggerated and appropriated by each group of people in the Fells to explain why they believe they are superior in every respect. The false versions of the story perpetuated by these different groups in the queendom have produced cultural arrogances that Nodelman (1988) argues are potentially dangerous, and he contends that "if we are not conscious that other cultures offer different and, for those who live within them, equally satisfactory definitions of meaning and value, and that consequently, these cultures postulate quite different but equally satisfactory realities, then we are doomed to a dangerous solitude, a blindness that amounts to an unconscious form of arrogance" (232). At the end of *The Seven Realms* series, many of the Demonai have been vilified, but so too have many of the Valefolk. This suggests that their downfall is not ethnically based but the result of cultural arrogance. Raisa and her eventual husband Han Alister's success, on the other hand, seems to be due to their ability to avoid cultural arrogance by accepting their own multiplicity. Ultimately, we feel that despite its potentially problematic ethnic constructions, at least from an American point of view, this series needs to be examined because it does promote the virtues and the necessity of multiplicity.

Throughout the series, patterns established by structural techniques— such as the motif of names and the use of a variety of settings—develop the theme of multiplicity. These elements help build a final narrative arc that concludes with a triumphant Raisa. The narrative and structure work together to produce a female protagonist who is not fragmented but whole, thereby supporting the advantages of claiming multiplicity and illustrating the intersectionalities of ethnicity, gender, and class. David Mittelberg and Mary C. Waters (1992) suggest that "ethnicity has been used to refer to distinctions based on national origin, language, religion, food—and other cultural markers" (425). No one denies that Raisa is the daughter of Marianna, queen of the Fells and a member of the Valefolk, and of Lord Averill Demonai, the patriarch of the Demonai camp. Yet neither her parents nor most of the other people in Raisa's life are willing to recognize that she has chosen to identify with the cultural markers of both her mother's and father's ethnicities. Doing so has created tension between her parents and strains her relationship with each parent separately. In *The Exiled Queen*, Marianna indicates that many of the machinations complicating Raisa's life are due to efforts to align her more toward one ethnicity or another. In a letter, Marianna tells her daughter, "He [Lord Averill] and the other Demonai see you as one of them, because of your Demonai blood. . . . A faction of warriors favors setting me aside and crowning you as a queen more to their liking" (Chima 2010, 462). Each parent only sees the fragmented component of Raisa's identity aligned to her or his own ethnicity. They both see their daughter as a pawn to be used for their own people's agendas rather than appreciating the possibilities created by the intersections of these ethnicities. Their inability to see Raisa's multiplicity is manifested through the names they ascribe to her.

Throughout the series, Raisa struggles to overcome the fragmented identity externally imposed by those who refuse to acknowledge both facets of her ancestry. Lincoln Fernandes (2006) argues that "names in many cultures act as signs" often providing associations and indicators connected to gender, class, history, nationality, and religion (46). Raisa is originally associated with two names that together indicate her mixed heritage. The name Raisa *ana*'Marianna ties her to her Vale heritage, while Briar Rose is a name formally given to her by the Demonai clan. These names serve a greater role than just linking her to a specific ethnicity; the use of the names indicates people's inability to accept Raisa's multiplicity. Dale Spender (1985) says "naming is of necessity biased" (164), and Raisa's parents use her names to indicate their own personal ethnic and cultural biases. As public figures, Marianna's and Averill's separate naming choices likewise provide cues to the people of the queendom as to whom her parents believe Raisa's allegiance should lie. Her parents are not unique in using her names to emphasize either ethnic preferences or desires to continue the separation of the Valefolk and the Spirit clans. Many of the people in Raisa's life, including her paternal grandmother, her sister, and most of the boys romantically interested in her, emphasize their own ethnic and cultural loyalties in calling her either Raisa or Briar Rose. In *The Crimson Crown*, Nightwalker, a Demonai warrior approved by her father, tells Raisa that she is more attractive than her nonclan ancestors. Indicating his own clan preference, he asks, "Who would choose a pale flatlander over a clan princess?" (Chima 2012, 18). Although he was attempting to flatter Raisa, his comment instead alienates himself from her by illustrating that he cannot wholly appreciate her as he only sees the fragmented part that is Briar Rose.

Raisa's feelings for Nightwalker wane as she realizes that his prejudices prevent him from sharing her goals to create a harmonious relationship between all of the people of the Fells. She starts small by trying to keep harmony between her parents. In *The Exiled Queen*, Raisa stresses that she does not want to choose between her parents and their desires (ibid. 2010, 61). She assumes that by not favoring one parent over the other she can avoid indicating any ethnic partiality. Eventually, Raisa discovers that by not picking sides no one wins, herself included. Instead, she realizes she can only claim her agency by embracing both sides of her ethnicity. In *The Gray Wolf Throne*, while fleeing for her safety, Raisa adopts the name Brianna Trailwalker because of both its ordinariness and its reference to her clan ancestry (ibid. 2011, 2). This name allows her to accept her complicated feelings about her mixed ancestry, but it also helps her better understand her desires about who she wants to be. According to Spender (1985), "Without a name it is difficult to accept the existence of . . . a feeling. Naming is the means whereby we attempt to order and structure the chaos and flux of existence" (163). Spender's argument is based on the assumption that names are more than meaningless words; naming is an intentional act to ascribe specific meanings through specific words. Choosing the name Brianna Trailwalker is a move toward a self-selected identity that is multifaceted rather than fragmented. The name Brianna Trailwalker is not used extensively in the series; however, Raisa's choice of this name shows that she is aware of the associate power of names. This self-selected moniker reveals Raisa's internal struggles to find a balance between her Spirit and Vale sides. Embracing both her given names, as well as the larger meaning behind her self-chosen name, Raisa admits that she values her multiplicity. Choosing her identity is an act of claiming agency that allows her to become a woman fantastic—a woman capable of being complex and empowered. Finally, she is ready to turn her personal revelations into positive change for her people. In *The Crimson Crown*, she tells Nightwalker that in order for the realm to thrive, its people "cannot continue on as we are, splintered and squabbling among ourselves" (Chima 2012, 19). She knows that her people are not Spirit *or* Vale, but they are *all* of the Fells just as she is *all* the names connected to her ethnicity.

The queendom consists of specific ethnic groups as well as highly striated social and class distinctions. In *The Seven Realms* series, the motif of naming serves to illustrate the intricacies of ethnic multiplicity, but it additionally indicates the ways that gender, power, and class intersect. *The Exiled Queen* opens with Raisa leaving the queendom for her own safety and assuming the role of Lady Rebecca Morley, the daughter of a minor noble. As Rebecca, Raisa travels the realm and neighboring lands freely before attending a military school as an average student. There she grows to appreciate a newfound independence based in part on how other people treat her when they assume she is a lady of a lower class. This guise also provides her with a desirable freedom from her responsibilities as a royal (Chima 2010, 417). Nevertheless, she begins to realize that selecting this pseudonym not only grants her freedom; it furthermore provides her with the opportunity to see the different facets of herself from a unique perspective. Being away from the influence of her parents and with the anonymity she gains as Rebecca, Raisa is able to learn more about herself and the responsibilities she has to her people (ibid. 2010, 417). Rather than further fragmenting herself, adopting the name Rebecca helps Raisa understand that her success as the future queen depends on her joining her own disparate parts while simultaneously uniting the very different groups in her queendom.

In order to become the woman fantastic, Raisa must navigate the dimensions of her identity by gleaning the knowledge offered through the adoption of her different names. Part of this process requires her to overcome the ways that people, even those closest to her, have used her names to limit her in terms of power and class. Amon Byrne, who transitions from childhood friend to romantic interest and eventual personal guard and advisor, frequently shifts between calling her "Your Highness," "Raisa," and "Rai," depending on the level of class distinction that he wants to make between them. He makes this switch in an effort to emphasize their closeness or produce a distance between them, depending on the power dynamics he wants in the relationship (ibid. 2009). Later at the military academy, those she befriends treat her less formally than they would if they knew she was a princess, but they too use variations of her assumed name (Lady Rebecca Morley) to indicate her elevated social class and to distinguish themselves from her. Eventually, her friends realize that she is just a fellow cadet and begin referring to her as "Morley" in an effort to show that she is one of them (ibid. 2010, 183). Their recognition of the artificiality of imposing class-related barriers through the act of naming is a realization Raisa herself has while at the military academy.

Raisa's acceptance and understanding of the ways her names highlight and draw together the components of her multiplicity is fully matched by just one other person: Han Alister. In *The Demon King*, Raisa wants to see what the Fells's capital and its people are like without the distance her rank would enforce, so she adopts the persona of Rebecca Morley, the name and character she returns to when she flees for her safety in *The Exiled Queen*. Han meets the princess while she is under the guise of Rebecca (ibid. 2009, 234). Unlike most people who know Raisa as Rebecca, Han is less interested in trying to force her into a specific category based on her class, her gender, or his relationship to her. He is aware that people do not fit into neat little boxes, but that some possess the ability to move fluidly between culturally constructed structures of identity. This awareness is based in part on his own multiplicity. Throughout the series, Han undergoes multiple transformations in which he ceases to view the various components of his identity—cutthroat street lord, adopted clan member, respectable student, and powerful wizard—as fragmented. Instead, appreciating the potential of intersections, he accepts his own multiplicity. It is for this reason that more than any other character, Han is able to see Raisa's multiplicity and cherish it. He welcomes the idea that the woman he loves is simultaneously scrappy and elegant, a fighter and a lady, passionate and circumspect. When Han learns the truth, that his love is actually Princess Raisa, the soon-to-be queen, and not Rebecca, a minor lady (ibid. 2012, 204), he uses her names to help him transition his thoughts. Calling her first Rebecca, then thinking of her as "Rebecca/Queen Raisa" (ibid. 2011, 229), before finally seeing her as Raisa (ibid., 234), Han quickly reconciles himself to the fact that despite possessing multiple names, she is still the same person. Han, much like Raisa herself, acknowledges that her multiple names are evidence of a multiplicity that makes her a stronger woman and future queen.

Many characters in this series possess the potential for multiplicity; however, Raisa and Han stand out as each willingly accepts her or his own multiplicity and succeeds in claiming agency by uniting the facets of her or his identity that others see as fragmented. Despite the similarities between Raisa and Han, Raisa's situation is uniquely juxtaposed against the choices made by her younger sister. Mellony is also a princess and a daughter of Queen Marianna and Lord Averill. Although she has both Vale and clan names, she does not embrace both of her ethnicities and chooses to solely associate with the Valefolk. At the clan celebration for Raisa's coronation, Averill says, "I have another daughter, Daylily, also called Mellony, but she does not feel the call of her clan blood. She has no desire to learn the Old Ways. She will not come to the uplands" (ibid. 2012, 6). Averill is providing this comparison to propose that his eldest daughter is a true clan queen. Yet his points inadvertently reflect Raisa's willingness to be multifaceted. The contrast between Raisa and Mellony stressed throughout the series suggests that it is not the circumstances, but their choices, that separate them. As Raisa becomes more unified by accepting her multiplicity, Mellony grows increasingly fragmented. Thinking to herself that "Mellony is trying so hard to claim her own place in the world" (204), Raisa is saddened by how lost her sister appears. Raisa knows that because Mellony cannot appreciate both parts of her heritage, she will be unable to find any place where she truly belongs. Whereas Raisa makes her own place, Mellony wants someone to make a place for her. Refusing to accept her multiplicity, Mellony lacks the ability to claim agency and to make a place for herself as a woman fantastic.

Unlike her sister, Raisa shapes her world in ways that allow her to develop and mature. Spender (1985) writes "that those who have the power to name the world are in a position to influence reality" (165). Raisa values how the different facets of her identity are influenced by the naming process, both by the claiming as well as creating of certain names. Though the extended use of the names Raisa, Briar Rose, and Rebecca Morley, she is able to explore her queendom from a variety of perspectives, and she gains insights and experiences that allow her to change herself and her world. As Raisa she learns court intrigue and politics, as Briar Rose she learns how to be a warrior and tradesperson, and as Rebecca Morley she learns discipline and how to understand her peoples' needs. Even though she gains different skills through these identities, she also discovers how to appreciate the ways that this knowledge and these perspectives intersect. Rather than producing a fragmented ruler, Raisa's diverse skill set and her multiplicity allow her to be the queen needed by her people in such tumultuous times (ibid., 435). Her general tells her that despite her short rule, Raisa has "launched the kinds of changes this queendom has needed for a long time—in the army, in the council, in dealing with the flatland refugees" (ibid.). Raisa's willingness to act on her conviction that there is strength within intersectionality allows her, in the final chapters of

The Crimson Crown, to begin the reconstructive work needed to make her queendom a place for all of her people.

A relationship between place and identity is enforced not only in the last book, but throughout *The Seven Realms* series. Places and geographical journeys serve as opportunities for Raisa and others to develop and accept their identities. The map of the Seven Realms included in the last three books reveals the degree to which these realms, particularly Raisa's queendom, are divided. While it shows the official borders between realms, the map additionally depicts the natural borders used by the different groups of people to erect cultural barriers. Land is a continual point of tension, particularly between the Spirit clans and the Valefolk. Both groups associate positive attributes with their particular domain and tend to see the other areas of the Fells as inferior spaces. Clare L. Twigger-Ross and David L. Uzzell (1996, 206) argue that place becomes a component of identification and creates a connection to a cultural group membership. For this reason, place plays a dominant role in *The Seven Realms* series. Many of the political dealings and established treaties in the Fells have revolved around issues of place. For example, as part of one ancient treaty, all future queens are required to spend time both at home in the capital and in the uplands where the Spirit clans dwell. Most princess heirs prior to Raisa fulfilled their duties begrudgingly and with as little time in the uplands as possible. Despite her mother's wishes, Raisa, however, has spent several years living in the Demonai camp with her father's family (Chima 2009, 25). Raisa's unique ethnicity ensures her time is more evenly divided between the Vale and uplands in an effort to appease both of her parents. Each parent attempts to situate Raisa within a specific place in an effort to foster one cultural identity over another, just as they used her names in an effort to call attention to one specific side of her heritage. Her parents know that place influences ideologies and each wants his or her respective place and its associated beliefs to dominate Raisa's way of thinking.

Although Raisa always had a connection to the Spirit clans, it was not until she fostered in the Demonai camp that she began to assimilate their culture into her own identity. After having lived in both the capital and the camps, Raisa feels attached to two separate cultural groups. Summarizing the ideas of Stefan E. Hormuth, Twigger-Ross and Uzzell (1996) state, "Place is considered to be an active part of the construction of a person's identity" (207). The capital and the camps have both served as active places in constructing Raisa's identity, particularly as it concerns her cultural identification. When the series begins, it is clear that her parents' independent efforts to connect her to the Valefork and the Spirit clans have been successful. By forcing her to live in two different places and associate with two different cultures, they have also enforced very different place attachments. Place attachment can be expressed as a sense of contentment experienced by someone who feels physically or emotionally close to a place (Giuliani 1991, 134). Raisa's developed attachment to the uplands makes her appreciate the land, the people, and their way of life. Raisa learned and grew to value many of the skills utilized by the Spirit clans—including hunting, trading, fighting, and negotiating—during her three years in the Demonai camp. In crossing a geographical border, Raisa has moreover permanently crossed a cultural border; her time in the camps has left an indelible mark on her worldview and ways of thinking. When she returns to the capital, Raisa sees how much this time has impacted her views and desires as she compares the capital's restraints and protocols to the freedoms of the camps (Chima 2009, 21–25). She has been taught to believe that, like the vast spatial separation between her parents' peoples, her cultural heritages should likewise be kept separate. Her parents' responses, especially her mother's, to Raisa's evolving place attachment to the uplands have reinforced this mode of thinking. In particular, Raisa's open affection for the Demonai way of life has put a strain on her relationship with her mother (ibid.). Her parents' focus on the borders that exist between these two groups leads to feelings of fragmentation. Raisa does not know how to resolve the problems created by both the physical and cultural distances that exist between these places and their peoples. Only when she travels throughout her queendom and beyond does she see how her attachments to places can intersect.

Starting in *The Exiled Queen*, for the first time Raisa travels largely unaccompanied through the queendom in an effort to flee from an increasingly corrupt court. Tim Cresswell (1996) maintains that place "forces us to make interpretations and act accordingly" (161). Raisa's interactions with the various places of her queendom affect her interpretations of the people as she develops a concrete understanding of the driving forces within the Fells that affect her citizens and the land (Chima 2010, 161). Her perception of an ideal queen changes after seeing the diversity of her people and their needs while on the road to Oden's Ford. Oden's Ford is at a crossroads outside of the queendom in a neighboring realm and is a neutral territory where people from all the different realms can gain the best education in a variety of subjects and disciplines. Here Raisa discovers that to truly understand her people, she must first learn to connect to them; in order for this to happen, she needs a specific education, one that can only be gained at Oden's Ford. In the capital she studied philosophy, art, and court etiquette, all useful information for navigating the world of court politics and palace proceedings. In the uplands camps she developed a work ethic and became disciplined, preparing her for ruling in difficult times. As she tells one of the teachers at Oden's Ford, "I came here to fill in the gaps in my education, to prepare for the times I will be making decisions all by myself, when knowledge of leadership, engineering, and military science may make the difference between success and failure" (ibid., 174). She knows that the military academy in Oden's Ford will offer the theories and experiences that she is lacking, including military tactics and combat skills. Being trained at the military academy proves to be a grueling, albeit rewarding, experience for Raisa as it teaches her how to make important decisions for herself. Choosing this education in this place becomes a critical step in claiming her agency because it is a step toward fully accepting her multiplicity.

Without the added pressures or responsibilities of being princess heir, Raisa is able to reflect while studying in Oden's Ford. She realizes that there are no disadvantages to incorporating all of the different facets of herself. However, Raisa must act on this acceptance of multiplicity in order to claim her agency. At the end of *The Exiled Queen*, a threat to remove Raisa from the succession to the throne catalyzes her decision to leave the sanctuary of the military academy. After a series of events disrupts her original plan for an escorted return to the capitol, Raisa embarks on a dangerous journey while hunted by multiple parties. This trek back home ends her practice of consciously keeping the various places of her life separate. It also allows her to bridge the gaps between the different viewpoints and concerns she had at court, in the uplands, and at the military academy as Raisa, Briar Rose, and Rebecca Morley, respectively. It is only by combining the knowledge, experience, and skill sets she has gained in these different locations that Raisa is able to outtalk, outfight, and outwit her opponents (ibid. 2011, 73–77). With such a rich store of information, she is able to mature into the young woman needed to lead her people. Raisa now appreciates the intersectionality of the places she has been. Knowing that she is stronger for her multiplicity, Raisa firmly claims her agency in time to develop into the queen best suited for her queendom.

The Fells needs a queen who understands that the fragmented world is ineffective and harms everyone, and it needs a consort for the queen who will support her efforts to unite these fragmented components. Raisa's other suitors possessed a single-place attachment and an accompanying cultural connection to one group. Han, however, has lived in the slums of the capital, in the uplands, at Oden's Ford, and in the palace. His willingness to embrace new places continues to allow him to form multiple place attachments and to appreciate different people, regardless of their gender, ethnicity, or class. Han uses his experiences from different places to learn how to accept and work with his multiplicity, and his actions parallel Raisa's own explorations. In discussing the power of place, Edward S. Casey (2001) says, "Places come into us lastingly; once having been in a particular place for any considerable time—or even briefly, if our experience there has been intense—we are forever marked by that place, which lingers in us indefinitely and in a thousand ways, many too attenuated to specify" (414). Despite having lived for an extended period of time in just three places—the capital, the Demonai camp, and Oden's Ford—Raisa is transformed into a more complex young woman because she has been forever marked by the places and people she encounters in her journeys. Yet she becomes a woman fantastic when she finally allows herself to be marked by the intersections of these places and changed by her multiplicity.

Raisa realizes that to save her queendom she must accept multiplicity, not only within herself and within the Fells, but also within the warring Seven Realms. Understanding the relationship between geography, economy, and culture, Raisa knows that it is senseless to keep everyone separate and to allow the fighting to continue. She thinks, "When the Seven Realms were joined together, goods, money and people flowed freely among them, making the whole stronger than its component parts" (Chima 2010, 161). Before she can help bring change to the Seven Realms, however, she must first teach her people to work together to accept the multiplicity within the Fells. At her mother's funeral, she addresses her people: "It is good to be home. I have missed these mountains and the people who dwell here—uplanders and Valefolk, the Spirit clans and charmcasters" (ibid. 2011, 338). Her speech demonstrates what she learned while away—there is a connection between the land and its people. Stuart Hall (1990) suggests that cultural identity is "a matter of 'becoming' as well as 'being.' It belongs as much to the future as to the past" (225). By including everyone together in her speech, Raisa shows her understanding that the future of the Fells will only be promising through accepting multiplicity. Raisa knows she must actively work to lead her people in creating the culture she believes they need.

The Seven Realms series explores the complications that can arise in a non-homogenized world. In this respect, the books stand out from other contemporary young adult fantasy. Generally, young adult literature has struggled to create diverse representations of young adults that reflect the actualities of real world diversity; this is particularly true as it concerns issues of ethnicity (Doll 2012). Yet Marc Aronson, quoted in an article by Jen Doll (ibid.), speculates that when it comes to producing more diversified young adult characters he "expect[s] the next wave to expand or overlap with fantasy/dystopia" (Doll 2012, paragraph 11). If *The Seven Realms* series is any indication, then Aronson's prediction seems to have merit. Through presentations of alternative worlds, the complexities of diversity can be explored safely within the fantasy genre without being bound by the contentious and limited realities of the existing world. If works of fantasy that explore multiplicity, like *The*

Seven Realms series, can both garner sufficient popularity and receive enough critical attention, then they could help create a paradigm shift in which representations of diversity are not elusive or infrequent but rather critical staples of young adult literature.

Raisa may not identify with ethnic groups found in the real world; however, her unique identity makes her a character needed to help transform young adult literature, in part because her struggles and triumphs in accepting multiplicity bridge literary concerns and current social trends. Vincent J. Cheng (2004, 133–34) argues that around the millennium, American culture began exhibiting a greater recognition of, as well as a pride in, multiracial and multiethnic identities. Raisa's mixed heritage combined with her appreciation of her multiethnicity makes her an ideal character for these times and for this culture. Furthermore, she is a character who reflects current social opinions through her understanding that multiplicity is valuable and that identity is formed at the intersections of not only ethnicity, but also of gender and of class. In discussing the role that girls have in creating social change and embracing their power, Sinikka Aapola, Marnina Gonick, and Anita Harris (2005) assert that "young women are forging new identities that promise exciting ways to imagine global citizenship. The old 'torn between two cultures' model of understanding diversity in cultural identity is being dismantled by young people who refuse to choose or be torn" (182–83). Raisa illustrates how this refusal to choose or be torn can be empowering. She accepts her multiplicity and refuses to be ruled by the cultural binaries that others want to impose upon her. Through these actions, Raisa transforms into a powerful young woman who claims her agency and who fights for change.

Throughout the final book in *The Seven Realms* series, Raisa works towards creating a new future for her queendom and her people. She takes a step toward claiming her agency each time she chooses to accept the challenges of uniting the fragmented components of her world. The process is fraught with difficulties, yet Raisa is pleased by the "chance, win or lose" to make her own mark in the world (Chima 2012, 325). *The Crimson Crown* ends with the celebration of Han and Raisa's wedding, but this moment is also a celebration of Raisa's victory in learning to embody her multiplicity. On their wedding day, Han watches Raisa walk down the aisle and thinks to himself that she is a "bewitching mix of clan and flatland beauty" (ibid., 591). The series ends shortly after the wedding with this image of Raisa, secure in her multiplicity. Cheng (2004) suggests that "we *create*—not merely inherit or 'retrieve'—culture. This is a powerful and empowering understanding, for it allows us to imagine and recognize ourselves as active agents participating in the making and shaping of our culture" (179). Raisa, at the end of the series, has created change within herself and is actively working toward shaping a new culture for the Fells. It is this final version of Raisa as a woman fantastic—triumphant in her ruling, secure in her multiplicity, and rewarded with true love—that lingers in the imaginations of the readers.

References

Aapola, Sinikka, Marnina Gonick, and Anita Harris. 2005. *Young Femininity: Girlhood, Power and Social Change*. Edited by Jo Campling. New York: Palgrave Macmillan.

Bradford, Clare, Kerry Mallan, John Stephens, and Robyn McCallum. 2008. *New World Orders in Contemporary Children's Literature*. New York: Palgrave MacMillan.

Casey, Edward S. 2001. "Body, Self, and Landscape: A Geophilosophical Inquiry into the Place-World." In *Textures of Place: Exploring Humanist Geographies*, edited by Paul C. Adams, Steven Hoelscher, and Karen E. Till, 403–425. Minneapolis: University of Minnesota Press.

Cheng. Vincent J. 2004. *Inauthentic: The Anxiety over Culture and Identity*. New Brunswick, NJ: Rutgers University Press.

Chima, Cinda Williams. 2009. *The Demon King*. New York: Hyperion.

——. 2010 *The Exiled Queen*. New York: Hyperion.

——. 2011. *The Gray Wolf Throne*. New York: Hyperion.

——. 2012. *The Crimson Crown*. New York: Hyperion.

——. 2014. E-mail to authors. May 12.

Crenshaw, Kimberle. 1991. "Mapping the Margins: Intersectionality, Identity Politics, and Violence against Women of Color." *Stanford Law Review* 43: 1241–99.

Cresswell, Tim. 1996. *In Place/Out of Place: Geography, Ideology, and Transgression*. Minneapolis: University of Minnesota Press.

Crosby, Janice C. 2000. *Cauldron of Changes: Feminist Spirituality in Fantastic Fiction*. Jefferson, NC: McFarland.

Doll, Jen. 2012. "The Ongoing Problem of Race in Y.A." *The Wire*. April 26. http://www.thewire.com/entertainment/2012/04/ongoing-problem-race-y/51574/ (accessed May 19, 2014).

Fernandes, Lincoln. 2006. "Translation of Names in Children's Fantasy Literature: Bringing the Young Reader into Play." *New Voices in Translation Studies* 2: 44–57.

Garry, Ann. 2012. "Who Is Included? Intersectionality, Metaphors, and the Multiplicity of Gender." In *Out from the Shadows: Analytical Feminist Contributions to Traditional Philosophy*, edited by Sharon L. Crasnow and Anita M. Superson, 493–530. Oxford: Oxford University Press.

Guiliani, Maria Vittoria. 1991. "Towards an Analysis of Mental Representations of Attachment to the Home." *Journal of Architectural and Planning Research* 8 (2): 133–46.

Hall. Stuart. 1990. "Cultural Identity and Diaspora." *Identity: Community, Culture, Difference*, edited by Jonathan Rutherford, 222–37. London: Lawrence and Wishart.

Lugones, María. 2003. *Pilgrimages/Peregrinajes: Theorizing Coalition against Multiple Oppressions*. New York: Rowman & Littlefield.

Mittelberg, David, and Mary C. Waters. 1992. "The Process of Ethnogenesis among Haitian and Israeli Immigrants in the United States." *Ethnic and Racial Studies* 15 (3): 412–35.

Nodelman, Perry. 1988. "Cultural Arrogance and Realism in Judy Blume's *Superfudge.*" *Children's Literature in Education* 19 (4): 230–41.

Spender, Dale. 1985. *Man Made Language.* 2nd ed. London: Routledge & Kegan Paul.

Swinfen, Ann. 1984. *In Defense of Fantasy: A Study of the Genre in English and American Literature since 1945.* Boston: Routledge & Kegan Paul.

Trites, Roberta Seelinger. 2000. *Disturbing the Universe: Power and Repression in Adolescent Literature.* Iowa City: University of Iowa Press.

Twigger-Ross, Clare L., and David L. Uzzell. 1996. "Place and Identity Process." *Journal of Environmental Psychology* 16: 205–20.

Forced Glory: Katniss Everdeen, Bella Swan, and Varieties of Virginity

—Rhonda V. Wilcox

"I only got engaged to save people's lives, and that completely backfired."
—Katniss Everdeen (Collins 2009, 185)

As the March 23, 2012, release of the first *Hunger Games* film approached, comparisons between Suzanne Collins's trilogy and Stephenie Meyer's *Twilight* series abounded in the popular press. Both stories feature self-sacrificing young female protagonists who must choose between two young men. Writers in magazines such as *Entertainment Weekly* and *Salon.com* and authors such as Stephen King, however, emphasized the difference between the two (Valby 2012; Miller 2010). Nina Jacobson, one of *The Hunger Games* film's producers, asserted, "This book is about so much more than, 'Gee, which boy do I like?'" (quoted in Valby 2012, 65), and *Entertainment Weekly*'s Karen Valby (2012) responded, "(Suck on that, *Twilight* comparisons)" (65). The *Twilight* books, as those who have not recently been living in Antarctica know, focus on a high school girl; she undergoes many dangers in the course of connecting with her true love and is torn between a handsome vampire and a hunky werewolf. *The Hunger Games*'s Katniss Everdeen, on the other hand, chooses between a hunter and a baker. *The Hunger Games*'s protagonist is a young woman who offers herself in place of her still younger sister for a dystopian, state-sponsored reality show in which teenagers are forced to compete until only one survives. With both a male and a female chosen from each of twelve poorer districts that support the Capitol, the drafted male contestant, the baker's son Peeta, tells her and the television world that he is in love with her, and Katniss must discover whether his feelings are real—as she tries to sort out her own feelings for him and for her handsome best friend and hunting partner Gale. Unquestionably, the differences in these stories are more important than the similarities.

But before reaching these differences, I want to explore the significance of some of the similarities, similarities that go beyond the love triangles. Bella and Katniss share signs of resistance to adulthood, but the depictions of their virginities are quite different, suggesting different models of heroism and different degrees of agency.

Before delving into the similarities, let me note a categorical difference: curiously enough, Bella Swan is a superhero, while Katniss Everdeen is not. Near the beginning of the *Twilight* series, we learn that the handsome vampire Edward Cullen, who belongs to a family of vampires that chooses not to consume humans, has the special power of being able to read minds—all minds but Bella's, which is closed to him. It later develops that Bella is able to resist any kind of mental assault, even from powerful supernatural creatures; this girl, who is self-effacing and clumsy, is nonetheless a powerful "shield," to use their term (Meyer 2008, 595). In contrast, Katniss Everdeen's life-preserving ability is a learned skill—the bow and arrow work she has practiced since age eleven in order to feed her starving mother and sister after her father dies. If we follow Kareem Harper's categorization of superheroes by origin, we can extend the definition to include Katniss: Harper lists in-born mutation, scientific experiment or mistake, technology (as with Iron Man), magic, and "natural origin characters ... that fine tun[e] their body to 'above average' levels" (quoted in Willis 2014). We could, if we wished, place Katniss in the last category. But in any case, Bella Swan's power is inborn, essentialist, while Katniss Everdeen's skill is something she gained by choosing to practice it day after day. This skill enables her to win the Hunger Games. Furthermore, it is a skill she has practiced in order to succeed in her own normal life, to gather food; unlike contestants who have volunteered from the relatively wealthier districts, the so-called Careers, Katniss has not been focused on the externally imposed Hunger Games themselves; there has been no "teaching to the test" for Katniss. She recognizes some innate talent in herself, but she has honed that talent for her own purposes. Bella, on the other hand, was born to be a shield.

Both young women do, to one degree or another, eventually save the day, and that is just one of many significant similarities. Both tales are first-person narratives, so we are privy to the mind of each protagonist. One of Bella Swan's most noteworthy characteristics is her low self-esteem, her lack of confidence, particularly in terms of her attractiveness to males. "I'm absolutely ordinary," she declares repeatedly; she also calls herself "shamefully plain" (Meyer 2005, 210; ibid. 2006, 65). And her assertions that she never had a boyfriend at her former school in Arizona seem to support this idea—which would make her a particularly helpful heroine for the more normal looking among her readers. But we never experience Bella (whose very name means beautiful) being normal in attractiveness; once she arrives in her new home in Forks, Washington, as the story begins, she is pursued by one male after another. The normal human boys Mike, Eric, and Tyler all want her to go to the dance with them; and then, of course, there are Edward the vampire and Jacob the budding werewolf. As Edward tells her, "You don't see yourself very clearly, you know. . . . You didn't hear what every human male in this school was thinking on your first day. . . . You are the opposite of ordinary" (Meyer 2005, 210). So she is not only beautiful, but modest, almost ferociously modest; insistently, blindly so. Similarly, though less insistently, Katniss Everdeen seems to underestimate her attractiveness. Her fellow District 12 contestant Peeta tells their mentor, "She has no idea. The effect she can have" (Collins 2008, 91). Two pages later, she finally starts to get a hint: "A tiny part of me wonders if this was a compliment. That he meant I was appealing in some way. It's weird." (93). Contestants, or tributes, as they are called, in the Hunger Games need support from sponsors watching the televised games, and it is clear that Katniss's attractiveness helps her gain sponsors. On the very first page of the story, she mentions her mother's reputed beauty; later in the trilogy, she sees recordings of her mother when she was young and acknowledges how extraordinarily beautiful she was—a beauty that she might reasonably have supposed would pass, in some measure, to her. (Her father is quite handsome, too.) But again and again through the books, Katniss rejects the idea of her own beauty, just as Bella does. Is it a danger for a young woman to see herself as beautiful? Would friends reject her? Would readers reject her? Perhaps it is simply normal for adolescents to see themselves as physically flawed—and therefore audiences can connect with this attitude. Perhaps it is a self-defense mechanism of psychology that is accurately represented by the authors. Perhaps it is an unhealthy internalization of the demand for perfection in appearance. In any case, it is a quality shared by Bella Swan and Katniss Everdeen.

Another, related similarity is their attitude toward and experience with clothing. In consonance with her view of herself as very normal, Bella enjoys wearing simple, everyday clothing—jeans and T-shirts. Once she becomes involved with the Cullen family,[1] however, she is repeatedly induced to wear much fancier clothing. In typical vampire fashion, the Cullens are extremely wealthy, and Edward's adopted sister Alice, who becomes Bella's best friend (a handy in-house relationship), takes every opportunity to dress Bella in expensive clothing—whether for her prom or her wedding. The impoverished Katniss, too, normally dresses in simple fashion, wearing clothes that allow her to move through the forest to hunt, and she prefers her normal style. When she reaches the Capitol to prepare for the Hunger Games, however, her mentor Haymitch instructs her to give herself over completely into the hands of her stylist, Cinna, as he dresses her for public events—and Cinna dresses her spectacularly; Alice Cullen's Paris designers could not do as well. In both Katniss's and Bella's cases, clothing is associated with wealth and power (and anyone who has watched the Academy Awards will not find it hard to make that connection). As Judith E. Johnson (1993) writes, "The powerful social position of the typical vampire is no accident. It tells us that part of the inherent material in society's dreams of vampires is social and involves questions of social justice, power, race, and class as well as the more obvious gender conflict" (4). Bella's disinclination to fancy clothes is one sign of her not being materialistic; she does not want Edward for his money. As she says, "I'd never had much money, and that had never bothered me. . . . Edward had a lot of money. . . . He, for some unfathomable reason, wanted to be with me. Anything he gave me on top of that just threw us more out of balance" (Meyer 2006, 13). Or, one might add, any clothes his sister gives her. And when Alice dresses her for the prom, she complains, "I'm not coming over any more if Alice is going to treat me like Guinea Pig Barbie" (ibid. 2005, 482). The extraordinary costumes Katniss wears in the Hunger Games are deeply connected to the system of power in her world—as are the Hunger Games themselves, which the central government forces on tributary districts that rebelled approximately seventy-five years before. Katniss loves the costumes that Cinna designs for her, in part because of his art and feeling for them, and in part because she knows they will help her craft an image and thus gain sponsors and be more likely to survive. These costumes are part of the books' very conscious exploration of the uses of rhetoric in communications media—or, to use an older term, the theme of appearance versus reality. There is a continuing struggle for the uses of beauty[2]: Will it be controlled by Cinna, who designs his clothes both to help save Katniss and to advance a rebellion? Or will it be controlled by the chilling President Snow, who requires Katniss to model wedding dresses for a marriage he is forcing on her? Abuse of power darkens beauty much more harshly in *The Hunger Games*. But both Bella and Katniss, when given a choice, reject fancy clothes in favor of simple garments. Nonetheless, both protagonists are forced, repeatedly, to wear extraordinarily beautiful clothes. Poor things. Thus readers who identify with them may simultaneously enjoy the sensual, aesthetic, and socioeconomic class pleasures of imagined couture, yet revel in the virtue of rejection of the corrupting material (an ambivalence that Laura Miller [2010] notes as well).

Even more noteworthy than the heroines' repudiation of fancy clothes, however, is their repudiation of marriage. With a hazy veneer of horror, the

Twilight novels are romances—but their heroine is emphatically antimarriage. Her beloved Edward is, on the other hand, dead set on it (if you'll forgive the expression). Having died at age seventeen during the 1918 influenza epidemic, Edward has old-fashioned attitudes toward marriage, and his preferences are, in the end, demonstrated to be sound (in the *Twilight* world). Bella, for her part, detests the idea of marriage in part because of her parents' failed marriage and also because of her mother's reiteration of the mistake it was to have married young, without an education: "She'd drilled it into me over and over—smart people took marriage seriously. Mature people went to college and started careers before they got deeply involved in a relationship. She knew I would never be as thoughtless and goofy and *small-town* as she'd been" (Meyer 2007, 45–46). The vampire's bite is widely associated with sexual penetration, of course, and despite her dislike of marriage, Bella wants to have both sex with Edward and his bite, to turn her into a vampire—a creature of marble invulnerability. Edward bargains with her for marriage to come first, and she ultimately agrees. Katniss, too, rejects marriage for herself, but for very different reasons. In her world, all District children are subject to the "reaping"—being drafted into the annual Hunger Games, from which only one emerges alive (Collins 2008, 3). She cannot bear the idea of bringing a child into the world only to see it killed in such a fashion. At one point she wonders, if Peeta had died the first time they were in the Hunger Games, would she have married her friend Gale? Would she have been "lulled by the security of [a winner's] money and food and the illusion of safety being a victor would bring? But there would still always be the reaping looming over us, over our children" (Collins 2009, 185). And moments later she adds, "Even if I had killed Peeta in the arena, I still wouldn't have wanted to marry anyone" (ibid., 185). Both young women, then, repudiate marriage for much of the narrative. This repudiation might convey an echo of the "independence" of the "spirited" heroine of traditional romance, as Janice Radway (1984, 123) describes her. Just as she is not motivated by money, so too she is not motivated by the simple desire for the social status of the married state; when at last she marries, it will be for love. In fact, Bella's mother implies that there is a loss of social status in marrying young. And Katniss has even darker reasons for resisting marriage: her recognition of the hardships of her world and the lack of real security provided by marriage. Even before she joins the games, she prefers her partnership with Gale to marriage with him. One might wonder whether there is a reflection here of a growing tendency among young people to eschew traditional marriage. Or, again, it could be a way to have the wedding cake and eat it, too: each heroine says no to marriage (thus proving her independence), but each, in the end, marries.

This willingness to be a single person, this variety of independence, is reflected in another shared quality of the two protagonists. As mentioned earlier, Bella Swan is the only person whom Edward Cullen cannot read telepathically, and he is baffled and astonished by that fact. Though Edward frequently enters her room, he cannot enter her mind, and thus she maintains an essential separateness, a room of her own, if you will—dependent on him though she may be in many ways.[3] Interestingly, Suzanne Collins writes of Katniss Everdeen in precisely similar fashion. On page six of the first book, Katniss tells us, "No one could ever read my thoughts" (Collins 2008, 6). Katniss is not literally referencing telepathy; this is a fictional future of our world, not a fantasy. And once again, while Bella's resistance to being read is inborn, part of her essential nature, Katniss's is something she has worked to achieve: in her world, it can be dangerous to be too transparent. She says, "When I was younger, I scared my mother to death, the things I would blurt out about [our] District 12, about the people who rule our country, Panem, from the far-off city called the Capitol. Eventually, I understood that this would only lead us to more trouble. So I learned to hold my tongue and to turn my features into an indifferent mask" (ibid.). Katniss's ability to hide her thoughts is a weapon as important as her arrows on many occasions, such as her interactions with television interviewer Caesar Flickerman or later with President Alma Coin. Of course, it is also true that both Bella and Katniss sometimes reveal themselves. Bella blushes to excess, and Katniss once in a while displays an impressive, if reckless, righteous anger, as when she shoots an arrow through the apple in the mouth of a pig on which the Hunger Games supervisors are feasting—a gesture that focuses on an emblem of their self-indulgence, skewered by a girl who comes from a world of want. As Dereck Coatney (2012) says, sometimes "she pays a high price for being authentic in an inauthentic world" (191). Both Katniss and Bella are generally bad liars. Nonetheless, both maintain an inner, protected core: neither can be "read"—except by us, the readers. Each young woman in some way keeps her inner self intact—though I will say more on this later.

Whether or not this unreachable inner self constitutes immature fear or mature individuation is another question—a question that connects to yet another parallel: the protagonists' relationships with their mothers. In her study of romance novels, Janice Radway (1984), building on Nancy Chodorow's work, has pointed out that "the heroine's and the reader's impulse towards individuation and autonomy [includes] a step that must be taken, at least within patriarchy, *against* the mother" (124). Both Bella and Katniss take that step. Bella's story begins as she separates from her loving mother, coming to live with her father in order to give her mother the space to develop her new marriage. Although Bella's mother Renee is affectionate, she is also hapless;

Bella is portrayed as the responsible person in the relationship, with her scatterbrained mother being described as "childlike" (Meyer 2005, 46), likely to forget bills or gas for her car—likely even to get lost (ibid., 4). Bella is the one who cooks and pays the bills: "My mom always says I was born thirty-five years old" (ibid., 106), she reports. Anna Krugovoy Silver (2010, 124) argues that Renee has chosen to leave Bella, but in fact Renee repeatedly urges Bella to stay with her (e.g., Meyer 2005, 4, 66, 466). Bella turns away from her mom for her mom's sake, but turn away she does; and in giving her mom's marriage room to grow, Bella gives herself room to grow as well.

This shift in roles from child to adult is even starker for Katniss. Katniss lives in the Appalachian part of the former United States, and her father works as a coal miner. Her mother has taken a social step down from the merchant class in order to marry this handsome, intelligent, loving man. When Katniss is eleven, her father is killed in a mining accident, and her mother collapses. She withdraws so thoroughly that her two daughters, Katniss and Primrose, or Prim, almost starve. It is eleven-year-old Katniss who manages to find food for them—through a gift of bread from the baker's son, Peeta, and the knowledge of bow hunting left by her father and developed by her new friend Gale, whose father also died in the mine. It is interesting to consider that Katniss's mother's reaction to her father's death is very like Bella's reaction to Edward's desertion of her in the second book, *New Moon*: months of blank emptiness. In *New Moon*, that emptiness is given as a sign of love—a problem, yes, but a sign of love nonetheless. In *The Hunger Games*, we see this reaction from the perspective of the daughter who should be able to depend on her—and Katniss's condemnation of her mother is unequivocal. Of course, Bella does not have young children depending on her when she collapses, whereas Katniss's mother (so far as I know, she is never given a name) does. Katniss takes over the job of providing food for the family and never trusts her mother again. As the story proceeds, we see her mother act as a healer, a physician, generously helping people over and over. But when the end of the story has nearly come and Katniss is devastated emotionally and physically by her sister's death, her mother deserts her once again. Katniss is motherless. As for Bella, she keeps on friendly, loving terms with Renee—indeed, naming her own daughter after her—but she becomes more and more distant. As Bella says of her absent mother at Christmas in *Breaking Dawn*, "I hadn't seen my mother since the wedding, but I found I could only be glad for the gradual distancing that had begun two years ago. She was too fragile for my world. I didn't want her to have any part of this. Charlie [her father] was stronger" (Meyer 2008, 654). Bella's distancing from her mother evinces both a sociological move to the higher class of her husband and an emotional separation.

As for their fathers, they are both present and absent, in different ways. Charlie is a loving father who fits the stereotype of the strong, silent man. He communicates through gestures, such as getting up early to put snow chains on her truck. However, in his noncommunicative fashion, he leaves her to herself; furthermore, as both the sheriff and a fisherman, he is often absent from their home. He is the most convenient of parents for a young woman who wants to entertain a vampire in her bedroom. Katniss's father never gets in her way, either, since he is dead; any patriarchal threat from him is evacuated. Yet his gifts to her are very present in her life. He is the one who started teaching her to use a bow and arrow, and he left behind handmade weapons for her. He is the one who taught her to sing old songs that she uses to comfort fellow tributes such as Rue and Peeta—and to connect with the audience that sponsors her. His love sustains her but never controls her. And both fathers are presented as having truly loved the girls' mothers, thus providing a model of male fidelity. Indeed, both these fathers could be seen as another element of wish fulfillment for some young readers: the loving father who is out of the way.

The role of the father indirectly impinges on the next similarity, and that is the major matter of the virginity of the heroines. And here is where the similarities get different, really different. As noted earlier, Edward Cullen can read everyone's mind but Bella's; indeed, this is the first thing about her that attracts his attention, across a crowded lunchroom, before they come close enough for him to identify her scent. The mental connection of telepathy, in fantasy and science fiction, can be used to represent sexual connection; as Anne Cranny-Francis (1997) says, telepathy, among other things, "enables the writer to describe . . . heterosexual intimacy" (254). Edward cannot mentally penetrate Bella. If telepathy can signify intercourse, her impermeability can signify her virginity. And just as the traditional romance hero is fascinated by the virgin heroine, so too Edward is fascinated by the inaccessible Bella, the impermeable virgin. Later in the story, we learn that she is not only resistant to Edward's mental powers but to those of other vampires as well. When they confront members of the Volturi, the Italian group of vampire tyrants, even the Volturi's touch telepath cannot invade her mind, nor can the vampire who deals in illusory but excruciating mental pain. If Bella's impermeability represents her virginity, then her virginity is in effect her superpower. She is the magic virgin, echoing the medieval lady who alone draws forth the phallic unicorn. The Cullens explain to her that some vampires have special, supernatural gifts: Edward's telepathy, Alices's glimpses of the future, Jasper's ability to calm emotions. Bella's special gift, her essential element, equates to virginity.

Bella has many other noteworthy qualities, some of which have been mentioned above. One should not forget that she is willing, at the end of the first book, to sacrifice her own life to save her mother (though one might wish that she had planned more carefully, since the gesture was unnecessary and in fact only endangered herself). She also is willing to brave death for other loved ones. But there is no question that Bella's status as impermeable virgin receives much emphasis in the narrative. Julia Kristeva (1987) refers to the "fascination . . . with the virgin daughter as guardian of paternal power" (237). Bella becomes fully absorbed into the family of her future husband and proceeds to protect it. As for Edward himself, he is pervasively presented as a father figure, with Bella in childlike relationship to him. "Their song" is a lullaby he has written for her; he sings her to sleep with it. He not only holds her on his lap; he also carries her piggyback. At the prom, with her foot in a cast, she dances by placing her feet on top of his—the little girl dancing with her daddy (Meyer 2005, 488). He is described as "gripping [her] like [she] was a toddler" (ibid., 297) and "cradling [her] in his arms like a small child" (ibid., 280). In the third novel, Edward restricts her movements by disabling her car—like a strict father or an abusive husband (ibid., 2007, 63). While Bella is sometimes portrayed as independent (at least in her pursuit of self-sacrifice), her behavior is often presented as charmingly childlike in contrast to the much older Edward—a quality which Radway (1984, 130–34) notes in the typical romance heroine, subject to patriarchy. Edward, as I am hardly the first to note,[4] clearly represents patriarchy, and Bella, the magic virgin, guards him.

At the end of the second novel, *New Moon*, it is the Volturi's recognition of her essential nature—her mental celibacy—that gains Bella, Alice, and Edward their freedom. Furthermore, once she marries and has sanctioned sex, she becomes able to extend her shield to members of her family and close friends—an almost feudal group that comes to reside with the Cullen family before a battle. Her family now includes her daughter, conceived on her honeymoon; interestingly, Bella becomes a mother and a vampire simultaneously. It should be noticed that this shield extension does require some active training on Bella's part, and so in a sense we are witnessing choice and agency. But the main import of the training is for her to recognize her own inner nature, as she does in the climactic battle. And her purpose is to protect her family:

The shield blew out from me in a bubble of sheer energy. . . . There was no recoil to the elastic fabric now; in that instant of raw force, I saw that the backlash I'd felt before was of my own making—I had been clinging to the invisible part of me in self-defense, subconsciously unwilling to let it go. Now I set it free, and my shield exploded a good fifty yards out from me effortlessly, taking only a fraction of my concentration. I could feel it flex like just another muscle, obedient to my will. . . . Everything underneath the flexible iron shield was suddenly a part of me. . . . I felt Edward's brilliant light within my protection. (Meyer 2008, 690–91)

The shield, then, is like her own muscle, a part of herself. Silver compares it to a womb (2010, 134). She has transitioned from virgin to mother, with almost no time being just a wife, since her pregnancy is supernaturally fast. As both virgin and mother, she protects her husband's family. She is first the magic virgin, then the magic mother (not the Virgin Mother, but the Vampire Mother). At the end of the story, in the "Happily Ever After," having succeeded in both of these functions, Bella at last lets Edward in completely; she discovers how to open her telepathic shield, and the story closes with her opening to him.

What is to me the most curious thing about Bella's virginity, however, is that it is of Edward's making. One of the elements of *Twilight* that I appreciate is the fact that these stories recognize sexual desire in the heroine without condemning her for that desire. Time and again Bella responds to Edward with intense sexual feeling—a normal human teenage response. On the other hand, Edward, though he is portrayed as desiring Bella in more than one way, responds to her with abnormal restraint. One wonders if the fourteen-year-old girls who read these novels will be expecting the same sort of response from their own very special true loves. As Christine Seifert (quoted in Silver 2010) says, Bella "is absolutely dependent on Edward's ability to save her life [and] her virginity" (7). The novel points out that Edward has absorbed the mores of a different era; furthermore, he has experienced over a hundred years of existence. In any case, it is Bella (Eve) who wishes to have sex[5] and Edward who refuses, who persuades her to wait until marriage. If, then, Bella's main power is that of the magic virgin, it is a power given to her by Edward, a role granted by patriarchy. Or to put it another way, however we may choose to interpret the possible significance of Bella's virginity, her virginity is not her choice.[6]

Katniss, on the other hand, makes a choice of virginity in a world that does not expect it of her—and, indeed, she pretends to be sexually active while secretly being chaste. The other Hunger Games contestants tease her, Peeta says, because she is "so . . . pure" compared to others in the Capitol (Collins 2009, 216). While Bella has a pregnancy and childbirth that is terrifyingly physical, Katniss endures a phony pregnancy, one that is completely unreal, for the sake of the games she must play to stay alive—and to help her loved ones stay alive. While *Twilight* focuses on a set of families—the Cullens, the Quileute wolf pack, perhaps even the Volturi—*The Hunger Games* extends through the web of a world. And it is a world very much like our own in that political relationships are grounded in media presentation; *The Hunger Games* does a remarkable job of showing how those political-media relations affect—indeed, control—the citizens of Panem. This control extends from the public face of the government all the way into the bedroom of a citizen.

As many know, the working title for the first *Hunger Games* movie was *Artemis*. And as many also know, Artemis is the Greek goddess of the hunt. The appropriateness for Katniss—whose image with her bow is shown in many posters—is clear. Artemis is also a virgin goddess—a quality equally worthy of remark. Marilyn Frye (1992) asserts that the word *virgin* has had changing implications, and once meant "a free woman, one not betrothed, not married, not bound to, not possessed by any man" (133).[7] As for the character's own name of Katniss—she, like numerous other young women from the District, is named for a plant. But while many, like her sister Primrose and her fellow tribute Rue, are named for flowers, Katniss is named for an edible plant which can be used for food. Her name might also connect her with the idea of the cat; indeed, it could be argued that Katniss is paralleled with a cat in the story, the scruffy and incongruously named Buttercup who, like Katniss, truly loves Prim, and who, like Katniss, keeps coming back alive despite all the desperate journeys she is forced through. In any case, their names are connected with nature, in opposition to the Roman names of the city folk who dwell in the Capitol. Katniss, the virginal Artemis-figure who communes with nature as she hunts, must learn to deal with the unnatural ways of the wider world.

From the very beginning, however, it is clear that access to nature is limited; the eyes of the Capitol are almost everywhere. As Katniss and her family prepare to face the annual reaping in the opening pages of the book, Capitol camera crews are "perched like buzzards on rooftops" (Collins 2008, 16); later she refers to reporters as "insect-like" (ibid., 40). When her twelve-year-old sister's name is drawn and Katniss volunteers to replace her, she is keenly aware, as she readies herself, of the necessity to avoid showing weakness: "I've had a lot of practice at wiping my face clean of emotions and I do this now" (ibid.). But she finds it easier to hide emotion than to actively convey false emotion. Her mentor, Haymitch, emphasizes that "it's all a big show. It's all how you're perceived" (ibid., 135). In order, it seems, to get more sponsors, Haymitch and her fellow tribute Peeta concoct a plan to have Peeta announce in the glare of a television interview that he has long had a crush on her. However, Katniss, knowing that only one tribute can survive, assumes that Peeta will, sooner or later, turn on her; how real can his declarations be? As the story continues, we learn that Peeta's love is real, but how tainted must it be by the uses to which they are forced to put it? Their first kiss must be on national television, and they know the world is watching; by the end of the first novel,

Peeta believes that Katniss has used him solely in order to stay alive, even though in truth her feelings for him are confused and, by the end of the story, transform into love.

Her relationship with Peeta, then, is damaged by being public and by being long deprived of choice. The root of their relationship is genuine: Peeta's father, in fact, loved Katniss's mother, but lost her to Katniss's father—and Peeta knew this—as, perhaps, did Peeta's bitter mother. When Katniss, at eleven, scrounged in the garbage for food, Peeta chose to get a beating from that mother for burning some loaves of bread so that he could then toss the bread out where the starving Katniss could retrieve it. From beginning to end, Peeta feeds Katniss in many ways. Nonetheless, coming from different classes—the coal miner's daughter and the merchant's son—they have never spoken until the Games. She is dismayed to learn that he has been chosen to be a fellow competitor, but at first she steels herself, choosing to live for Prim's sake. In the end of the first book, however, Katniss and Peeta combine their understanding of the "big show" with their choice not to kill each other in order to survive; having succeeded in outlasting all the other tributes, they choose to simultaneously eat poisonous berries. This is a complex action. They know that the mechanism of the political machine, the circus part of the bread and circuses, demands a winner; so they gamble that those in power will not let the supposed "star-crossed lovers" both die. However, they also know that they themselves cannot be seen as gaming the system, so they must pretend to feel the kind of love that could not go on without the other. In fact, Katniss must pretend to feel the kind of despair that besets Bella when Edward leaves—but she is using this pretense to try to save both herself and Peeta and to live for her own sake and her family's. The layers of deception weigh down the feeling underneath.

Wishing herself away from the public, Katniss later turns to her best friend Gale, kissing him in their place, the forest. Here is a person who has hunted with her, has been close to nature with her; he and she have made a pact to help feed the other's family should either of them be reaped. Like hers, his name suggests nature; indeed, his suggests a natural force. Like Edward Cullen, Gale is beautiful and strong and catches the eye of many a girl. But even her relationship with him is not free. President Snow, when he visits her home in the second book, tells her, "I know about the kiss" (Collins 2009, 29). Somehow, that private moment with Gale was not private. And because the president refuses to look foolish, she must carry out the show that she and Peeta began: she must marry Peeta. When Gale suggests that she and he could run away together, she knows their families are hostage.

As mentioned earlier, Katniss does not wish to marry anyone. And soon after the president's visit, she recalls, "One of the few freedoms we have in District 12 is the right to marry who we want or not marry at all" (ibid., 45). Now she prepares to marry Peeta, but any fondness she has for him is darkened by her being forced by the president. She also, sadly, recalls that in District 12, the former sheriff had a "habit of luring starving young women into his bed for money" (ibid., 114) and recognizes the precariousness of her position in the past as well: "Had I been older when my father died, I might have been among them. Instead I learned to hunt" (ibid., 115). The last book also divulges the secret prostitution of earlier victors: when an attractive tribute has won the games in the past, President Snow (who has apparently been in office for many years) sells their sexual services to the highest bidder. If the victor resists, the president begins killing off the victor's loved ones, driving some to madness, others to degradation. Katniss is poised at the edge of a continuum of rape.

One can hardly imagine the gentle Peeta demanding conjugal rights, however—nor Katniss accepting such a demand; and in fact, Katniss exerts her freedom by continuing to choose not to have sex until the last three pages of the trilogy. Ironically, one way they maintain their freedom is the pretense of sexual activity—part of the public narrative, part of the big show. When Peeta and Katniss both, with the odds ever against them, survive the Games at the end of the first book, he devises a story to spare her: her mother says that she is too young to marry. But when they travel as victors, as part of the publicity machine for the Games, they sleep together so that Peeta can comfort her when she has nightmares. Katniss says, "Every night I let him into my bed. We manage the darkness as we did in the arena, wrapped in each other's arms, guarding against dangers that can descend at any moment. Nothing else happens, but our arrangement quickly becomes a subject of gossip on the train" (Collins 2009, 72). This true moment of connection allows them to perpetrate another life-saving lie. When the president arranges for them to be forced back into the next year's deadly Games, Peeta, in one of their television interviews, tells the world they have been secretly married and that Katniss is pregnant. His declaration helps give the audience some inkling of the barbarity of the Games; it also is an attempt to invoke sympathy and therefore sponsors and protection. But it also highlights Katniss's own choice not to marry, not to have sex, not to have children, because of the uses to which they would be put. As she tells Peeta in the last book, "Our whole relationship has been tainted by the games" (ibid. 2010, 162). Though she survives the second set of Games, she realizes she has never left the arena—and readers may be working their way to that same realization.

Only when Katniss brings the Games to an end—only when she stops the grossest of the media manipulations and the political maneuverings—does she finally choose to enter into a relationship with one of her two young men, and then only after a time of healing has passed. While Bella loves a character who clearly represents patriarchy, Katniss makes another choice. Both Peeta and Gale are strong in many ways—not least among them, in their ability to succeed through the media. Peeta is noted for his words, and Gale is admired for his looks. Both of them are physically strong as well. But in other ways they are very different. Peeta is almost maternal in his nurturing (cf. Jessica Miller 2012, 154–55); he is the baker who supplies bread and gentle embraces, the artist who supplies beauty. Gale, on the other hand, is filled with anger; he is good with weapons and a leader in the rebel army that develops in the last part of the story. He is willing to kill and to accept collateral damage. Peeta is connected, in Katniss's history, with the maternal side of the family: his father loved her mother. Gale is connected with the paternal side of the family: their fathers worked together, and Gale continues the training in the hunt that her father began. In the end, Katniss chooses the gentle, damaged Peeta, whose lost leg might be seen as a castration symbol. Katniss, who in the Games has been called The Girl on Fire, says, "What I need to survive is not Gale's fire, kindled with rage and hatred. I have plenty of fire myself" (Collins 2010, 388).

So for Katniss, it is a matter of choice—both her virginity and, eventually, her marriage. She and Peeta have children who are not threatened by the Games—those particular games no longer exist, thanks to Katniss. Both Katniss and Peeta pass through their own separate kinds of madness to reach each other, and the mantra of their love is the question, "You love me. Real or not real?" "Real," is the answer (ibid.); no game-playing here. After years of trials, they thoughtfully, carefully choose each other.

Bella and Edward, however, are not pro-choice. When in the original novel Bella retreats to the woods (yes, both she and Katniss find themselves there), Bella in the woods first comes to the realization that Edward is a vampire; but she also knows that she wants to be with him: "I didn't know if there ever was a choice, really" (Meyer 2005, 139). Not much later in the same book, Edward agrees: "I don't know if I have a choice anymore" (ibid., 173). Again and again throughout the novels, Bella and Edward convey this idea. Many a teenager has used the same logic on the way to an unplanned pregnancy.

Such a remark may seem unfair, given that the *Twilight* novels present no premarital sex for either Bella or her marble-hard beloved. But, again, the choice of virginity is not Bella's. It is, however, Katniss's. Though in *The Hunger Games* the stress of all the social and emotional forces leaves Katniss's sexual desire seeming almost vestigial, still, in the end, she makes her own choices. And having grown wise enough to play the game, she is able to shoot down the possibility of a renewal of the Hunger Games by shooting down the new president, Alma Coin, whose name, in Hebrew, means virgin.[8] Only after she kills the games does she choose to bring children into her life. By the end of the stories, these virgins have both become mothers. But Katniss has changed the world, while Bella has become beautiful but unchanging stone.[9]

Notes

1. Anna Krugovoy Silver (2010) argues that Bella's engagement with the Cullen family is at least as significant as her romance with Edward Cullen.

2. One could also discuss Peeta's role as an artist.

3. I must confess that the idea of connecting Virginia Woolf with Bella Swan made me pause.

4. See, for example, Silver (2010), McClimans and Wisnewski (2009), and Mukherjea (2011).

5. The novels contain much Adam and Eve imagery; also, consider the well-known book cover for *Twilight* (Meyer 2005), with its image of the woman's hand cupping an apple. Eve is, among other things, traditionally a figure of sexual temptation. The first novel begins by directly referencing the subject with an epigraph from Genesis 2:17. There are also clear references within the text, such as Bella's comment, "He didn't know me from Eve" (ibid., 24).

6. At the end of *Eclipse*, just before their marriage, she finally decides that he is right, and that she will do "everything in the right order" (Meyer 2007, 619).

7. My thanks to Ariel Dingus for calling Frye's comment to my attention. See also Kristeva 1987, 236–37.

8. As with the term *virgin* itself, there is discussion over the meaning; "Almah" is variously translated as "virgin" or "young woman." In discussing *Twilight*, Silver quotes the Church of Jesus Christ of Latter-day Saints as saying, "The prophet Alma taught that sexual sins are more serious than any sins except murder and denying the Holy Spirit" (2010, 128); in other words, the name Alma has links to virginity in more than one context.

9. An earlier version of this essay, with the same title, was the keynote for the conference "From Catwoman to Katniss: Villainnesses and Heroines of Fantasy and Science Fiction," March 15–16, 2012. Middle Tennessee State University, Murfreesboro, Tennessee.

References

Coatney, Dereck. 2012. "Why Does Katniss Fail at Everything She Fakes?: Being Versus Seeming to Be in the Hunger Games Trilogy." In The Hunger Games *and Philosophy: A Critique of Pure Treason*, edited by George A. Dunn and Nicolas Michaud, 178–92. Blackwell Philosophy and Pop Culture Series. Hoboken, NJ: Wiley.

Collins, Suzanne. 2008. *The Hunger Games*. New York: Scholastic.

———. 2009. *Catching Fire*. New York: Scholastic.

———. 2010. *Mockingjay*. New York: Scholastic.

Cranny-Francis, Anne. 1997. "Different Identities, Different Voices: Possibilities and Pleasures in Some of Jean Lorrah's *Star Trek* Novels." *Science Fiction Studies* 72 (2): 245–55. MLA International Bibliography (online database) (accessed March 5, 2012).

Frye, Marilyn. 1992. *Willful Virgins: Essays on Feminism, 1976–1992*. Berkeley, CA: Crossing Press.

Johnson, Judith E. 1993. "Women and Vampires: Nightmare or Utopia?" *Kenyon Review* 15 (1): 72–80. Academic Search Premier (online database) (accessed March 27, 2009).

Kristeva, Julia. 1987. "Stabat Mater." In *Tales of Love*, translated by Leon S. Roudiez, 234–63. New York: Columbia University Press.

McClimans, Leah, and J. Jeremy Wisnewski. 2009. "Undead Patriarchy and the Possibility of Love." In Twilight *and Philosophy: Vampires, Vegetarians, and the Pursuit of Immortality*, edited by Rebecca Housel and J. Jeremy Wisnewski, 163–75. Blackwell Philosophy and Pop Culture Series. Hoboken, NJ: Wiley.

Meyer, Stephenie. 2005. *Twilight: A Novel*. New York and Boston: Little, Brown.

———. 2006. *New Moon*. New York: Little, Brown.

———. 2007. *Eclipse*. New York: Little, Brown.

———. 2008. *Breaking Dawn*. New York: Little, Brown.

Miller, Jessica. 2012. "'She Has No Idea. The Effect She Can Have': Katniss and the Politics of Gender." In The Hunger Games *and Philosophy: A Critique of Pure Treason*, edited by George A. Dunn and Nicolas Michaud, 145–61. Blackwell Philosophy and Pop Culture Series. Hoboken, NJ: Wiley.

Miller, Laura. 2010. "'The Hunger Games' vs. 'Twilight.'" *Salon*, September 5, 2010 http://www.salon.com (accessed March 9, 2012).

Mukherjea, Ananya. 2011. "My Vampire Boyfriend: Postfeminism, 'Perfect' Masculinity, and the Contemporary Appeal of Paranormal Romance." *Studies in Popular Culture* 33 (2): 1–20.

Radway, Janice A. 1984. *Reading the Romance: Women, Patriarchy, and Popular Literature*. Chapel Hill: University of North Carolina Press.

Silver, Anna Krugovoy. 2010. "'Twilight Is Not Good for Maidens': Gender, Sexuality, and the Family in Stephenie Meyer's *Twilight* Series." *Studies in the Novel* 42 (1–2): 121–38. MLA International Bibliography (online database) (accessed March 8, 2012).

Valby, Karen. 2012. "*The Hunger Games*: Game On!" *Entertainment Weekly*, March 9, 55–65.

Willis, Victoria. 2014. "Joining the Evil League of Evil: The Rhetoric of Post-Human Negotiation in *Dr. Horrible's Sing-Along Blog*." In *Reading Joss Whedon*, edited by Rhonda V. Wilcox, Tanya R. Cochran, Cynthea Masson, et al. Syracuse, NY: Syracuse University Press.

Contributors

Marleen S. Barr is known for her pioneering work in feminist science fiction and teaches English at the City University of New York. In 1997, she won the Science Fiction Research Association Pilgrim Award for lifetime achievement in science fiction criticism. Barr is the author of *Alien to Femininity: Speculative Fiction and Feminist Theory* (1987), *Lost in Space: Probing Feminist Science Fiction and Beyond* (1993), *Feminist Fabulation: Space/Postmodern Fiction* (1992), *Genre Fission: A New Discourse Practice for Cultural Studies* (2000), and *Oy Pioneer!: A Novel* (2003). Barr has edited many anthologies and co-edited the special science fiction issue of PMLA, the journal of the Modern Language Association of America.

Elyce Rae Helford is professor of English, faculty in Women's and Gender Studies, and director of Jewish and Holocaust Studies at Middle Tennessee State University. She teaches and publishes research on issues of gender, sexuality, and ethnicity in twentieth- and twenty-first century American media culture. Helford is currently completing a book on Hollywood director George Cukor, forthcoming from Wayne State University Press.

Ewan Kirkland teaches Film and Screen Studies at the University of Brighton, UK. His research interests include videogames, children's culture, and representations of gender, race, and sexuality in popular media. Publications in this area include articles on masculinity in horror videogames, heterosexuality in romantic comedy cinema, and whiteness in popular television. Ewan has also written extensively on the videogame series *Silent Hill*, exploring the franchise's relationship to Gothic and horror fiction in terms of narrative, gender representation, and self-reflexivity. Currently, Kirkland is organizing the first academic conference on the *My Little Pony* series.

Nicola Mann is assistant professor of Communications and Visual Cultures at Richmond, The American International University in London. She received a PhD and MA in Visual and Cultural Studies from the University of Rochester, New York, and an MA in Painting from the Royal College of Art,

London. Her dissertation explores the destructive nature of popular visual representations of Chicago's public housing in light of the city's recent urban renewal initiative. She recasts negative stereotypes through a consideration of community-driven strategies, including blogs, newspapers, and public art. Mann also works for the Arts Council of the England-funded organization, The Happy Museum Project (http: www.happymuseumproject.org).

Megan McDonough is pursuing a PhD in Humanities at the University of Louisville in Kentucky. Her interests include children's and young adult fantasy, dystopic fiction, fairytales, adaptation studies, ecocriticism, and cultural studies. Her dissertation explores female agency in young adult fantasy texts and their film adaptations. McDonough's most recent research projects address the evolution of Disney princesses, the uncanny in horror and fairytale, and Katniss's agency in *Catching Fire*. Her coauthored publication with Katherine A. Wagner, "Rebellious Natures: The Role of Nature in Young Adult Dystopian Female Protagonists' Awakenings and Agency," can be found in the collection *Female Rebellion in Young Adult Dystopian Fiction*, edited by Sarah K. Day, Miranda A. Green-barteet, and Amy L. Montz (Farnham, UK: Ashgate, 2014).

Alex Naylor is lecturer in film and visual culture at the University of Greenwich, UK. She graduated from University College London with a PhD. Her dissertation addresses discourses of affect in the 1930s horror film cycle. Her research interests include SF and horror cinema, anime, censorship, fan cultures, and social media. She has book chapters forthcoming on memory and the traumatized body in *Cat People* (1942) and brutalist architecture as dystopic space in Kubrick's *A Clockwork Orange*. Naylor is also coeditor of a special issue on anime in the *Journal of Science Fiction Film and Television 7*, no. 3 (2014).

Rhonda Nicol is instructional assistant professor of English and Women's and Gender Studies at Illinois State University. Her research focuses upon issues of gender, power, and identity in contemporary fantasy, and she has published essays on works such as Harry Potter, Twilight, Supernatural, and Buffy the Vampire Slayer.

Joan Ormrod is senior lecturer at Manchester Metropolitan University, UK. Her research is in popular culture, particularly gender, fantasy, and science fiction. She is editor of the *Journal of Graphic Novels and Comics* and organizes The International Conference of Graphic Novels and Comics with David Huxley. Her recent publications include the coedited collection *Superheroes and Identities* (Routledge 2014) and essays on Wonder Woman and the Cold War and Roger Corman's adaptations of Edgar Allan Poe and vampire fandom.

J. Richard Stevens is assistant professor in Media Studies at the University of Colorado, Boulder. Dr. Stevens's research delves into the intersection of ideological formation and media message dissemination. This work comprises studies such as how cultural messages are formed and passed through popular culture, how technology infrastructure affects the delivery of media messages, communication technology policy, and how media and technology platforms are changing American public discourse.

Tosha Taylor is a PhD candidate at Loughborough University, UK, where she is studying American captivity in contemporary horror film. Her recent and forthcoming publications include essays on female comics readership, gender relations in Batman comics and movies, and sexuality in *American Horror Story*. She leads seminars for first-year university students on introductory linguistics and film studies.

Katherine A. Wagner is a doctoral candidate in Humanities at the University of Louisville. She has a coauthored chapter with Megan McDonough in the edited collection *Female Rebellion in Young Adult Dystopian Fiction* (Ashgate 2014). Her article "Haven't We Been Here Before?: *The Cabin in the Woods*, the Horror Genre, and Placelessness" was published in *Slayage: The Journal of the Whedon Studies Association*. She has also contributed to the Marseilles, Prague, and Boston volumes of the *World Film Locations* series. Her dissertation explores how representations of placelessness within post–World War II American horror literature and film articulate larger cultural fears about globalization. Her other research interests include issues of identity, place, and the carnivalesque within fantasy, speculative fiction, and horror. Wagner also publishes fiction under the name Katherine A. W. Troyer. Her story "Selling Happiness" can be found in the Winter 2012/2013 issue of *Calliope*.

Rhonda V. Wilcox, PhD, is professor of English at Gordon State College in Georgia. She is editor of *Studies in Popular Culture* and *Slayage: The Journal of Whedon Studies*. She is the author of *Why Buffy Matters: The Art of Buffy the Vampire Slayer* (2005); coeditor, with David Lavery, of *Fighting the Forces: What's at Stake in Buffy the Vampire Slayer* (2002); coeditor, with Tanya R. Cochran, of *Investigating Firefly and Serenity: Science Fiction on the Frontier*

(2008); coeditor, with Sue Turnbull, of *Investigating Veronica Mars: Essays on the Teen Detective Series* (2011); and coeditor, with Lavery, Cochran, and Cynthea Masson, of *Reading Joss Whedon* (2014). She is a cofounding editor of *Critical Studies in Television*, cofounder and past president of the Whedon Studies Association, and past president of the Popular Culture Association in the South.

Index

abuse, 47, 51, 91, 122, 124, 129; domestic, 92, 94, 102, 135, 201; of power, 46, 125, 196; sexual, 47, 93–94, 124; substance, 154n5; survival of, 49, 53

African American(s), 7, 8, 101–2, 105, 116n1, 133

agency, 3, 7, 9, 19, 30, 50, 63, 105, 129, 131, 179; clothing and, 68–71; ethnicity and, 68–71, 73, 182–83; female, 89, 105, 115, 116, 120–21, 129, 177, 201; identity and, 67, 177, 183–85; male, 67; multiplicity and, 182–83, 184–85, 188, 190; in young adult novels, 177–91

Alien/Aliens, 7, 8, 85, 87, 88, 89, 90, 92, 143

Arabic, 7, 61–62, 64, 65, 66, 68, 69, 70, 71, 73, 74, 75, 77–78; -Chinese, 72; fantasy, 71; -Oriental, 67

archetype, 52, 61, 87, 110; Amazon, 13–14, 21–22, 24, 26, 28, 31, 32–33; Final Girl, 87, 89; Jungle Queen, 6, 13–14, 16, 19, 21–22, 24, 28, 30, 31, 32–33

artificiality, 3, 5, 184

Asian(s), 61, 62, 66, 68, 72–73, 74, 75; and Arabic, 7, 61; East Asian, 7, 62, 63, 64, 67–68, 69–70, 71, 72–73, 75, 78

auteur, 4, 84

Avatar, 8, 143

Avengers, The (television series), 4, 134

Bakhtin, Mikhail (*Rabelais and His World*), 172

Banner, Bruce, 15, 30

Batman, 6, 61–77, 79n2, 79n15, 106, 114, 160. *See also* DC comics/universe

Barr, Marleen S., 4–5, 8, 144, 152; *Future Females: A Critical Anthology*, 4; *Future Females: The Next Generation*, 4

Battlestar Galactica, 7, 82–95

black/"blackness," 7, 48, 66, 101, 104, 106, 140–41, 178. *See also* African American(s)

boundaries, 4–5; gender, 9, 10, 32, 88–90; genre, 4, 166; racial, 9, 105; social, 9, 13, 104, 105; somatic, 174–75

Buffy the Vampire Slayer, 84, 85, 87, 93, 94, 123, 141

Butler, Judith, 5, 139, 162; "Gender Insubordination," 162; "Is Kinship Always Already Heterosexual?," 139

Charlie's Angels, 83, 85, 141

class (social), 5, 9, 177–79, 181, 183–84, 188, 190, 196, 199, 204; constructions of, 177; politics, 7; race and, 8, 105

classism. *See* class

Clinton, Bill, 144, 147, 148, 149, 151, 152

Clinton, Hillary Rodham, 8, 143–54

Clover, Carol (*Men, Women, and Chainsaws*), 87, 89

community, 8, 33, 42, 45, 48, 122, 125, 128, 210; activism, 111; alternative, 45; blogging, 55; boundaries, 13; female, 32; feminist online, 56n3; international, 27; leaders, 111; reality-based, 144; scholarly, 130; superhero, 27; supernatural, 123, 125, 127, 128; Urban Fantasy (UF), 119

compulsory heterosexuality. *See* heteronormativity

www.ingramcontent.com/pod-product-compliance
Lightning Source LLC
Chambersburg PA
CBHW031130270326
41929CB00011B/1573